SECOND

FLAGS
OF THE WORLD

FIREFLY BOOKS

A FIREFLY BOOK

Published by Firefly Books Ltd. 2012

National flags copyright © 2012 The Flag Institute
Subnational flags and flags of international
  organizations copyright © 2012 Raymond Turvey
Signal flags copyright © 2012 Philip's
Cartography copyright © 2012 Philip's

First printing

Publisher Cataloging-in-Publication Data (U.S.)

Flags of the world.
2nd ed.
Originally published as: Firefly guide to flags of
the world, 2003.
[232] p. : col. ill., col. maps ; cm.
Includes index.
ISBN-13: 978-1-77085-157-3 (pbk.)
1. Flags – Handbooks, manuals, etc. I. Title.
929.92 dc23   CR101.F434 2012

Library and Archives Canada Cataloguing in
Publication

A CIP record for this title is available from Library
and Archives Canada

Published in the United States by
Firefly Books (U.S.) Inc.
P.O. Box 1338, Ellicott Station
Buffalo, New York 14205

Published in Canada by
Firefly Books Ltd.
66 Leek Crescent
Richmond Hill, Ontario L4B 1H1

This book was developed by Philip's,
a division of Octopus Publishing Group Ltd,
Endeavour House, 189 Shaftesbury Avenue,
London WC2H 8JY
An Hachette UK Company

FRONT COVER (clockwise from top left):
East Timor, Swaziland, Papua New Guinea,
Zambia, Antigua and Barbuda, Central
African Republic

Picture credits: p6 INTERFOTO / Sammlung
Rauch / Mary Evans, p8 Mary Evans/AISA
Media, p9 NASA

Printed in China

CONTENTS

World Flags

World Maps

National Flags

Subnational Flags

International Organization Flags

Signal Flags

National Flag Days

A HISTORY OF FLAGS

The first visually documented uses of flags come from two Roman coins dating from 89 and 42 BC. The decoration of these coins includes images of soldiers carrying a spear or staff with a square piece of cloth hanging from a cross-bar. This piece of cloth was known as a *vexillum* (meaning a small sail, from the Latin for sail, *velum*). This is the source of the term for the study of flags, vexillology. The *vexillum* formed part of the regalia of the Roman legions, along with such symbols as imperial eagles, and could be a plain color (most commonly red) or decorated, often with the abbreviation "SPQR" (*Senatus Populusque Romanus*, the Senate and People of Rome), the motto of Rome.

The word "vexillum" is still sometimes used as a term for vertical flags, such as the

***A Roman* vexillum** *with an imperial eagle. A wide variety of symbols were used on vexilla to denote such things as a particular legion.*

banners (*labara*) used in some Christian processions, and the gonfalons of the Pope and Italian villages, towns, and cities.

THE ANCIENT WORLD

The Roman use of banners, however, is not the earliest known example of the use of emblems or colors as a means of personal, tribal, or military identification. For example, the Hittite Museum in Ankara, Turkey, holds a sculpture with the image of a standard of an Assyrian ruler, Ashurnazirpal II (r. 883–859 BC), and the first Persian Aechminid Emperor, Cyrus the Great (r. 559–530 BC), had a stylized falcon as a standard. Farther back, there are references to banners in several ancient Egyptian descriptions dating to *c.* 2650 BC. There are also mentions in the Bible of banners being used for tribal identification and as rallying points in battle.

In ancient China, flags are thought to have been in use as early as 1500 BC, and probably before, but seem to have functioned as indicators of position in the social scale rather than as personal emblems.

An early example of a flag displaying national pride is the Derafsh Kaviani flag of the Sassanid kings (AD 224–651), which represented independence after their empire's legendary foundation and struggle against a foreign, demonic ruler.

Farther west, in October AD 312, the forces of the rival Roman emperors Constantine and Maxentius fought at the Battle of Milvian Bridge, near Rome. According to the contemporary chronicler Eusebius, Constantine had a vision of a cross above the Sun, together with the phrase (in Greek) "In this sign, conquer." The following night, he dreamed that Christ said he should use the sign against his enemies. Legend has it that he had his soldiers paint the sign on their shields. He was victorious, and these events led him to adopt the Chi-Rho (the first two letters in the Greek spelling of Christ's name) in place of the imperial eagle on his personal *vexillum*.

THE MIDDLE AGES

The Roman Empire in Western Europe collapsed in the 5th century AD, although the idea of the Empire was revived in 800 when Pope Leo III crowned Charlemagne emperor of territories that stretched over much of central Europe. As heads of Catholic Christian countries, all the rulers of Europe were answerable to the pope, as well as to their feudal overlords, and popes often sought to influence political events. For example, in 1066, Pope Alexander II granted Duke William II of Normandy his blessing and a standard of St Peter in support for his bid for the English throne. It is thought that this standard may be represented on the famous Bayeux Tapestry.

Popes also had the right to call upon countries to supply armies to fight in "holy wars," including the Crusades. One theory of the origin of the flag of England is that during the First Crusade (1096–99) Pope Urban II required the soldiers of different countries to display crosses of various colors so that they could be easily distinguished. Originally, the

cross worn by the English was white on red and that of the French red on white, although the two countries soon exchanged colors. Other theories include the idea that English ships in the Mediterranean during the Third Crusade (1189–91) displayed the Genoese flag in order to gain safe passage through that city-state's waters. A flag depicting the Cross of St George is carried by Christ's mother in King Richard II's portable altar – known as the *Wilton Diptych* (National Gallery, London, *c*. 1395–99), but at this stage it is a symbol of the king and country's allegiance to St George, not a national flag.

Other countries also adopted the emblems of patron saints as symbols, such as the St Andrew's Cross of Scotland, which was probably adopted as a national symbol in the 13th century, although it may not have been used on a flag until the 15th.

During the Middle Ages, chivalry and heraldry became highly important in Europe. Knightly orders, such as the Order of the Golden Fleece and the Order of St Michael, were ways for rulers to create and formalize ties of loyalty with their important subjects or with other monarchs. In battle, knights were identified by their personal battle standards.

THE PAN-ARAB FLAG

In the early Islamic world, the first caliphate, the Rashidun (AD 632–661), adopted Muhammad's black banner, while the second caliphate, the Umayyad (AD 661–750), used a plain white one. The third caliphate, the Abbasid (*c*. 750–1258, 1261–1517), reverted to Muhammad's flag to indicate that the dynasty was founded by the descendants of one of the Prophet's family and that they were his true spiritual heirs. The fourth caliphate,

the Fatimid (909–1171), used a green banner. Together with the red of the flags of leaders in the Maghreb (North Africa) and Al-Andalus (711–1492, North Africa and the Iberian peninsula), these make up the pan-Arab colors that were first used under that name in the flag of the Arab revolt of 1916. The colors are still used in combinations of two, three, or four in the flags of many Islamic countries today – for example, Iraq, Bahrain, and Kuwait.

Henri VII of Luxembourg *defeating a revolt by the Milanese in 1311. The emblems of the leaders of his forces fly on the lances.*

Personalized, inherited, coats of arms appear to have been introduced in the early to mid-12th century, and heraldry eventually became a highly complex system of rules about who was entitled to which emblems. The terminology used for the parts of flags and coats of arms derives from heraldry.

SYMBOLS IN FLAGS

Religious symbolism – especially of the Cross in association with battles – features in many countries' national flags to this day, such as that of Denmark, the Daneborg, which is thought to be the oldest national flag in continuous use and to derive from a vision seen by King Waldemar II in 1219.

Although the French kings' battle standard between 1124 and 1415, the Oriflamme, had no overt religious symbols, it was a religious symbol in itself. Originally the standard of the Abbey of St Denis north of Paris, it was orange-red or red, representing the blood of the country's patron saint, and flown from a lance in times of war. In contrast, the royal standard consisted of a blue ground with

golden *fleurs-de-lis*. They were both replaced by the white flag with golden *fleurs-de-lis* of Joan of Arc in the 15th century.

Religious and imperial symbolism also occurs in another group of flags: those displaying a double-headed eagle. Depictions of both double-headed and single-headed eagles, often clasping symbols of power, go back even farther than the falcon on Cyrus the Great's standard, and examples have been found at Sumerian archeological sites in modern-day Iraq. The double-headed eagle dates back to *c.* 3800 BC and was a symbol of Ninurta, the god of Lagash. The Hittites in what is now Anatolia, Turkey, also used it as a religious symbol during the early period of their empire (*c.* 1900–1250 BC).

The Byzantine Empire (AD 395–1453) continued the use of the single-headed Roman eagle long after it had been abandoned in the West, but this was dropped in favor of the double-headed version in the mid-11th century. The exact reasons for the change are unknown, but one of the most probable theories is that it was adopted by

Emperor Isaac I Komnenos (r. 1057–59), from Paphlagonia in northern Anatolia, who had heard local legends of a powerful double-headed giant eagle. Hundreds of miles to the east, it appears to have been adopted by the Seljuk Turks, who would soon come to conquer Constantinople, at more or less the same time. In both cases, the two heads of the eagle represented power in both East and West.

The crescent that now appears on the Turkish flag and those of many Islamic countries was first used on the flag of the Ottoman Empire in 1453, while the star first appears on the Ottoman naval ensign in 1793 and the imperial flag in 1844.

The banner of the Holy Roman Emperor. This version was in use from c.1430 to 1806.

The double-headed eagle is known to have begun to be adopted in the Holy Roman Empire by about 1250, and its use spread to many German cities and members of the aristocracy. It was retained on the flag of the Austrian (1804–67) and Austro-Hungarian (1867–1918) empires, after which Germany

The Spanish Armada battle the English fleet in the harbor at Gravelines, Flanders, on August 8, 1588. The cross of St George is on the English ships. The yellow cross on a red field on the Spanish ships may be a variant of the Spanish naval ensign, which was a saltire.

The French flag *raised on Malakoff Redoubt, 1855, during the Crimean War. The flag is used as a clear symbol of a national victory.*

NATIONAL FLAGS

While many flags were adopted for military purposes in the Middle Ages, it was the development of trade, empires, and naval power that would eventually lead to their becoming national emblems. With the development of cannon, warfare at sea was no longer restricted to hand-to-hand fighting at close quarters, and it became necessary to find a way to identify which ships were whose. By the time of the attempted naval invasion of England by the Spanish Armada in 1588, the English ships bore both the cross of St George and a red-and-white striped naval ensign – the design of which led to the stripes of the United States' flag. After the union of England and Scotland in 1603, this cross was incorporated with that of the Scottish saltire to form the first Union Flag.

One of the most common forms of national flag is the tricolor, with either horizontal or vertical bands of color. The first revolutionary flag, the tricolor of the Netherlands, was adopted by those struggling for independence from Spain in the late 16th century. It was originally orange, white, and blue to reflect the colors of the coat of arms of the revolt's leader, the Prince of Orange, but the orange was later changed to red.

Other revolutionary movements have also chosen tricolor flags, such as in France, Ireland, and Russia. The reasons for the Russian adoption of the colors of the Dutch flag in the mid-17th century are unclear and may be entirely coincidental. In turn, however, its blue, white, and red became the "pan-Slavic" colors used by countries such as Slovenia and Croatia.

In the era of colonial expansion, planting a national flag on territory being claimed or conquered became widespread. In 1770, on his first voyage, Captain Cook planted the Union Flag at several sites, including Possession Island north of what is now Queensland, Australia, as he noted in his journal:

and Austria both reverted to single-headed eagles. The Russian royal family adopted the double eagle through marriage in the early 16th century, and it was used on the royal standard in various forms until the Russian Revolution and deposition of the Tsar in 1917. It re-emerged in 1994 on the flag of the President of Russia.

The white double eagle on the flag of Serbia was originally adopted under the Nemanjic dynasty (1166–1371) during its struggle for independence from the Ottoman Empire, while the black double eagle of Albania was the symbol of George Skanderbeg, a 15th-century national hero who led the struggle against the same power. The gold double eagle on the flag of Montenegro relates to its close ties with Russia during the 19th century.

Notwithstand[ing] I had in the Name of His Majesty taken possession of several places upon this coast, I now once more hoisted English Coulers and in the Name of His Majesty King George the Third took possession of the whole Eastern Coast...

Even when no claim to a territory is being staked, the tradition by which the first people to arrive at a site plant a flag continues, as in July 1969 when the astronauts of Apollo 11 planted the United States' flag on the surface of the Moon at Tranquility Base as a marker of their brief visit. At the time there were concerns about how this act would be viewed in other countries, although the United States was a signatory to the Outer Space Treaty of 1967, which specifically outlaws any country making a territorial claim to any celestial object. According to Russian foreign minister Sergey Lavrov, the Russian flag planted on the sea floor at the North Pole in 2007 had the same symbolic value.

By contrast, the desecration of national flags – often by burning – has become an increasingly prominent means of protest, although it dates back at least a century to when Croatian patriots burned the flag of the kingdom of Hungary in 1895.

THE MODERN ERA

Modern flag designs are no longer chosen because they happen to represent the most powerful or important person in the country, but are carefully thought through and are often full of symbolism about the country's history, people, culture, and aims. As important national emblems, they have frequently been used in propaganda, such as in Soviet-era posters and Nazi-era Germany.

Many of the countries in Africa that gained independence from colonial rule in the 20th century adopted one, two, or more of the "pan-African" colors of green, yellow, and red as the basis of their flag designs. Newly free islands in the Caribbean also did so as a reflection of their people's heritage.

After the breakup of the Soviet Union, several states, such as Poland, Lithuania, Ukraine, and Estonia, reverted to older flag designs; others, including Uzbekistan and Kazakhstan, adopted new ones.

Several countries, such as Australia and Canada, threw the design open to competition. The result in the case of the Australian flag was a design that contained both a reminder of the country's links with the United Kingdom in the shape of the Union Flag in one quarter and – in the stars of the Southern Cross – a pattern that had been used as a symbol for Australia for about 150 years. The maple leaf had been a national emblem of Canada for 105 years when the country's new flag was adopted in 1965 to replace the Canadian red ensign that had been used unofficially since the 19th century.

The US flag on the lunar surface, July 20, 1969, during the Apollo 11 mission.

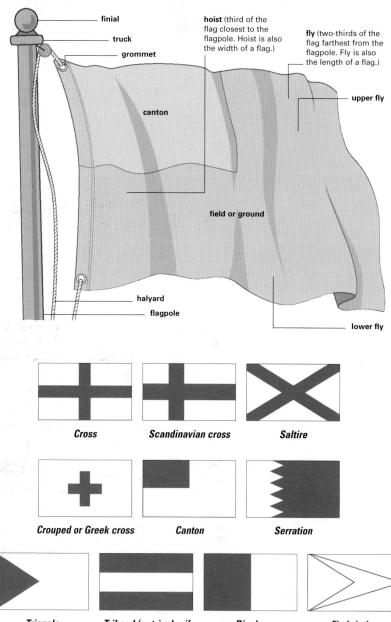

finial

truck

grommet

hoist (third of the flag closest to the flagpole. Hoist is also the width of a flag.)

fly (two-thirds of the flag farthest from the flagpole. Fly is also the length of a flag.)

canton

upper fly

field or ground

halyard

flagpole

lower fly

Cross

Scandinavian cross

Saltire

Crouped or Greek cross

Canton

Serration

Triangle

Triband (or tricolor if three colors used)

Bicolor

Fimbriation

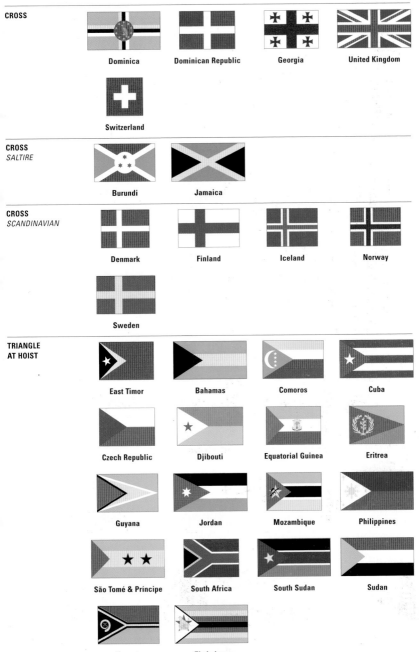

CROSS

Dominica   Dominican Republic   Georgia   United Kingdom

Switzerland

CROSS
SALTIRE

Burundi   Jamaica

CROSS
SCANDINAVIAN

Denmark   Finland   Iceland   Norway

Sweden

**TRIANGLE
AT HOIST**

East Timor   Bahamas   Comoros   Cuba

Czech Republic   Djibouti   Equatorial Guinea   Eritrea

Guyana   Jordan   Mozambique   Philippines

São Tomé & Príncipe   South Africa   South Sudan   Sudan

Vanuatu   Zimbabwe

WORLD FLAGS *STYLES*

SERRATION

Bahrain

Qatar

**VERTICAL STRIPE
AT HOIST WITH
HORIZONTAL
STRIPES**

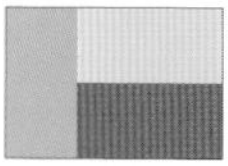

Benin

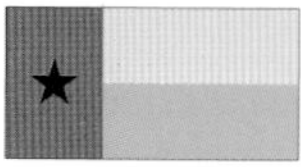

Guinea-Bissau

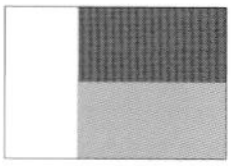

Madagascar

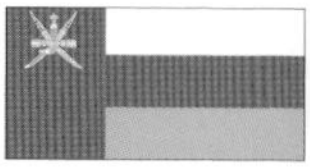

Oman

United Arab Emirates

**CENTRAL
DIAGONAL
STRIPE(S)**

Brunei

Congo

Congo (Dem. Rep.)

Namibia

Solomon Islands

St Kitts & Nevis

Tanzania

Trinidad & Tobago

**SINGLE-COLOR
FIELD** *WITH OR
WITHOUT DEVICE*

Albania

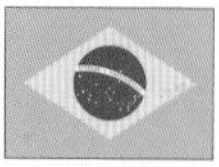

Brazil

Cyprus

Kazakstan

Kosovo

Kyrgyzstan

Maldives

Mauritania

Micronesia

Morocco

Saudi Arabia

Somalia

St Lucia

Tunisia

Turkey

Turkmenistan

Vietnam

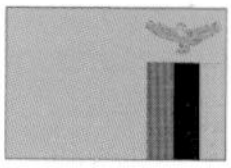

Zambia

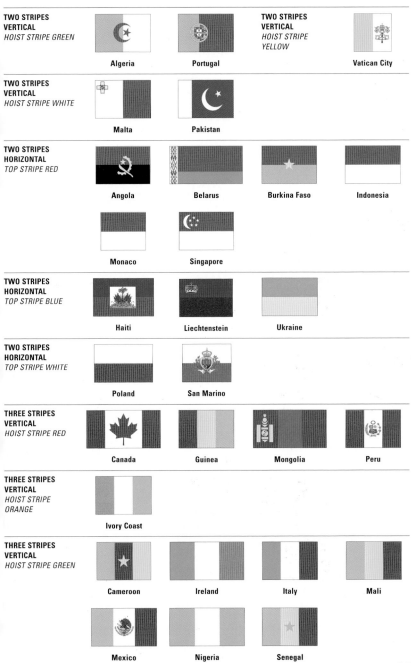

TWO STRIPES VERTICAL
HOIST STRIPE GREEN

Algeria

Portugal

TWO STRIPES VERTICAL
HOIST STRIPE YELLOW

Vatican City

TWO STRIPES VERTICAL
HOIST STRIPE WHITE

Malta

Pakistan

TWO STRIPES HORIZONTAL
TOP STRIPE RED

Angola

Belarus

Burkina Faso

Indonesia

Monaco

Singapore

TWO STRIPES HORIZONTAL
TOP STRIPE BLUE

Haiti

Liechtenstein

Ukraine

TWO STRIPES HORIZONTAL
TOP STRIPE WHITE

Poland

San Marino

THREE STRIPES VERTICAL
HOIST STRIPE RED

Canada

Guinea

Mongolia

Peru

THREE STRIPES VERTICAL
HOIST STRIPE ORANGE

Ivory Coast

THREE STRIPES VERTICAL
HOIST STRIPE GREEN

Cameroon

Ireland

Italy

Mali

Mexico

Nigeria

Senegal

13

WORLD FLAGS *STYLES*

THREE STRIPES
VERTICAL
HOIST STRIPE BLUE

Andorra

Barbados

Chad

France

Guatemala

Moldova

Romania

St Vincent

THREE STRIPES
VERTICAL
HOIST STRIPE BLACK

Afghanistan

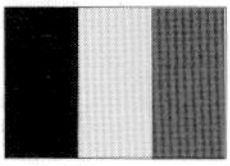

Belgium

THREE STRIPES
HORIZONTAL
TOP STRIPE RED

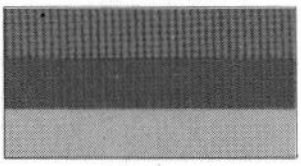

Armenia

Austria

Belize

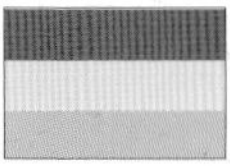

Bolivia

Croatia

Egypt

Ghana

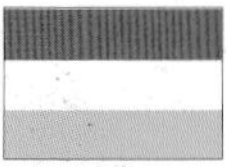

Hungary

Iraq

Laos

Latvia

Lebanon

Libya

Luxembourg

Malawi

Netherlands

Paraguay

Spain

Serbia

Syria

Tajikistan

Yemen

THREE STRIPES
HORIZONTAL
TOP STRIPE ORANGE

India

Niger

THREE STRIPES
HORIZONTAL
TOP STRIPE BLACK

Germany

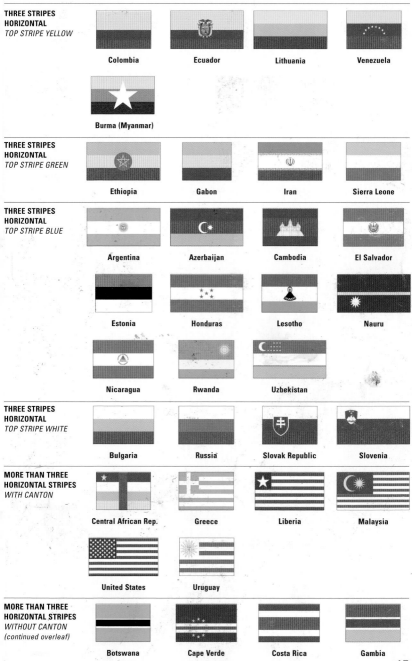

THREE STRIPES HORIZONTAL
TOP STRIPE YELLOW

Colombia | Ecuador | Lithuania | Venezuela

Burma (Myanmar)

THREE STRIPES HORIZONTAL
TOP STRIPE GREEN

Ethiopia | Gabon | Iran | Sierra Leone

THREE STRIPES HORIZONTAL
TOP STRIPE BLUE

Argentina | Azerbaijan | Cambodia | El Salvador

Estonia | Honduras | Lesotho | Nauru

Nicaragua | Rwanda | Uzbekistan

THREE STRIPES HORIZONTAL
TOP STRIPE WHITE

Bulgaria | Russia | Slovak Republic | Slovenia

MORE THAN THREE HORIZONTAL STRIPES
WITH CANTON

Central African Rep. | Greece | Liberia | Malaysia

United States | Uruguay

MORE THAN THREE HORIZONTAL STRIPES
WITHOUT CANTON
(continued overleaf)

Botswana | Cape Verde | Costa Rica | Gambia

15

WORLD FLAGS *STYLES*

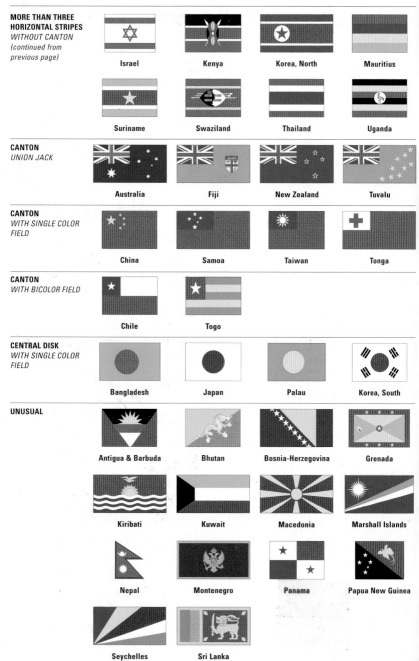

MORE THAN THREE HORIZONTAL STRIPES
WITHOUT CANTON
(continued from previous page)

Israel

Kenya

Korea, North

Mauritius

Suriname

Swaziland

Thailand

Uganda

CANTON
UNION JACK

Australia

Fiji

New Zealand

Tuvalu

CANTON
WITH SINGLE COLOR FIELD

China

Samoa

Taiwan

Tonga

CANTON
WITH BICOLOR FIELD

Chile

Togo

CENTRAL DISK
WITH SINGLE COLOR FIELD

Bangladesh

Japan

Palau

Korea, South

UNUSUAL

Antigua & Barbuda

Bhutan

Bosnia-Herzegovina

Grenada

Kiribati

Kuwait

Macedonia

Marshall Islands

Nepal

Montenegro

Panama

Papua New Guinea

Seychelles

Sri Lanka

PAN AFRICAN

Red, Gold, Green
Benin
Burkina Faso
Cameroon
Central African Republic
Congo
Eritrea
Ethiopia
Ghana
Grenada
Guinea
Guinea-Bissau
Guyana
Mali
Mozambique
São Tomé and Príncipe
Senegal
Togo

FLAG NAMES

Canada	Maple Leaf Flag
Croatia	*Trobojnica/ Crven-Bijeli-Plavi/ S'ahovnica*
Cuba	*La Estrella Solitaria*
Denmark	*Dannebrog*
France	*Tricolore*
Germany	*Schwarz-Rot-Gold*
Greece	*Galanolefki*
Guyana	Golden Arrow
Indonesia	*Sang Saka/ Merah Putih*
Italy	*Tricolore*
Japan	*Hinomaru*
Netherlands	*Prinsenvlag*
Portugal	*Verde e Rubra*
South Korea	*Tae-Gheuk-Ghi*
Spain	*Rojigualda*
St Vincent	The Gems
Switzerland	Federal Cross
Thailand	*Trairong*
Turkey	*Ayyildiz*
UK	Union Jack
	Union Flag
USA	Stars and Stripes
	Star Spangled Banner
	Old Glory
	Red, White, and Blue

PAN ARAB

Red, White, Black, Green
Afghanistan
Iraq
Jordan
Kuwait
Sudan
Syria
United Arab Emirates

Red, White, Black
Egypt
Yemen

PAN SLAVIC

Red, White, Blue
Croatia
Czech Republic
Russia
Serbia
Slovak Republic
Slovenia

ORGANIZATIONS

International Federation of
Vexilological Associations
*Fédération internationale des
associations vexillologiques* (FIAV)
www.fiav.org

The Canadian Flag Association
*L'Association Canadienne de
Vexillologie*
www.facebook.com/pages/
canadian-flag-association-
lassociation-canadienne-de-
vexillologie/317266027131

The Flag Research Center (United
States)
www.flagresearchcenter.com

The Flag Institute (United Kingdom)
www.flaginstitute.org

Flag Society of Australia
www.flagsaustralia.com.au

WORLD MAPS

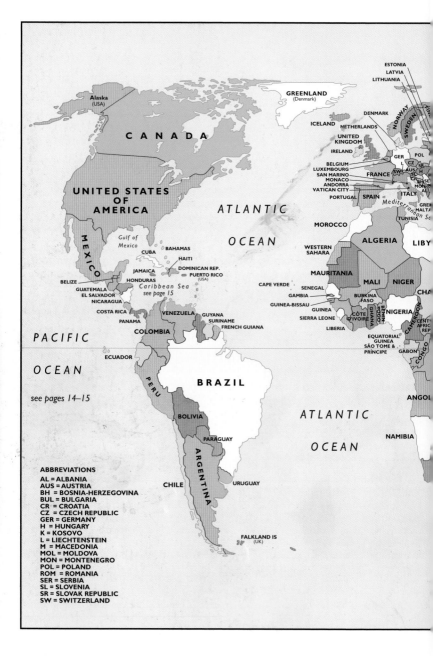

ESTONIA
LATVIA
LITHUANIA

GREENLAND
(Denmark)

DENMARK

ICELAND

NETHERLANDS
UNITED KINGDOM
IRELAND

NORWAY
SWEDEN

Alaska (USA)

CANADA

GER
POL
CZ
BELGIUM
LUXEMBOURG
SAN MARINO
MONACO
ANDORRA
VATICAN CITY

L
AUS
SW
SL
BH
SER
MON
AL

FRANCE
ITALY

UNITED STATES
OF
AMERICA

ATLANTIC

OCEAN

PORTUGAL
SPAIN

Mediterranean Sea

GRE
MALTA

MEXICO

Gulf of Mexico

MOROCCO

TUNISIA

CUBA
BAHAMAS

WESTERN
SAHARA

ALGERIA

LIBY

HAITI
JAMAICA
DOMINICAN REP.
PUERTO RICO (USA)

Caribbean Sea
see page 15

MAURITANIA

MALI

NIGER

CHA

BELIZE
GUATEMALA
EL SALVADOR
HONDURAS
NICARAGUA

CAPE VERDE

SENEGAL

BURKINA
FASO

GAMBIA
GUINEA-BISSAU
GUINEA
SIERRA LEONE
CÔTE
D'IVOIRE

BENIN
TOGO
GHANA

NIGERIA

COSTA RICA
PANAMA

VENEZUELA
GUYANA
SURINAME
FRENCH GUIANA

LIBERIA

CAMEROON

COLOMBIA

EQUATORIAL
GUINEA
SÃO TOMÉ &
PRÍNCIPE

CENT.
AFRIC.
REP

GABON

CONGO

PACIFIC

ECUADOR

OCEAN

see pages 14–15

PERU

BRAZIL

ATLANTIC

ANGOL

BOLIVIA

PARAGUAY

OCEAN

NAMIBIA

ABBREVIATIONS
AL = ALBANIA
AUS = AUSTRIA
BH = BOSNIA-HERZEGOVINA
BUL = BULGARIA
CR = CROATIA
CZ = CZECH REPUBLIC
GER = GERMANY
H = HUNGARY
K = KOSOVO
L = LIECHTENSTEIN
M = MACEDONIA
MOL = MOLDOVA
MON = MONTENEGRO
POL = POLAND
ROM = ROMANIA
SER = SERBIA
SL = SLOVENIA
SR = SLOVAK REPUBLIC
SW = SWITZERLAND

CHILE

ARGENTINA

URUGUAY

FALKLAND IS
(UK)

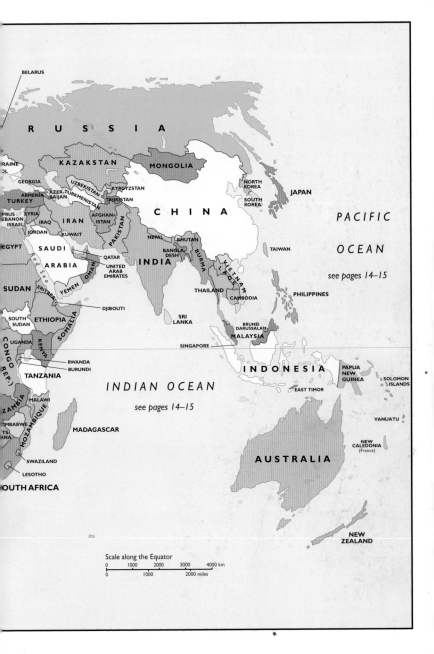

BELARUS

R U S S I A

KAZAKSTAN

MONGOLIA

RAINE
GEORGIA
ARMENIA UZBEKISTAN
AZER-TURKMENISTAN KYRGYZSTAN
BAIJAN
TURKEY TAJIKISTAN
PRUS SYRIA
LEBANON IRAQ IRAN AFGHAN-
ISRAEL ISTAN
JORDAN KUWAIT PAKISTAN
EGYPT SAUDI NEPAL
ARABIA QATAR BANGLA-
UNITED DESH
ARAB INDIA
EMIRATES
SUDAN OMAN
ERITREA YEMEN
DJIBOUTI
SOUTH ETHIOPIA
SUDAN SRI
CONGO SOMALIA LANKA
UGANDA KENYA
REP.) RWANDA
BURUNDI
TANZANIA
ZAMBIA MALAWI MADAGASCAR
IMBABWE
TS
ANA MOZAMBIQUE
SWAZILAND
LESOTHO
OUTH AFRICA

CHINA

NORTH
KOREA
JAPAN
SOUTH
KOREA

BHUTAN
BURMA
VIETNAM
LAOS
THAILAND
CAMBODIA
TAIWAN

PACIFIC

OCEAN

see pages 14–15

PHILIPPINES

BRUNEI
DARUSSALAM
MALAYSIA
SINGAPORE

INDONESIA

EAST TIMOR

PAPUA
NEW
GUINEA

SOLOMON
ISLANDS

INDIAN OCEAN

see pages 14–15

VANUATU

NEW
CALEDONIA
(France)

AUSTRALIA

NEW
ZEALAND

Red Sea

Scale along the Equator
0   1000   2000   3000   4000 km
0   1000   2000 miles

19

WORLD MAPS

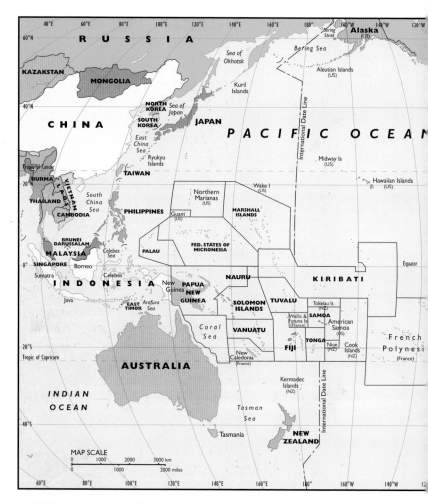

MAP SCALE

Kilometres: 0 — 1000 — 2000 — 3000 km
Miles: 0 — 1000 — 2000 miles

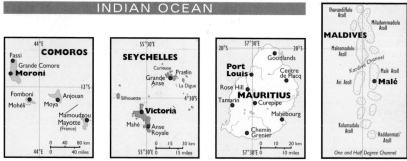

INDIAN OCEAN

COMOROS
44°E
Fassi
Grande Comore
● Moroni
12°S
Fomboni
Mohéli
Anjouan
Moya
Mamoudzou
Mayotte
(France)
0 — 40 — 80 km
0 — 40 miles
44°E

SEYCHELLES
55°30′E
Curieuse
Praslin
Grande Anse
La Digue
Silhouette
4°30′S
● Victoria
Mahé
Anse Royale
0 — 15 — 30 km
0 — 15 miles
55°30′E

MAURITIUS
20°S — 57°30′E — 20°S
Goodlands
Port Louis
Centre de Flacq
Rose Hill
Tamarin
Curepipe
Mahebourg
Chemin Grenier
0 — 10 — 20 km
0 — 10 miles
57°30′E

MALDIVES
Ihavandiffulu Atoll
Miladummadulu Atoll
Malosmadulu Atoll
Kardiva Channel
Malé Atoll
Ari Atoll
● Malé
Kolumadulu Atoll
Haddunmati Atoll
One and Half Degree Channel

20

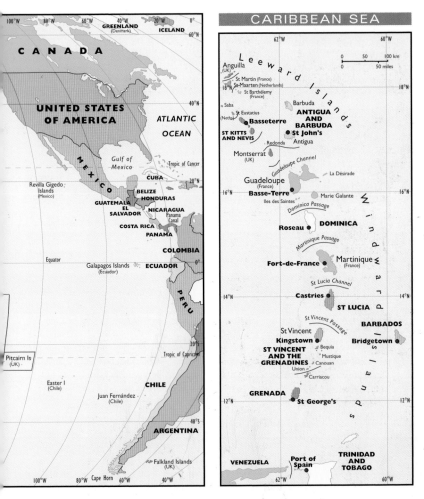

The world map shows the Americas including CANADA, GREENLAND (Denmark), ICELAND, UNITED STATES OF AMERICA, MEXICO, ATLANTIC OCEAN, Gulf of Mexico, Tropic of Cancer, CUBA, BELIZE, HONDURAS, GUATEMALA, EL SALVADOR, NICARAGUA, Panama Canal, COSTA RICA, PANAMA, COLOMBIA, Revilla Gigedo Islands (Mexico), Equator, Galapagos Islands (Ecuador), ECUADOR, PERU, Pitcairn Is (UK), Tropic of Capricorn, Easter I (Chile), Juan Fernández (Chile), CHILE, ARGENTINA, Falkland Islands (UK), Cape Horn.

The Caribbean Sea inset shows: Leeward Islands, Anguilla (UK), St Martin (France), St-Maarten (Netherlands), St Barthélemy (France), Saba (Neth), St Eustatius (Neth), Barbuda, ANTIGUA AND BARBUDA, Basseterre, ST KITTS AND NEVIS, St John's, Redonda, Antigua, Montserrat (UK), Guadeloupe Channel, La Désirade, Guadeloupe, Basse-Terre, Marie Galante, Iles des Saintes, Dominica Passage, Roseau, DOMINICA, Martinique Passage, Fort-de-France, Martinique (France), St Lucia Channel, Castries, ST LUCIA, BARBADOS, St Vincent Passage, St Vincent, Kingstown, Bridgetown, Bequia, ST VINCENT AND THE GRENADINES, Mustique, Union, Canouan, Carriacou, GRENADA, St George's, Windward Islands, VENEZUELA, Port of Spain, TRINIDAD AND TOBAGO.

The lower map shows: SUDAN, DJIBOUTI, Cape Guardafui, Laccadive Islands (India), Nicobar Islands (India), Gulf of Thailand, CAMBODIA, SOUTH SUDAN, ETHIOPIA, SOMALIA, SRI LANKA, MALAYSIA, MALDIVES, SINGAPORE, Borneo, UGANDA, KENYA, Equator, Sumatra, INDONESIA, RWANDA, BURUNDI, Chagos Archipelago (UK), Java Sea, Java, TANZANIA, Amirante Is, SEYCHELLES, Diego Garcia, Sunda Islands, ZAMBIA, COMOROS, Cocos I (Keeling Is) (Australia), Christmas I (Australia), ZIMBABWE, MOZAMBIQUE, MADAGASCAR, Rodrigues, MAURITIUS, Reunion (France), Tropic of Capricorn, AUSTRALIA, BOTSWANA.

AFGHANISTAN

FLAG RATIO: 1:2 USE: National DATE ADOPTED: 1992 LAST MODIFIED: 2001

The **tricolor** of **black**, **red** and **green** **vertical stripes** returned as the flag of Afghanistan after the defeat of the Taliban in 2001. First adopted in 1992, the flag uses the colors of the *Mujaheddin* ("holy warriors") who fought against the Marxist regime and Soviet forces in the Afghanistan War (1979–89). Green represents **Islam**, **red** stands for the blood shed in war, and **black** denotes the country's dark past. The **coat of arms** consists of a **mosque** and a wreath of **wheat ears**. The wheat recalls the crowning of Afghan monarchs with wreaths of wheat. Above the coat of arms is the *shahada*, the declaration of Muslim faith, and "*Allah-u Aqbar*" ("God is Great").

AREA 252,000 sq mi (652,000 sq km)
POPULATION 29,835,000
CAPITAL Kabul
GOVERNMENT Islamic republic
ETHNIC GROUPS Pashtun (Pathan) 44%, Tajik 25%, Hazara 10%, Uzbek 8%, others 8%
LANGUAGES Pashtu, Dari/Persian (both official), Uzbek
RELIGIONS Islam (Sunni Muslim 84%, Shiite Muslim 15%), others
NATIONAL ANTHEM (DATE)
"*Sououd-e-melli*" (1978)

HISTORY

Buddhism arrived in the 2nd century BC, while Arab armies brought **Islam** in the 7th century. **Shah Nadir** extended Persian rule to most of Afghanistan. His successor, **Ahmad Durrani** established the first unified state in 1747. **Britain** fought three wars for control of the region. In 1919 Afghanistan regained its **independence**. In 1933 **Muhammad Zahir** became Shah. In 1964 Zahir proclaimed a constitutional monarchy. In 1996 the fundamentalist **Taliban** seized Kabul. In 2001 the **United States** launched airstrikes after the Taliban refused to hand over **Osama Bin Laden**. In December 2001, Afghan opposition forces, led by **Hamid Karzai**, overthrew the Taliban and set up a coalition government. International forces remained in the country for well over a decade.

Afghan stamp *from 1987, showing a dove of peace over the outline of Afghanistan.*

A lbania's flag is a striking **red field** with a **black, double-headed eagle**. The two-headed eagle was the seal of Albanian national hero Gjergj Kastrioti. Taken hostage by the Turks, Kastrioti converted to Islam, was renamed Iskander, and given the title of bey (hence his byname Skanderbeg). In 1444, after embracing Christianity, Kastrioti successfully organized Albanian resistance against the Turks.

HISTORY

The **Balkan** republic of Albania is mountainous and prone to earthquakes. It formed part of ancient **Illyria**. In 167 BC, Albania was subsumed into the **Roman Empire**. Between 1469 and 1912, Albania was part of the **Ottoman Empire**. In 1939 Italy invaded and **King Zog** fled into exile. In 1943 **Germany** occupied Albania. In 1944 Albanian Communists, led by **Enver Hoxha**, took power. Hoxha, who remained in office until his death in 1985, built a **Stalinist**, isolationist state. In 1967 Albania became the world's first **atheist** nation. In 1992 Democratic Party leader **Sali Berisha** became Albania's first non-communist president. In 1997, the collapse of nationwide **pyramid finance schemes** sparked a large-scale rebellion in southern Albania. The government resigned and **Fatos Nano** became prime minister. In 1999, nearly 500,000 ethnic **Albanian refugees** fled to Albania from the Serbian province of **Kosovo**.

AREA 11,100 sq mi (28,700 sq km)
POPULATION 2,995,000
CAPITAL Tirana
GOVERNMENT Multiparty republic
ETHNIC GROUPS Albanian 95%, Greek 3%, Macedonian, Vlachs, Gypsy
LANGUAGES Albanian (official)
RELIGIONS of those who state a belief, 70% Muslim, 30% Christian (Orthodox 20%, Roman Catholic 10%)
NATIONAL ANTHEM (DATE) *"Himni i Flamurit"* "Hymn to Our Flag" (1912)

Shqiperia, the Albanian name for the country, means "Land of the eagle."

23

ALGERIA

FLAG RATIO: 2:3 USE: National/Civil DATE ADOPTED: 1962 LAST MODIFIED: 1962

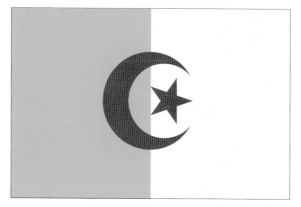

The **red star** and **crescent** at the center of Algeria's flag are common symbols of Islam. **Green** is also traditionally associated with Islam. **White** stands for purity and also recalls the banner of Abd al-Kadir, an early hero of the liberation movement. The National Liberation Front (FLN), which led the struggle for independence from France, adopted the present flag in 1954. From 1958 to 1962 it was the flag of the government in exile. On July 3, 1962, it was hoisted as the national flag of an independent Algeria.

HISTORY

Algeria is the second largest country in **Africa**. In the 9th century BC, coastal Algeria (**Numidia**) formed part of the empire of **Carthage**. **Berbers** controlled Algeria until the arrival of the Arabs in the late 7th century AD. The Arabs converted Algeria to Islam. In the early 10th century, the **Fatimids** built an empire from their base in northeast Algeria. In 1830 **France** invaded. **Abd al-Kadir** led resistance to French colonization. In 1954 the **National Liberation Front (FLN)** launched a war of liberation that claimed more than 350,000 lives. In 1962 Algeria gained **independence**. In 1965 **Houari Boumédienne** overthrew **Ahmed Ben Bella** in an army coup. **Chadli Benjedid** served as president from 1978 to 1991. In 1999 a civil concord promised an end to a **civil war** between government forces and Islamic militants that claimed more than 100,000 lives, but terrorist attacks, some by **al Qaeda**, continued.

AREA 920,000 sq mi (2,382,000 sq km)
POPULATION 34,995,000
CAPITAL Algiers
GOVERNMENT Socialist republic
ETHNIC GROUPS Arab-Berber 99%
LANGUAGES Arabic and Berber (both official), French
RELIGIONS Sunni Muslim 99%
NATIONAL ANTHEM (DATE) *"Qassaman"* "The Pledge" (1963)

This stamp celebrates elections to Algeria's parliament, the Conseil de la Nation.

FLAG RATIO: 2:3   USE: National   DATE ADOPTED: 1866   LAST MODIFIED: 1866

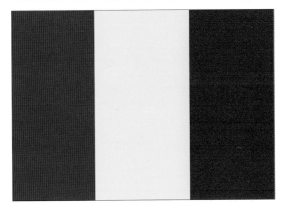

Andorra's (French, *Andorre*) **tricolor** flag of **vertical stripes** links with its neighboring countries. The **blue** and **red** stripes associate it with France, the **red** and **yellow** with Spain. At the center of the yellow stripe is the **coat of arms**. The **shield** divides into four quarters. The first quarter stands for the bishopric, depicted by a **golden miter** and **crosier**. The **three red stripes** symbolize the Counts of Foix. The **four stripes** signify Catalonia, while the **cows** are a symbol of the French province of Béarn. The **civil flag** omits the arms.

HISTORY

Andorra is a small state situated high in the eastern **Pyrenees** between France and Spain. In 803 **Charlemagne** regained Andorra from its Moorish rulers. In 843 Charlemagne's grandson, **Charles II (the Bald)**, granted Andorra to the Count of Urgell. In 1278 and 1288, the **Bishop of Urgell** and the **Count of Foix** signed two *Pariatges* agreeing to share sovereignty of Andorra in return for an annual tribute (*quèstia*) from Andorra. This feudal arrangement between the Spanish Bishops of Urgell and the French Counts of Foix persisted almost unchanged for 715 years. In 1589 Henry II of Foix became **Henry IV of France** and the title of joint ruler passed to the French head of state. In 1993 Andorrans approved a **democratic constitution** and the creation of a "parliamentary co-principality".

Stamp *honoring the 25th anniversary of Andorra's Society of Arts and Letters in 1993.*

AREA 180 sq mi (470 sq km)
POPULATION 85,000
CAPITAL (POPULATION) Andorra La Vella
GOVERNMENT Co-principality
ETHNIC GROUPS Spanish 43%, Andorran 33%, Portuguese 11%, French 7%
LANGUAGES Catalan (official)
RELIGIONS Mainly Roman Catholic
NATIONAL MOTTO *"Virtus Unita Fortior"* "Virtue United in Strength"
NATIONAL ANTHEM (DATE) *"El Gran Carlemany"* "The Great Charlemagne" (1914)

ANGOLA

FLAG RATIO: 2:3 USE: National/Civil DATE ADOPTED: 1975 LAST MODIFIED: 1992

Angola's flag derives from the flag of the MPLA (*Movimento Popular de Libertacão de Angola*), leaders of the struggle for liberation from Portugal. The flag has **two horizontal stripes**. The **red** stripe symbolizes the blood shed in Angola's fight for independence. The **black stripe** represents Africa. The central motif, a **cogwheel**, **machete** and **star**, is reminiscent of communist symbolism. The cogwheel stands for industrial workers, and the machete represents the peasants. The star signifies socialism and progress. The **gold** color of the symbol represents Angola's mineral wealth.

HISTORY

Bantu-speaking people settled in Angola *c*. 2000 years ago. In the early 1600s, Angola became an important source of **slaves** for the Portuguese colony of Brazil. After the decline in the slave trade, Portuguese settlers began to develop the land. Portuguese immigration increased dramatically in the early 20th century. In 1961 the **MPLA** led a revolt in Luanda, the capital. In 1966 southern peoples, including many Ovimbundu, formed the National Union for the Total Independence of Angola (**UNITA**). In **1975** Portugal granted **independence**, and **civil war** ensued between the MPLA government, led by **Agostinho Neto**, and UNITA forces led by **Jonas Savimbi**. The **Lusaka Protocol** (1994) led to a lull in the civil war. In 2002 government troops killed Savimbi and UNITA declared a ceasefire. Rebuilding the country has been a slow process.

AREA 481,000 sq mi (1,247,000 sq km)
POPULATION 13,339,000
CAPITAL Luanda
GOVERNMENT Multiparty republic
ETHNIC GROUPS Ovimbundu 37%, Kimbundu 25%, Bakongo 13%, others 25%
LANGUAGES Portuguese (official), many others
RELIGIONS Traditional beliefs 47%, Roman Catholic 38%, Protestant 15%
NATIONAL ANTHEM (DATE) "Angola, avante!" "Angola, advance!" (1975)

***Angolan** stamp celebrating the 50th anniversary of the United Nations in 1995.*

ANTIGUA AND BARBUDA

FLAG RATIO: 2:3   **USE:** National/Civil   **DATE ADOPTED:** 1967   **LAST MODIFIED:** 1967

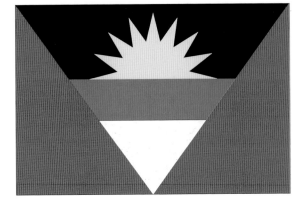

In 1967 Antigua and Barbuda became self-governing and held a competition to design the national flag. The 16-pointed **golden star** at the center of the flag represents the rising sun, symbolizing the dawning of a new era in Antigua and Barbuda's history. The red **triangles** mark a "V" for victory. **Red** stands for the energy of its people, **blue** signifies hope, and **black** recalls the African heritage of its people. The sun rising above the blue band and **white** triangle is a stylized representation of the sun, sea, and sand that attract visitors to Antigua and Barbuda.

HISTORY

In 1493 **Christopher Columbus** landed on Antigua, naming it after Santa Maria la Antigua, Saint of Seville. The indigenous **Caribs** resisted European settlement. England colonized Antigua in 1632, and the smaller island of Barbuda in 1666. In 1684 **Sir Christopher Codrington** established the first **sugar plantation**. The English brought in **slaves** from Africa to work on the plantations. In 1784 **Horatio Nelson** built a naval base on Antigua. In 1834 Britain abolished slavery. From 1871 to 1956 the islands formed part of the British colony of the **Leeward Islands**. **Vere Bird**, of the Antiguan Labor Party (ALP), led the nation to **independence** in 1981. His son succeeded him in 1994, and the party remained in power for a further 20 years.

Antigua and Barbuda is 2100 kilometers (1300 miles) from the coast of Florida.

AREA 170 sq mi (440 sq km)
POPULATION 88,000
CAPITAL St John's
GOVERNMENT Constitutional monarchy
ETHNIC GROUPS Black 91%, Mixed race 4%, White 2%
LANGUAGES English (official), Creole
RELIGIONS Anglican 40%, Methodist 33%, other Protestant 12%, Roman Catholic 5%
MOTTO "Each Endeavouring, All Achieving"
NATIONAL ANTHEM (DATE) "Fair Antigua, We Salute Thee" (1967)

ARGENTINA

FLAG RATIO: 1:2 USE: National/Civil DATE ADOPTED: 1818 LAST MODIFIED: 1818

General Manuel Belgrano, leader of Argentina's independence struggle against the Spanish, designed the **triband** flag shortly before the Battle of Rosario (1812). He based the design on the celeste (**sky-blue**) and **white** colors worn by the patriotic forces. In 1818 Congress approved the addition of a **32-rayed golden sun** on the center of the white band. It is called the "**Sun of May**" in honor of the sun shining through the clouds above Buenos Aires on May 25, 1810, when rebels overthrew the Spanish Viceroy. The sun, an Inca symbol, has **alternate straight** and **flaming rays** and a **human face** on its disk.

HISTORY

Argentina is the second-largest country in South America and the eighth-largest in the world. In 1516 Spanish explorers reached the coast, and settlers followed in search of silver and gold. Spanish rule continued until 1810. In 1816 Argentina declared independence. After General Juan Manuel de Rosas' dictatorship (1835–52), Argentina adopted a federal constitution in 1853. In 1944 Juan Perón toppled the pro-Axis government of Ramón Castillo. With the aid of his wife, Eva, Perón established a popular dictatorship. In 1955 a military junta ousted Perón. In 1973 Perón returned from exile to head a civilian government. Torture, "disappearances", and arbitrary imprisonment characterized the military "rule of the generals" (1976–83). Economic turmoil dominated the early 21st century.

AREA 1,074,000 sq mi (2,780,000 sq km)
POPULATION 41,770,000
CAPITAL Buenos Aires
GOVERNMENT Federal republic
ETHNIC GROUPS European 97%, Mestizo, Amerindian
LANGUAGES Spanish (official)
RELIGIONS Roman Catholic 92%, Protestant 2%, Jewish 2%, others
NATIONAL ANTHEM (DATE) "Himno Nacional Argentino" (1813)

Stamp *celebrating the 50th anniversary of the Universal Declaration of Human Rights.*

ARMENIA

FLAG RATIO: 1:2 USE: National/Civil DATE ADOPTED: 1990 LAST MODIFIED: 1990

Armenia's flag is **tricolor**, comprised of **horizontal stripes** of **red**, **blue**, and **orange**. Red stands for the blood spilled by Armenians fighting for independence and religious freedom. **Blue** symbolizes the sky and hope for the future, and orange represents Armenia's fertile lands.

HISTORY

Armenia lies in the southern **Caucasus** Mountains. In 303 it became the first country to adopt **Christianity** as a state religion. From the 11th to the 15th century, the **Mongols** were the greatest power in the region. By the 16th century the **Ottoman Empire** controlled Armenia. In 1828 **Russia** gained Persian Armenia. During **World War I**, Armenia was a battleground for the Turkish and Russian armies. Turkish troops killed more than 600,000 Armenians, and deported 1.75 million people. In 1918 Russian Armenia became the **Armenian Autonomous Republic**, the western part remained part of Turkey, and the northwestern region became part of Iran. In 1922 Armenia, Azerbaijan, and Georgia federated to form the **Transcaucasian Soviet Socialist Republic**, one of the four original republics of the Soviet Union. In 1936 Armenia became a separate **republic. Earthquakes** in 1984 and 1988 killed more than 80,000 people. Armenia gained **independence** from the Soviet Union in 1990. In 1992 war broke out between Armenia and Azerbaijan over the Armenian enclave of Nagorno-Karabakh. Relations with Turkey and Azerbaijan thawed in the first decade of the 21st century.

AREA 11,500 sq mi (29,800 sq km)
POPULATION 2,968,000
CAPITAL Yerevan
GOVERNMENT Multiparty republic
ETHNIC GROUPS Armenian 93%,
Russian 2%, Azeri 1%, others (mostly
Kurds) 4%
LANGUAGES Armenian (official)
RELIGIONS Armenian Apostolic 94%
NATIONAL ANTHEM (DATE) "Mer Hayrenik"
"Our Fatherland" (1991)

Stamp *marking the millennium of Grigor Narekatsi's* "A Record of Lamentations."

AUSTRALIA

FLAG RATIO: 1:2 **USE:** National/Civil **DATE ADOPTED:** 1909 **LAST MODIFIED:** 1912

In 1901 the new federal nation of Australia held a competition to design a national flag. The **British "Union Jack"** flag in the top left corner reflects Australia's historic ties with Britain. The **"Star of Federation"** on the lower hoist has seven points, one point representing each of the six Australian states and one for its territories. On the right half of the flag is the kite-shaped constellation of the "**Southern Cross**" or Crux, which can be seen in the night sky above all States and territories. In 1995 the government gave legal recognition to the **Native Australian flag** and the **Torres Strait Islander flag**.

AREA 2,989,000 sq mi (7,741,000 sq km)
POPULATION 21,767,000
CAPITAL Canberra
GOVERNMENT Federal constitutional monarchy
ETHNIC GROUPS Caucasian 92%. Asian 7%. Aboriginal 1%
LANGUAGES English (official)
RELIGIONS Roman Catholic 26%, Anglican 26%, other Christian 24%, non-Christian 24%
NATIONAL MOTTO "Advance Australia"
NATIONAL ANTHEM (DATE) "Advance Australia Fair" (1984)

HISTORY

Native Australians (**Aborigines**) arrived from southeast Asia more than 50,000 years ago. They remained isolated from the world until the arrival of the first European explorers. In 1770 British explorer **Captain James Cook** reached Botany Bay and claimed the east coast for Great Britain. In 1788 Britain built its first settlement (for convicts), on the site of present-day **Sydney**. In 1901 the states of Queensland, Victoria, Tasmania, New South Wales, South Australia, and Western Australia united to form the **Commonwealth of Australia**. In 1911 Northern Territory joined the federation. In 1999 Australians narrowly voted against becoming a republic. Years of economically damaging drought ended in 2011 with widespread flooding in Queensland and New South Wales.

Stamp *marking the opening of the National Museum of Australia in 2001.*

AUSTRIA

FLAG RATIO: 2:3 USE: National DATE ADOPTED: 1919 LAST MODIFIED: 1984

Austria's flag dates to 1230. It derives from the seal of **Duke Frederick II**, the last **Babenberg** ruler of Austria (1230–46). According to legend, the first Babenberg ruler **Duke Leopold V** (r.1177–1194) received the **red-white-red** colors at the Battle of Ptolemais (1191), when his tunic became so blood-stained that the only white remaining was the band covered by his sword belt. At the center of the **state flag** is a **coat of arms**, derived from the **double-headed eagle** of the Hapsburg Empire. The crowned, one-headed eagle grasps a **hammer** and **sickle** in its talons. In 1945 the Second Republic added **broken chains** to the eagle's legs, symbolizing liberation from the shackles of Nazism.

HISTORY

Once part of the **Holy Roman Empire**, Austria united with Bohemia and Hungary in 1526. Under Hapsburg rule it was the greatest state in the Empire. The succession of **Maria Theresa** led to the **War of the Austrian Succession** (1740–48). Austrian power declined after the **Austro-Prussian War** (1866). The Austro-Hungarian Empire collapsed after World War I (1914–18) and the **First Republic** was born. In 1938 **Adolf Hitler unified** Germany and Austria. Defeat in World War II (1939–45) led to the creation of the Second Republic. In 1955 Austria became a **neutral** republic. In 1995 it joined the **European Union**.

***Austria** celebrated the 150th anniversary of its stamps in 2000.*

AREA 32,400 sq mi (83,900 sq km)
POPULATION 8,217,000
CAPITAL Vienna
GOVERNMENT Federal republic
ETHNIC GROUPS Austrian 90%, Croatian, Slovene, others
LANGUAGES German (official)
RELIGIONS Roman Catholic 78%, Protestant 5%, Islam and others 17%
NATIONAL ANTHEM (DATE) *"Land der Berge, Land am Strome"* "Land of Mountains, Land on the River" (1947)

31

AZERBAIJAN

FLAG RATIO: 1:2 **USE:** National/Civil **DATE ADOPTED:** 1991 **LAST MODIFIED:** 1991

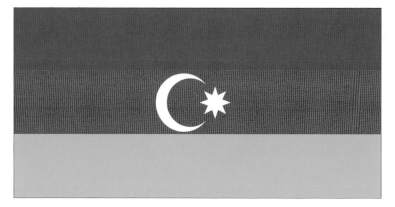

Azerbaijan's **tricolor** flag dates to 1918, the start of a brief period of independence before Russian occupation in 1920. In 1991 Azerbaijan regained independence and readopted the flag. The flag reflects the Azerbaijani motto. **Light blue** is a traditional Turkic color. At the center of the middle, red stripe is a **white crescent and star**, traditional symbols of **Islam**. The **star** has **eight points** to represent each of Azerbaijan's Turkic peoples. **Red** stands for modernity and progress. **Green** is a traditional color of Islam.

AREA 33,400 sq mi (86,600 sq km)

POPULATION 8,372,000

CAPITAL Baku

GOVERNMENT Federal multiparty republic

ETHNIC GROUPS Azeri 90%, Dagestani 3%, Russian, Armenian, others

LANGUAGES Azerbaijani (official),Russian, Armenian

RELIGIONS Islam 93%, Russian Orthodox 2%, Armenian Orthodox

NATIONAL MOTTO "Turkify, Islamize, and Europeanize"

NATIONAL ANTHEM (DATE) *"Azärbaycan Respublikasinin Dövlat Himni"* "Azerbaijani National Hymn" (1992)

HISTORY

Azerbaijan is the world's oldest center of **oil** production. In the late 7th century Arabs conquered the region, and Islam became the main religion. In the mid-11th century **Seljuk Turks** occupied present-day Azerbaijan. The **Mongols** ruled the region in the 13th century. In the 16th century the **Iranian Safavid dynasty** assumed control. By the early 19th century Azerbaijan formed part of the **Russian Empire**. In 1920 the Bolsheviks invaded the fledgling nation and, in 1922, Azerbaijan became part of the **Soviet Union**. In 1991, the Soviet Union collapsed and Azerbaijan gained **independence**. In 1992 war broke out between Azerbaijan and **Armenia** over **Nagorno-Karabakh**, an Armenian enclave within Azerbaijan.

Azerbaijan *stamp from 1992, showing a view of the Caspian Sea.*

BAHAMAS

FLAG RATIO: 1:2 USE: National DATE ADOPTED: 1973 LAST MODIFIED: 1973

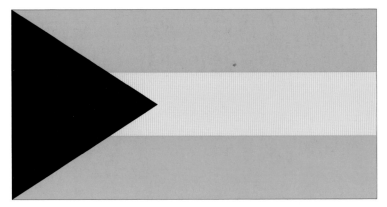

The Bahamian flag emerged from a combination of winning entries to a national competition in 1973. The central **gold stripe** recalls Bahama's sandy beaches, while the **aquamarine** bands represent the clear Atlantic waters that surround the Bahamas. The **black triangle** on the hoist side stands for the strength and pride of the Bahamians.

HISTORY

A popular tourist destination, the Bahamas consists of 700 islands in the West Indies, off the coast of southeast Florida. In 1492 Christopher Columbus landed on San Salvador island. He called the Atlantic waters "baja mar" (Spanish, "low sea"). The 40,000 native Lucayan Indians died within 25 years of Spain's arrival. In 1648 the English Puritan Eleutherian Adventurers built the first European settlement. In the 17th century, the islands became notorious for piracy. By 1783 Britain had full control of the Bahamas. The islands prospered on trade with the Confederacy during the American Civil War and smuggling alcohol during Prohibition. In 1964 the Bahamas gained self-government as a prelude to full independence in 1973. In 2004, **hurricanes Frances** and **Jeanne** caused widespread damage.

AREA 5,400 sq mi (13,900 sq km)

POPULATION 313,000

CAPITAL Nassau

GOVERNMENT Constitutional monarchy

ETHNIC GROUPS Black 85%, White 12%, Asian and Hispanic 3%

LANGUAGES English, Creole (among Haitian immigrants)

RELIGIONS Baptist 32%, Anglican 20%, Roman Catholic 19%, Methodist 6%, Church of God 6%, other Protestant 12%

MOTTO "Forward, Upward, Onward, Together"

NATIONAL ANTHEM (DATE) "March on, Bahamaland" (1973)

The flamingo is the national bird of the Bahamas.

33

BAHRAIN

FLAG RATIO: 3:5 USE: National/Civil DATE ADOPTED: 1933 LAST MODIFIED: 2002

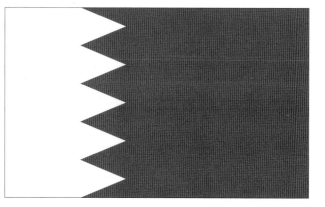

Bahrain's flag is **red** with a vertical, **serrated white** border on the hoist side. Red and white are traditional colors of the **Gulf States**. The **vertical white** stripe dates from the General Maritime Treaty with the British East India Company in 1820. The treaty sought to prevent piracy in the Persian (Arabian) Gulf, and the white stripe identified the friendly Arab States. In 1932 the stripe acquired a serrated edge to distinguish it from the flag of **Dubai**. The flag is identical to **Qatar**'s flag, except for the shade of red and the number of steps in the serration. Bahrain's flag has **five steps**, signifying the five Pillars of **Islam**.

HISTORY

Bahrain is an Emirate archipelago in the Persian Gulf. Bahrain has been **Arab** and Muslim since the Arab conquest in the 7th century. The **Khalifa** dynasty, a branch of the Bani Utbah tribe, has ruled the islands since 1783. In 1861 Bahrain became a **British Protectorate**. In 1932 Standard Oil made the first discovery of **oil** on the Arabian Peninsula in Bahrain. In **1971** Bahrain declared **independence** and **Sheikh Isa** became Emir. In 1999 Sheikh **Hamad bin Isa al-Khalifa** succeeded Isa, his father, as Emir. Tensions exist between the Sunni and the majority Shi'a populations. In 2002 Bahrain became a **constitutional monarchy** and held its first elections for 27 years. In 2011 widespread pro-democracy protests sparked a harsh government response.

AREA 270 sq mi (690 sq km)
POPULATION 1,215,000
CAPITAL Manama
GOVERNMENT Constitutional monarchy
ETHNIC GROUPS Bahraini 62%, others
LANGUAGES Arabic, English, Farsi, Urdu
RELIGIONS Muslim (Shi'a and Sunni) 81%, Christian 9%, other
NATIONAL ANTHEM (DATE) "*Bahrainona*" "Our Bahrain" (1971)

Bahrain *stamp marking the 21st Supreme Council of the Gulf Cooperation Council.*

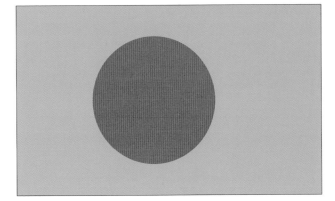

Bangladesh's flag is a simple **red disk** on a **green field**. Adopted following independence in 1971, the red disk represents the dawn of independence and commemorates the blood shed in the struggle for freedom. Green stands for the lush landscape of Bangladesh and is also traditionally associated with **Islam**, the country's principal religion. The red disk is set slightly toward the hoist of the flag so that when the flag is flying it appears central.

HISTORY

Bangladesh is the most densely populated country in the world (834 people per square kilometer). It is prone to flooding. Its early history is synonymous with that of Bengal. In 1576 Bengal became part of the vast Mogul Empire under Akbar I (the Great). In the late-18th century, the British East India Company assumed control of Bengal. In 1947 British India was partitioned between the mainly Hindu India and Muslim Pakistan. Present-day Bangladesh became the Pakistan province of East Bengal. In March 1971, the Awami League, led by Sheikh Mujibur Rahman, declared independence. More than 1 million East Bengalis died in the ensuing nine months of civil war. With Indian military aid, East Bengal defeated Pakistan and gained independence as Bangladesh. Political violence and terrorist attacks marked the early 21st century. Economic diversification remains a priority.

Nearly two-thirds of Bangladeshis work in the agricultural sector.

AREA 55,600 sq mi (144,000 sq km)
POPULATION 158,571,000
CAPITAL Dhaka
GOVERNMENT Multiparty republic
ETHNIC GROUPS Bengali 98%, tribal groups
LANGUAGES Bengali (official), English
RELIGIONS Islam 83%, Hinduism 16%
NATIONAL ANTHEM (DATE) *"Amar Sonar Bangla"* "My Golden Bengal" (1972)

BARBADOS

FLAG RATIO: 2:3   **USE:** National/Civil   **DATE ADOPTED:** 1966   **LAST MODIFIED:** 1966

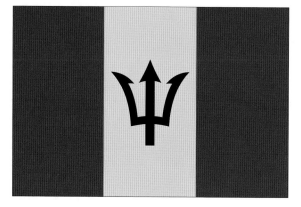

Barbados held a competition to design a national flag upon gaining independence in 1966. The flag has **three vertical stripes** (ultramarine-gold-ultramarine) and a **black trident** in the center of the middle gold band. The **two ultramarine** bands stand for the sky and the sea, the **gold** band represents the sun. Barbados' colonial flag, which featured the sea-god Neptune wielding a trident, inspired the symbol at the center of the new national flag. On the new flag the shaft of the trident is broken, symbolising the break with Britain at independence.

HISTORY

The **Windward Island** of Barbados is the easternmost island of the **West Indies**. The first European explorer, Portuguese navigator **Pedro Campos**, landed in 1536. Campos named the island *Los Barbados* (Portuguese, "bearded ones"), after its bearded fig trees. The Spanish enslaved the island's **Carib** population, which quickly died out. In 1627 **Britain** settled the island. The British used **slaves** from West Africa to work on the **sugar plantations**. In 1816 Bussa inspired a **slave revolt**. Britain finally abolished slavery in 1834. From 1958 to 1962 Barbados formed part of the Federation of the West Indies, led by Barbadian politician **Grantley Adams**. In 1961 Barbados gained **self-government**. In 1966 **Errol Barrow** led the nation to independence. **Owen Arthur** became prime minister in 1994 elections. Barbados is among the wealthiest Caribbean nations and has reserves of fossil fuels offshore.

AREA 170 sq mi (430 sq km)
POPULATION 287,000
CAPITAL Bridgetown
GOVERNMENT Parliamentary democracy
ETHNIC GROUPS African descent 96%, white 4%
LANGUAGES English
RELIGIONS Anglican 40%, Pentecostal 8%, Methodist 7%, other Protestant 12%, Roman Catholic 4%
NATIONAL ANTHEM (DATE) "National Anthem of Barbados" (1966)

In 1627 the William and John, *captained by William Powell, landed on Barbados.*

BELARUS

FLAG RATIO: 1:2 USE: National/Civil DATE ADOPTED: 1995 LAST MODIFIED: 1995

The current flag is almost identical to that of 1951–91, when Belarus was a Soviet republic. From 1991–95 Belarus had a white-red-white striped flag. In 1995 it readopted the **red** and **green** **horizontal stripes** of the Soviet-era flag, omitting the communist symbols and adding a **decorative white band** on the hoist to represent Belarus' cultural heritage. Red was the color of the standards of the Belarussian regiments that defeated the Teutonic Knights at the Battle of Tannenberg (1410) and of the Soviet Red Army and Belarusian guerrilla forces that fought fascism. Green symbolizes hope for the future and the fields and forests.

HISTORY

In 1529 the Grand Duchy of **Lithuania** recognized Belarus. Russia acquired Belarus in the **Partitions of Poland** (1772, 1793, 1795). In 1919 the Bolsheviks established the Belorussian Soviet Republic. **Poland** gained western Belorussia in the Treaty of Riga (1921). A quarter of Belarusians died under Nazi German occupation during World War II. Belarus achieved **independence** after the collapse of the Soviet Union in 1990. Repeated government landslides in elections, Alexander Lukashenko's autocratic rule and the country's poor human rights record led to international sanctions during the first decade of the 21st century. In 2011 Belarus received major loans from the International Monetary Fund.

Golden cross *of Saint Euphrosyne of Polotsk crafted in the 12th century.*

AREA 80,200 sq mi (208,000 sq km)
POPULATION 9,578,000
CAPITAL Minsk
GOVERNMENT Multiparty republic
ETHNIC GROUPS Belarusian 81%, Russian 11%, Polish, Ukrainian, others
LANGUAGES Belarusian, Russian (both official)
RELIGIONS Eastern Orthodox 80%, others 20%
NATIONAL ANTHEM (DATE) *"Maladaya Belarus"* "Young Belarus" (1955)

BELGIUM

FLAG RATIO: 13:15 USE: National/Civil DATE ADOPTED: 1831 LAST MODIFIED: 1831

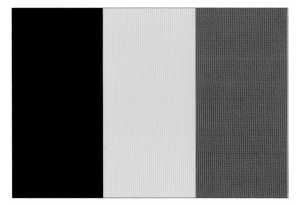

The colors of Belgium's flag date back to the 13th-century seal of Count Philip of Flanders, which featured a **black** lion on a **gold** field. In 1234 the Duchy of Brabant's flag consisted of a gold lion with **red** tongue and claws set against a black background. Rebels displayed the colors in the failed Brabant Revolt (1787–89) against Austrian rule. In 1830 revolutionaries raised the colors in a successful rebellion against the rule of William I of the Netherlands. In 1831 Belgium adopted its present flag, with the arrangement of the colors based on the French *tricolore*.

HISTORY

From 1363 to 1467 the **Dukes of** **Burgundy** ruled the Low Countries. In 1585 the southern **Spanish Netherlands** (now Belgium) separated from the northern United Provinces of the **Netherlands**. After the War of the Spanish Succession (1701–14) the Spanish Netherlands became the **Austrian Netherlands**. The French Revolutionary Wars resulted in the united **Kingdom of the Netherlands** in 1815. Dutch discrimination led to rebellion and Belgium declared **independence** in 1830. In August 1914, **Germany** invaded Belgium, prompting British entry into World War I. Germany captured Belgium in World War II. In 1989 Wallonia, Flanders and Brussels gained regional autonomy, but tensions between the Flemish and Walloon communities continued to cause political instability.

AREA 11,800 sq mi (30,500 sq km)
POPULATION 10,431,000
CAPITAL Brussels
GOVERNMENT 8sq km [11,787sq mi]
ETHNIC GROUPS Belgian 89% (Fleming 58%, Walloon 31%), others
LANGUAGES Dutch, French, German(all official)
RELIGIONS Roman Catholic 75%, others 25%
NATIONAL MOTTO *"Union fait la force"* or *"Eendracht maakt"* "Strength Lies In Unity"
NATIONAL ANTHEM (DATE) *"La Brabançonne"* "The Brabant Song" (1938)

Belgium *has been famous for producing luxury chocolate since the 17th century.*

At the center of Belize's flag is a white disk featuring the **coat of arms**. The **tripartite shield** contains **tools** and **products** of the timber trade. Above the shield grows a **mahogany tree**. Beside the shield stand **two woodcutters**, representing the nation's two main ethnic groups. A ring of **50 laurel leaves** surrounds the disk, marking 1950, the start of the liberation struggle. Belize's motto appears below the shield. The motto refers to Belize's former dependence on Britain. In 1981 a national committee chose a design that added **red stripes** to the top and bottom of the **royal blue** field.

HISTORY

Between *c*. 300 BC and AD 1000, Belize was part of the Maya Empire. In c. 1638 shipwrecked British sailors founded the first European settlement. Although the region was subject to regular Spanish incursions, Britain gradually took control of what became known as British Honduras. The British used slave labor for logging and on the sugar plantations. In 1871 British Honduras became a British Crown Colony. In 1950 currency devaluation prompted the birth of the People's United Party (PUP). Renamed Belize in 1973, the country gained independence in 1981. British troops stayed to prevent possible invasion by Guatemala, leaving in 1992. Unemployment and the drugs trade are major problems.

Belize has 300 species of orchid, including this Maxillaria elatior.

AREA 8,900 sq mi (23,000 sq km)
POPULATION 321,000
CAPITAL Belmopan
GOVERNMENT Constitutional monarchy
ETHNIC GROUPS Mestizo 49%, Creole 25%, Mayan Indian 11%, Garifuna 6%, others 9%
LANGUAGES English (official), Spanish, Creole
RELIGIONS Roman Catholic 50%, Protestant 27%, others
NATIONAL MOTTO *"Sub Umbra Florero"* "I Flourish in the Shadow"
NATIONAL ANTHEM (DATE) "Land of the Free" (1981)

BENIN

FLAG RATIO: 2:3 USE: National/Civil DATE ADOPTED: 1959 REINTRODUCED: 1990

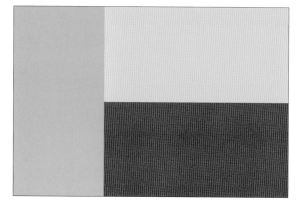

B enin, then called Dahomey, adopted its current flag in 1959. In 1975 Dahomey became the People's Republic of Benin and acquired a new flag, consisting of a green star against a red field. In 1990 Benin introduced a new constitution and reverted to the previous flag. Red, yellow and green are colors of the **Pan-African** movement and thus symbolize African unity. In addition, **green** stands for the palm groves in southern Benin. The **yellow** represents the savannahs in the north, while **red** signifies the blood shed in the struggle for independence.

HISTORY

Benin is one of Africa's smallest nations.

AREA 43,500 sq mi (113,000 sq km)
POPULATION 9,325,000
CAPITAL Porto-Novo
GOVERNMENT Multiparty republic
ETHNIC GROUPS Fon, Adja, Bariba, Yoruba, Fulani
LANGUAGES French (official), Fon, Adja, Yoruba
RELIGIONS Traditional beliefs 50%, Christianity 30%, Islam 20%
NATIONAL MOTTO *"Fraternité, Justice, Travail"* "Brotherhood, Justice, Work"
NATIONAL ANTHEM (DATE) *"L'Aube Nouvelle"* "The Dawn of a New Day" (1960)

The ancient Kingdom of **Dahomey** had its capital at **Abomey**, in what is now southern Benin. In the 17th century, the Kings of Dahomey became involved in the lucrative **slave trade**, and by 1700 more than 200,000 slaves were transported annually from the "**Slave Coast**." Despite British abolition in 1834, slavery persisted well into the 19th century. By 1894 France had conquered Dahomey. In 1904 it became part of the huge Federation of **French West Africa**. In 1958 Dahomey achieved self-government as a prelude to full **independence** in 1960. In 1972 General **Mathieu Kérékou** seized power in a military coup. In 1975 Dahomey became the **People's Republic of Benin** and adopted Marxism-Leninism as the state ideology. In 1990 Benin abandoned communism in favor of multiparty democracy.

Dugout canoes *deliver mail to some rural areas of Benin.*

FLAG RATIO: 2:3 USE: National/Civil DATE ADOPTED: 1969 LAST MODIFIED: 1969

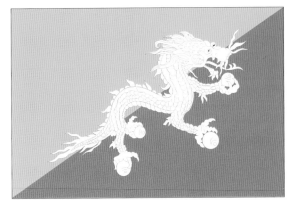

The Bhutanese often call their country *Druk Yul* ("Land of the Thunder Dragon"). The **dragon** used on the national flag dates to the 17th-century introduction of the Drukpa Kagyu school of Tantric Mahayana Buddhism. The **jewels** in the dragon's claws represent Bhutan's wealth. The **white** of the dragon symbolizes purity. The ground is divided diagonally into **gold** and **orange** triangles. Gold represents the secular power of the *Druk Gyalpo* ("Dragon King"), and **orange** the spiritual power of Buddhism.

HISTORY

In 1616 the Buddhist monk **Ngawang Namgyal** unified Bhutan and established Drukpa Kagyu as the state religion. He also founded a dual system of government (temporal and theocratic), which lasted until 1907. Villages developed around the *dzong* (castle-monastery). The *Tashichho Dzong* ("Monastery of Auspicious Religion") in Thimphu is the seat of government. War with Britain led to the British annexation of southern Bhutan in 1865. In 1907, with British support, **Ugyen Wangchuck** became the first **hereditary monarch** of Bhutan. In 1968 King **Jigme Dorji Wangchuk** (r.1952–72) abolished slavery. Bhutan joined the United Nations (UN) in 1971. In the 1990s racial tension forced nearly 100,000 ethnic **Nepalese** into refugee camps in Nepal. **Jigme Khesar Namguel Wanchuck** succeeded his father as king in 2006.

AREA 18,100 sq mi (47,000 sq km)
POPULATION 708,000
CAPITAL Thimphu
GOVERNMENT Constitutional monarchy
ETHNIC GROUPS Bhutanese 50%, Nepalese 35%
LANGUAGES Dzongkha (official), Bhotes speak various Tibetan dialects, Nepalese speak various Nepalese dialects
RELIGIONS Buddhism 75%, Hinduism 25%
NATIONAL ANTHEM (DATE) "Druk Tsendhen" "Thunder-Dragon Kingdom" (1953)

"Four Friends" (elephant, monkey, rabbit, bird) is a popular Bhutanese folk tale.

BOLIVIA

FLAG RATIO: 2:3   USE: National   DATE ADOPTED: 1851   CODIFIED: 1888

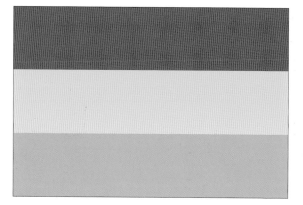

The colors on the Bolivian flag are traditional colors of the Aymará and Quechua peoples. In 1826, after gaining independence from Spain, Bolivia adopted a **tricolor** flag with **horizontal stripes** of (from the top) **yellow**, **red** and **green**. In 1851 Bolivia reversed the positions of the yellow and red stripes. Red represents the blood shed in the liberation struggle. Yellow symbolizes its mineral wealth. **Green** stands for the fertile land and agricultural wealth. The **state flag** has the coat of arms at the center.

HISTORY

Bolivia was home to one of the great **pre-Colombian** civilizations. Before the **Spanish** invasion in 1532, the **Quechua** had subsumed the **Aymará** into the **Inca Empire**. Spain exploited the Andean silver mines with native forced-labor. In 1824 **Antonio José de Sucre**, **Simon Bolívar's** general, liberated the country. **War** with Paraguay (1932–35) cost *c.* 100,000 lives. **Victor Paz Estenssoro** of the National Revolutionary Movement (MNR) was president for much of the late 20th century (1952–56, 1960–64, 1985–89, 2001). In 1952 he nationalized the **mines**. In 1964 a military coup toppled Paz's government. From 1964 to 1982, military dictators, most notably Colonel **Hugo Banzer Suárez** (1971–78), ruled Bolivia. Violent protests over the fuel policies of successive governments marked the early 21st century.

AREA 424,000 sq mi (1,099,000 sq km)
POPULATION 10,119,000
CAPITAL La Paz/Sucre
GOVERNMENT Multiparty republic
ETHNIC GROUPS Mestizo 30%, Quechua 30%, Aymara 25%, White 15%
LANGUAGES 8,581sq km [424,162sq mi]
RELIGIONS Roman Catholic 95%
NATIONAL ANTHEM (DATE) *"Himno Nacional"* "National Hymn" (1842)

Centennial stamp *featuring the Andean condor, Bolivia's national symbol.*

BOSNIA-HERZEGOVINA

FLAG RATIO: 1:2 USE: National/Civil DATE ADOPTED: 1998 LAST MODIFIED: 1998

In 1998 Bosnia-Herzegovina adopted a new flag because Croats and Serbs argued that the previous flag was synonymous with the wartime Muslim regime. The **blue background** and **white stars** derive from the flag of the **European Union**, while the **yellow triangle** stands for equality between the three main ethnic groups within Bosnia.

HISTORY

Bosnia-Herzegovina is one of five republics that emerged from the breakup of the former **Yugoslavia**. In 1946 Bosnia-Herzegovina became a constituent republic of **Tito**'s socialist federal republic. In 1991 the republic disintegrated with the secession of Croatia, Slovenia, and Macedonia. Fearing the creation of a Greater Serbia, Croats and Muslims pushed for independence. In March 1992 a referendum, boycotted by Serbian parties, voted for **independence**. **Alija Izetbegović** became president of the new nation. **War** broke out between Bosnian government forces and the Serb-dominated **Federal Yugoslav Army (JNA)**. Bosnian Serbs established a separate Serb republic led by **Radovan Karadžić** (1992). Serbs forced Muslims from their villages in a deliberate act of "**ethnic cleansing**." The three-year conflict claimed more than 200,000 lives. The **Dayton Peace Accord** (1995) preserved Bosnia-Herzegovina as a single state, but partitioned it between the Muslim-Croat Federation and Bosnian Serbs (**Republika Srpska**). Bosnia has a **tripartite**, ethnically based presidency.

Bosnian stamp *featuring Croat folk attire from the region of Kraljeva Sutjeska.*

AREA 19,800 sq mi (51,200 sq km)
POPULATION 4,622,000
CAPITAL Sarajevo
GOVERNMENT Federal republic
ETHNIC GROUPS km [19,767sq mi]
LANGUAGES Bosnian, Serbian, Croatian
RELIGIONS Islam 40%, Serbian Orthodox 31%, Roman Catholic 15%, others 14
NATIONAL ANTHEM (DATE) *"Hymna Republica Bosnia in Herzogovina"* (1999)

43

BOTSWANA

FLAG RATIO: 2:3 USE: National DATE ADOPTED: 1966 LAST MODIFIED: 1966

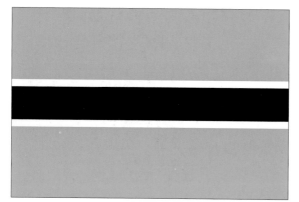

Botswana adopted its present national flag upon independence in 1966. The **white-black-white stripes** at the center of the flag signify racial harmony. The colors are also symbolic of the zebra, Botswana's national animal. The **blue bands** symbolize water, vitally important to the arid land of Botswana.

HISTORY

The cattle-owning **Tswana**, modern Botswana's majority population, first settled in eastern Botswana more than 1000 years ago. The Tswana gradually forced the native **San** (Bushmen) into the **Kalahari Desert**. In 1885 Britain made the **Bechuanaland Protectorate** to prevent incursions by Afrikaners and discourage German colonialism. In 1966 Bechuanaland achieved **independence** as **Botswana**. One of the "front-line states," Botswana provided a haven for refugees from South Africa's **apartheid** government. Botswana is a stable multiparty democracy. It is the world's largest exporter of gem-quality diamonds. Botswana has one of the world's highest rates of **HIV** infection; before stringent health measures were adopted more than one-third of adults had HIV. Economic and political crisis in Zimbabwe has led to an influx of economic migrants.

AREA 225,000 sq mi (582,000 sq km)
POPULATION 2,065,000
CAPITAL Gaborone
GOVERNMENT Multiparty republic
ETHNIC GROUPS Tswana (or Setswana) 79%, Kalanga 11%, Basarwa 3%, others
LANGUAGES English (official), Setswana
RELIGIONS Traditional beliefs 85%, Christianity 15%
NATIONAL MOTTO *"Pula"* "Let there be rain"
NATIONAL ANTHEM (DATE) *"Fatshe la Rona"* "Our Country" (1966)

Northwest Botswana is famous for its basket weaving, using the mokola palm tree.

In the 19th century, Brazil adopted green and yellow as national colors to symbolize the union of the House of Bragança with the House of Hapsburg. The **yellow diamond** on a **green field** became the national flag upon independence in 1882. In 1889 the government added the **blue disk** and **motto**. The blue disk represents the sky over Rio de Janeiro on the night of independence and includes the constellation of the **Southern Cross**. There are **27 stars**, one for the capital and one for each State. The **green** of the modern flag represents the rain forests, while **yellow** stands for gold and mineral wealth.

HISTORY

In 1500 explorer **Pedro Alvarez Cabral** claimed Brazil for **Portugal**. Portugal employed Native Americans and *c*. 4 mil-lion African **slaves** to work on the sugar plantations and in the mines. In 1807 **Napoleon**'s invasion of Portugal led King John VI to flee to Brazil. In 1822 he returned to Portugal, and his son **Pedro I** declared Brazil an **independent Empire**. In a bloodless revolution (1889), Brazil became a **republic** and Marshal **Manuel Deodoro da Fonseca** became the first president. In 1964 the military seized power, maintaining control through torture and death squads. Civilian government returned in 1985. Rapid economic growth has led Brazil to be one of the world's ten largest economies.

AREA 3,287,000 sq mi (8,514,000 sq km)

POPULATION 203,430,000

CAPITAL Brasília

GOVERNMENT Federal republic

ETHNIC GROUPS White 55%, Mulatto 38%, Black 6%, others 1%

LANGUAGES Portuguese (official), Spanish, English, French

RELIGIONS Roman Catholic 80%, Protestant, African/syncretist

MOTTO *"Ordem e Progresso"* "Order and Progress"

NATIONAL ANTHEM (DATE) *"Hino Nacional do Brasil"* "National Anthem of Brazil" (1922)

The azure jay (gralha azul) is the State bird of Paraná, southern Brazil.

BRUNEI DARUSSALAM

FLAG RATIO: 1:2 **USE:** National/Civil **DATE ADOPTED:** 1906 **LAST MODIFIED:** 1959

In 1906 Brunei became a British dependency and added two **diagonal stripes** to the previously all-yellow flag. The **yellow** represents the Sultan of Brunei, while the **white** and **black** stripes denote his two chief ministers. The constitution of 1959 added the **red coat of arms** to the flag. The crest has a parasol, wings, hands, and crescent. The **parasol** is a national symbol for royalty. The **wing** has four feathers, symbolizing the protection of justice, tranquillity, prosperity and peace. The **hands** signify the government's pledge to promote welfare, peace and prosperity. The **crescent** is a traditional symbol of **Islam**. Written in **yellow Arabic script** on the crescent is the national motto, "Always Render Service by God's Guidance." The **scroll** beneath the crest reads "*Brunei Darussalam*" ("Brunei, the abode of peace").

HISTORY

During the 16th century, Brunei was the seat of a powerful **Sultanate** that ruled over the whole of **Borneo** and parts of the Philippines. In 1888 Brunei became a **British Protectorate. Omar Ali Saifuddin** was succeeded as Sultan by his son **Hassanal Bolikiah** in 1967. In 1984 Brunei gained **independence**.

AREA 2,200 sq mi (5,800 sq km)
POPULATION 395,000
CAPITAL Bandar Seri Begawan
GOVERNMENT Multiparty republic
ETHNIC GROUPS Fang 20%, Bamileke and Bamum 19%, Duala, Luanda and Basa 15%, Fulani 10%
LANGUAGES French and English (both official), many others
RELIGIONS Christianity 40%, traditional beliefs 40%, Islam 20%
NATIONAL MOTTO *"Paix, Travail, Patrie"* "Peace, Work, Fatherland"
NATIONAL ANTHEM (DATE) *"Chant da Ralliement"* "Rallying Song" (1957)

Brunei *stamp celebrating the opening of the Malay Technology Museum in 1988.*

BULGARIA

FLAG RATIO: 3:5 USE: National/Civil DATE ADOPTED: 1879 REINTRODUCED: 1990

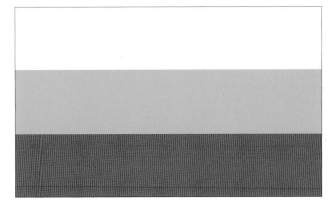

Bulgaria is the only Slavic nation to have **white**, **green** and **red** as its national colors rather than the Pan-Slavic colors of blue, white and red. Bulgaria adopted the **tricolor** flag of **horizontal stripes** in 1879. In 1947 Bulgaria's communist government added socialist symbols such as a red star to the coat of arms (a rampant golden lion), which it placed on the upper hoist of the flag. In 1990, after the collapse of the communist regime, the old flag returned. White stands for peace, love and freedom. Green represents agriculture. Red symbolizes the fight for independence.

HISTORY

The first Bulgarian Empire (681–1018) was a major power in the **Balkans**. In 1018 Basil II annexed it to the **Byzantine Empire**. A second Bulgarian Empire (1186–1396) encompassed the whole of the Balkans before it fell to the **Ottoman Empire**. The crushing of a Bulgar rebellion (1876) brought **Russian** assistance, and Bulgaria gained **autonomy** in 1879. In 1908 Czar Ferdinand declared Bulgaria an **independent monarchy**. It allied with Nazi Germany in **World War II**. In 1944 the **Soviet** army overran Bulgaria. From 1954 to 1989 **Todor Zhivkov** led a communist government. Bulgaria joined the **European Union** in 2007.

Stamp *featuring a painting by the Bulgarian modern artist Tzanko Lavrenov.*

AREA 42,800 sq mi (111,000 sq km)
POPULATION 7,149,000
CAPITAL Sofia
GOVERNMENT Multiparty republic
ETHNIC GROUPS Bulgarian 84%, Turkish 9%, Gypsy 5%, Macedonian, Armenian, others
LANGUAGES Bulgarian (official), Turkish
RELIGIONS Bulgarian Orthodox 83%, Islam 12%, Roman Catholic 2%, others
NATIONAL MOTTO *"Obedinenieto Pravi Silno"* "Unity is Strength"
NATIONAL ANTHEM (DATE) *"Mila Rodino"* "Dear Native Land" (1964)

BURKINA FASO

FLAG RATIO: 2:3 **USE:** National/Civil **ADOPTED:** 1984 **ESTABLISHED BY LAW:** 1997

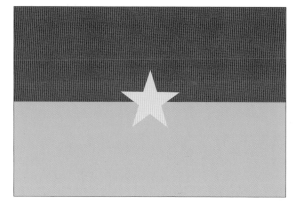

In 1984 **Upper Volta** was renamed Burkina Faso ("Land of the Incorruptible"). It adopted a new flag with **Pan-African** colors to celebrate the break from its colonial past and to champion unity among African nations. The upper, **red horizontal band** represents the blood shed in the liberation struggle. The **green horizontal band** symbolizes Burkina Faso's fertile agricultural land. The central **yellow five-pointed star** represents the nation's revolutionary ideals.

HISTORY

From *c*. 1100 the **Mossi** migrated north to what is now Burkina Faso. They established small, highly complex kingdoms.

The Moro Naba, an absolute monarch, ruled the state of **Ougadougou**, which defeated invasions by the mighty **Songhai Empire**. By 1897 **France** had conquered virtually the whole of Burkina Faso. In 1919 it became the French **colony** of Upper Volta. In 1958 Upper Volta became an autonomous republic – a prelude to full **independence** in 1960. In 1966 General **Sengoulé Lamizana** led a successful military coup against the elected government. Lamizana dominated the politics of Upper Volta until his overthrow in 1980. In 1983 **Thomas Sankara** seized office. **Blaise Campaoré** captured power after Sankara's assassination in 1987. Campaoré won elections in 1992, 1998, 2005, and 2010.

AREA 106,000 sq mi (274,000 sq km)
POPULATION 16,751,000
CAPITAL Ouagadougou
GOVERNMENT Multiparty republic
ETHNIC GROUPS Mossi 40%, Gurunsi, Senufo, Lobi, Bobo, Mande, Fulani
LANGUAGES French (official), Mossi, Fulani
RELIGIONS Islam 50%, traditional beliefs 40%, Christianity 10%
NATIONAL MOTTO *"Unité, Progrès, Justice"* "Unity, Progress, Justice"
NATIONAL ANTHEM (DATE) *"Ditanyé"* "Hymn of Victory" (1984)

Burkinabe *stamp celebrating International Women's Day.*

BURMA (MYANMAR)

FLAG RATIO: 2:3   USE: National/Civil   DATE ADOPTED: 2010   LAST MODIFIED: 2010

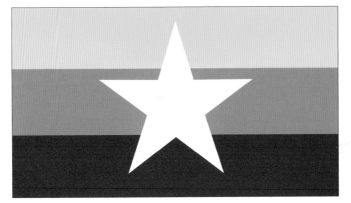

Burma's flag is a horizontal tricolor of **yellow**, **green**, and **red** stripes with a **white five-pointed star**. Yellow indicates solidarity, green tranquility, peace, and lush greenery, and red courage and determination. The flag is similar to that used under Japanese occupation, but with the star symbolizing the union of Myanmar replacing the royal peacock.

HISTORY

Conflict between the **Burmans** and **Mons** dominated Burma's early history and with **British India** the 19th century. In the first war (1824) Britain gained the coastal areas of Tenasserim and Arakan, in the second it acquired the **Irrawaddy** delta (1852), and in the third (1885) it took Burma. In 1942 Japan conquered Burma. **Aung San** led resistance to Japanese control. In 1947 he was murdered. Burma achieved **independence** in 1948. **U Nu** was the first prime minister. The military dictatorship of General **Ne Win** ruled Burma from 1962 to 1988. In 1989 Burma changed its name to the **Union of Myanmar**. The National League for Democracy (NLD) led by Aung San Suu Kyi won elections in 1990, but the military annulled the result. The country was renamed the Republic of the Union of Myanmar after a constitutional referendum in 2008. After more reforms, the NLD won most parliamentary seats available in byelections in 2012.

UNION OF MYANMAR

Golden lions flank the human pyramid set against the outline of Burma.

AREA 261,000 sq mi (677,000 sq km)
POPULATION 53,414,000
CAPITAL Rangoon/Naypyidaw
GOVERNMENT Unitary constitutional presidential republic
ETHNIC GROUPS Burman 68%, Shan 9%, Karen 7%, Rakhine 4%, Chinese, Indian, Mon
LANGUAGES Burmese (official), minority ethnic groups have their own languages
RELIGIONS Buddhism 89%, Christianity, Islam
NATIONAL ANTHEM (DATE) *"Gby majay Bma pyay"* "We shall always love Burma" (1948)

BURUNDI

FLAG RATIO: 3:5   **USE:** National/Civil   **DATE ADOPTED:** 1967   **LAST MODIFIED:** 1982

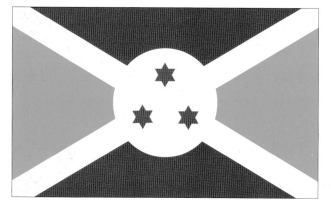

B urundi adopted its present flag after becoming a republic in 1967. In 1982 it altered the **ratio** from 2:3 to 3:5. A **white diagonal cross** divides the flag. A central **disk** contains **three red stars**, each representing an element of the national motto "*Unité, Travail, Progrès*," and also each of the three main ethnic groups in Burundi. The **red** symbolizes the blood shed in the fight for independence. **Green** stands for hope, while the **white** cross and disk signify peace.

HISTORY

About 1000 years ago, Bantu-speaking **Hutus** began to settle in the area. From the 15th century the **Tutsi**, a tall, cattle-owning people, gradually gained control. The Tutsi forced the Hutu majority into serfdom. In the 1890s **Germany** conquered the region. In 1916 **Belgium** occupied what was known as **Ruanda-Urundi**. In 1962 Burundi gained **independence**, ruled by a Tutsi king. In 1966 a **republic** was established. An attempted coup led to the creation of a **one-party state** in 1969. A Hutu president, **Melchior Ndadaye**, became president in 1993 multi-party elections. Ndadaye was assassinated in a military coup. Two months of **civil war** killed more than 50,000 people and created 500,000 refugees, mainly Hutus. In 1994 President Cyprien Ntaryamira died in an attack and **genocide** continued. In 1996 the Tutsi army seized power. A power-sharing government was set up in 2001 and elections took place in 2005.

AREA 10,700 sq mi (27,800 sq km)
POPULATION 10,216,000
CAPITAL Bujumbura
GOVERNMENT Republic
ETHNIC GROUPS Hutu 85%, Tutsi 14%, Twa (Pygmy)
LANGUAGES French, Kirundi (both official)
RELIGIONS Roman Catholic 62%, traditional beliefs 23%, Islam 10%, Protestant 5%
NATIONAL MOTTO *"Unité, Travail, Progrès"* "Unity, Work, Progress"
NATIONAL ANTHEM (DATE) *"Uburundi Bwacu"* "Beloved Burundi" (1962)

On July 1, 1962, *Burundi gained independence under King Mwambutsa IV.*

CAMBODIA

FLAG RATIO: 2:3 USE: National/Civil DATE ADOPTED: 1948 REINTRODUCED: 1993

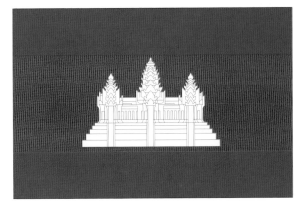

Cambodia adopted the present national flag in 1948. In 1970 the **Khmer** introduced a new flag with three white stars. In 1993 the monarchy and old flag were restored. The central emblem, a stylized representation of the temple of **Angkor Wat** has been a symbol of the Khmer monarchy since the 19th century. **Red** is the traditional color of Cambodia. The **blue** is said to represent the wealth of the land. The flag reflects the Khmer royal motto of "Nation, Religion, King."

HISTORY

The **Angkor period** (889–1434) was the "golden age" of Khmer civilization. In 1434 the **Thai** captured Angkor and the capital moved to **Phnom Penh**. In 1887 Cambodia became part of the French Union of **Indochina**. Japan occupied it during World War II. In 1953 Cambodia gained **independence** and **Norodom Sihanouk** became King. The **Vietnam War** (1954–75) dominated Cambodian politics. In 1970 Lon Nol overthrew Norodom and US and South Vietnamese troops entered Cambodia and provoked civil war. In 1975 the **Khmer Rouge** seized control and renamed the country **Kampuchea**. They killed between 1 and 4 million people, before being overthrown in 1979. After years of civil war, a peace agreement was signed and democratic reforms followed national elections in 1993. The first multiparty elections took place in 2002. Sihanouk abdicated in 2004 in favor of his son, Norodom Sihamoni.

Khmer dancers at the temple mountain of Bayon, built at Angkor by Jayavarman VII.

AREA 69,900 sq mi (181,000 sq km)
POPULATION 14,702,000
CAPITAL Phnom Penh
GOVERNMENT Constitutional monarchy
ETHNIC GROUPS Khmer 90%, Vietnamese 5%, Chinese 1%, others
LANGUAGES Khmer (official), French, English
RELIGIONS Buddhism 95%, others 5%
NATIONAL MOTTO "Nation, Religion, King"
NATIONAL ANTHEM (DATE) *"Nokoreach"* (1941, restored 1993)

51

CAMEROON

FLAG RATIO: 2:3   **USE:** National/Civil   **DATE ADOPTED:** 1975   **LAST MODIFIED:** 1975

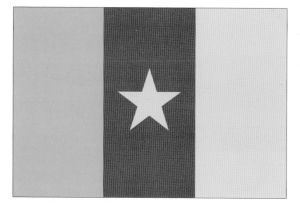

Cameroon's tricolor flag uses the Pan-African colors of **red**, **green**, and **yellow**. They represent freedom from colonialism and a united Africa. The colors also represent the vegetation of the south (green) and the savannahs of the north (yellow). Red stands for union and freedom. In 1975 a **five-pointed yellow star** replaced the two stars that had been on the flag's green stripe since 1961. The star stands for national unity.

HISTORY

In 1472 **Portuguese** explorers reached the coast. Cameroon gets its name from the explorers, who fished for *camarões* (prawns). From the 17th century, southern Cameroon was a center of the **slave trade**. In the early 19th century, Britain abolished slavery and established the **ivory** trade. After World War I, Cameroon divided into two zones, ruled by **Britain** and **France**. In 1960, following civil unrest, **French Cameroon** gained **independence**. In 1961 **northern British Cameroon** voted to join French Cameroon, forming the Federal Republic of Cameroon. **Ahmadou Ahidjo** served as president from 1960 to 1982. In 1966 Cameroon became a one-party state. In 1972 the federation became a unitary state. In 1984 **Paul Biya** made Cameroon a republic. In 1995 Cameroon joined the **Commonwealth of Nations**.

AREA 184,000 sq mi (475,000 sq km)

POPULATION 19,711,000

CAPITAL Yaoundé

GOVERNMENT Multiparty republic

ETHNIC GROUPS Cameroon Highlanders 31%, Bantu 27%, Kirdi 11%, Fulani 10%, others

LANGUAGES French and English (both official), many others

RELIGIONS Christianity 40%, traditional beliefs 40%, Islam 20%

NATIONAL MOTTO *"Paix, Travail, Patrie"* "Peace, Work, Fatherland"

NATIONAL ANTHEM (DATE) *"Chant da Ralliement"* "Rallying Song" (1957)

Cacao, grown mainly in the south and center, is Cameroon's major cash crop.

CANADA

FLAG RATIO: 1:2   USE: National/Civil   DATE ADOPTED: 1965   LAST MODIFIED: 1965

In 1965 Canada raised its **red** and **white** flag with a central, stylized **11-pointed red maple leaf** as the national flag. It replaced the Canadian Red Ensign, which featured the British Union Flag and Canada's coat of arms on a red field. The new flag sought to promote unity among Canadians. The maple leaf has been a national symbol since 1860. In 1921 King George VI proclaimed red and white as Canada's national colors and added the maple leaf to its coat of arms in recognition of Canadian sacrifice in World War I.

HISTORY

Ancestors of today's **Native Americans** arrived from Asia *c*. 20,000 years ago. In the 10th century, **Vikings** landed. In 1534 explorer **Jacques Cartier** claimed the region for **France**. The French established the first European settlement in 1605, and founded **Québec** in 1608. In 1759 Britain captured Québec, and gained French Canada at the end of the **French and Indian War** (1754–63). Canada remained loyal to Britain during the American Revolution (1775–83). The British North America Act (1867) established the Dominion of Canada. In 1982 **Pierre Trudeau** passed the Canada Act making it a sovereign nation. In 1999, the territory of Nunavut was formed in the north-west, and in 2006 parliamentary agreement was reached in favor of considering the Quebecois a "nation within Canada."

AREA 3,850,000 sq mi (9,971,000 sq km)
POPULATION 34,031,000
CAPITAL Ottawa
GOVERNMENT Federal multiparty constitutional monarchy
ETHNIC GROUPS British origin 28%, French origin 23%, other European 15%, Amerindian/Inuit 2%, others
LANGUAGES English and French (both official)
RELIGIONS Roman Catholic 46%, Protestant 36%, Judaism, Islam, Hinduism
NATIONAL MOTTO *"Mare usque ad mare"* "From sea to sea"
NATIONAL ANTHEM (DATE) "O Canada" (1980)

The Great Peace of Montréal *(1701) ended the Iroquois Wars with the French.*

53

CAPE VERDE

FLAG RATIO: Not fixed   USE: National/Civil   DATE ADOPTED: 1992   LAST MODIFIED: 1992

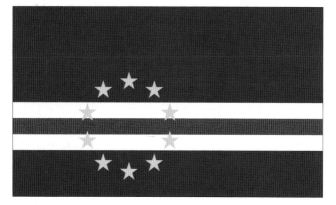

In 1992 Cape Verde, off the west coast of Africa, finally abandoned attempts to unite with Guinea-Bissau and adopted a new national flag. The **blue**, **white** and **red striped** flag replaced the design that had been in use since independence in 1975, and which was almost identical to the flag of Guinea-Bissau. Both were based on the flag of the *Partido Africano da Independência da Guiné e Cabo Verde* (PAIGC), which led the struggle for independence, and used the Pan-African colors. The blue symbolizes the sea and sky. The **ten, yellow five-pointed stars** represents each of Cape Verde's ten main islands. The **circle** stands for the unity of Cape Verde. White signifies peace, and red denotes national effort.

HISTORY

In 1462 **Portugal** began to settle the uninhabited islands of Cape Verde. The Portuguese imported **slaves** from west Africa to work on sugar plantations, and the islands prospered as a staging post in the Atlantic slave trade. In the 19th century, the abolition of slavery and persistent drought brought economic collapse and starvation. In 1956 the Cape Verdean **Amilcar Cabral** cofounded the PAIGC, which fought against Portuguese colonialism from Portuguese Guinea (now **Guinea-Bissau**). In 1975 Cape Verde gained **independence**. The first free elections were held in 1991 and a democratic constitution introduced in 1992.

AREA 1,600 sq mi (4,000 sq km)

POPULATION 516,000

CAPITAL Praia

GOVERNMENT Multiparty republic

ETHNIC GROUPS Creole (mulatto) 71%, African 28%, European 1%

LANGUAGES Portuguese, Crioulo (a blend of Portuguese and West African)

RELIGIONS Roman Catholic (infused with indigenous beliefs) 95%, Protestant (mostly Church of the Nazarene) 5%

NATIONAL ANTHEM (DATE) "*Cântico da Liberdade*" "Song of Liberty" (1975)

In 1898 Mindelo, on São Vicente island, was the world's fourth largest coaling station.

CENTRAL AFRICAN REPUBLIC

FLAG RATIO: 3:5 USE: National/Civil DATE ADOPTED: 1958 LAST MODIFIED: 1958

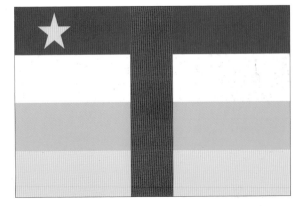

In 1958 the Central African Republic became a self-governing republic within the French Community and adopted its present flag. By combining the **yellow**, **green** and **red** colors of the **Pan-African** movement with the **blue** of the French flag, it acknowledges the history of the Central African Republic while looking forward to a united Africa. The **red** vertical stripe running through the center of the flag symbolizes the common blood of humanity. The **yellow, five-pointed star** in the blue stripe stands for progress and unity.

HISTORY

Between the 16th and 19th centuries slavery greatly reduced the population of what is now the Central African Republic. In 1887 **France** occupied the area, and in 1894 established the colony of Ubangi-Shari at **Bangui**. In 1906 the colony united with Chad, and in 1910 it joined **French Equatorial Africa**. Post-1945, the colony received representation in the French parliament. In 1960 the Central African Republic declared **independence** but remained unstable and one of the world's poorest countries. Widespread conflict caused the **displacement** of large numbers of citizens. Several rebel groups agreed a **ceasefire** in 2008, but the activities of the **Lords Resistance Army** from Uganda caused further problems by creating many thousands of refugees.

AREA 241,000 sq mi (623,000 sq km)
POPULATION 4,950,000
CAPITAL Bangui
GOVERNMENT Multiparty republic
ETHNIC GROUPS Baya 33%, Banda 27%, Mandjia 13%, Sara 10%, Mboum 7% Mbaka 4%, others
LANGUAGES French (official), Sangho
RELIGIONS Traditional beliefs 35%, Protestant 25%, Roman Catholic 25%, Islam 15%
NATIONAL MOTTO *"Unité, Dignité, Travail"* "Unity, Dignity, Work"
NATIONAL ANTHEM (DATE) *"La Renaissance"* "The Revival" (1960)

Subsistence agriculture dominates the economy of Central African Republic.

55

CHAD

FLAG RATIO: 2:3   **USE:** National/Civil   **DATE ADOPTED:** 1959   **LAST MODIFIED:** 1959

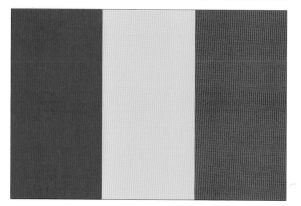

Chad's flag is identical to the flags of Andorra and Romania. It combines the **blue** of the French *tricolore* with the **yellow** and **red** of the **Pan-African** movement. The blue represents the sky and hope. Yellow symbolizes the Sahara Desert, and red stands for the blood shed for national liberation.

HISTORY

Chad straddles two, often conflicting worlds: the **Muslim** north and the sedentary **Christian** or animist south. In *c.* AD 700 North African nomads founded the **Kanem Empire**. In the 14th century, the kingdom of **Bornu** expanded to incorporate Kanem. In the late 19th century, the region fell to **Sudan**. In 1900 **France** defeated Sudan, and in 1908 Chad became the largest province of **French Equatorial Africa**. In 1920 it became a separate colony and in 1960 gained **independence**. In 1965 northern Muslims, led by the Chad National Liberation Front (**Frolinat**) rebelled against the government of **François Tombalbaye**. By 1973 the government, helped by the French, quashed the revolt. In 1980 **Libya** occupied northern Chad. In 1982 **Hisséne Habre** and Goukouni Oueddi formed rival regimes. Libya's bombing of Chad in 1983 saw the deployment of French troops. From 2003 the **Darfur** conflict in **Sudan** brought an influx of refugees.

AREA 496,000 sq mi (1,284,000 sq km)
POPULATION 10,759,000
CAPITAL Ndjamena
GOVERNMENT Multiparty republic
ETHNIC GROUPS 200 distinct groups: mostly Muslim in the north and centre; mostly Christian or animist in the south
LANGUAGES French and Arabic (both official), many others
RELIGIONS Islam 51%, Christianity 35%, animist 7%
NATIONAL ANTHEM (DATE) *"La Tchadienne"* "The Song of Chad" (1960)

***Armor**, clothes and weapon of a Moundang warrior from southern Chad.*

CHILE

FLAG RATIO: 2:3 USE: National/Civil DATE ADOPTED: 1817 LAST MODIFIED: 1912

Chile's flag dates from 1817, during the war of independence against Spain. Adopted by the government of Bernardo O'Higgins, it was apparently designed by the Minister of War José Ignacio Zenteno. The **blue canton** represents the sky. The **white** symbolizes the snow-capped **Andes** Mountains, while the **red** stands for the blood shed by the nation's patriots. The **white five-pointed star** stands for unity, progress and honor.

HISTORY

In 1520, the Portuguese navigator **Ferdinand Magellan** became the first European to sight Chile. In 1541 **Pedro de Valdivia** founded **Santiago**. Chile became a **Spanish colony**, ruled as part of the Viceroyalty of Peru. In 1817 an army, led by **José de San Martín**, surprised the Spanish by crossing the Andes. In 1818 **Bernardo O'Higgins** proclaimed Chilean **independence**. Chile gained mineral-rich land from Peru and Bolivia in the **War of the Pacific** (1879–84). In 1973 soaring inflation and public disturbances led to a military coup, with covert US support, against the government of **Salvador Allende**. The coup left more than 3000 people dead or missing, and **General Augusto Pinochet** assumed control. In 1977 Pinochet banned all political parties. His regime was characterized by repression and human rights' violations. In 2010 **Sebastian Pinera** became the first right-wing president since Pinochet.

AREA 292,000 sq mi (757,000 sq km)
POPULATION 16,889,000
CAPITAL Santiago
GOVERNMENT Multiparty republic
ETHNIC GROUPS Mestizo 95%, Amerindian 3%
LANGUAGES Spanish (official)
RELIGIONS Roman Catholic 89%, Protestant 11%
NATIONAL MOTTO *"Por la razon o la fuerza"* "By reason or by force"
NATIONAL ANTHEM (DATE) *"Himno Nacional de Chile"* "National Song of Chile" (1941)

The Mapuche of central Chile are renowned for their textile handicraft.

57

CHINA

FLAG RATIO: 2:3 USE: National/Civil DATE ADOPTED: 1949 LAST MODIFIED: 1949

China adopted its present flag in 1949, when Mao Zedong founded a communist republic. **Red** is a traditional color of China and communism. The **large gold star** represents the leading role of the **Communist Party of China**. The **four smaller gold stars** symbolize the main social classes: workers, peasants, bourgeoisie, and capitalists.

HISTORY

Qin Shihuangdi unified China. The **Qin** dynasty (221–206 BC) also built the majority of the **Great Wall**. The **Han** dynasty (202 BC–AD 220) developed the Empire, a bureaucracy based on **Confucianism**, and introduced **Buddhism**. **Genghis Khan** conquered most of China in the 1210s, and established the **Mongol Empire**. **Kublai Khan** founded the **Yüan** dynasty (1271–1368), an era of dialogue with Europe. The **Ming** dynasty (1368–1644) reestablished Chinese rule. The Manchu **Qing** dynasty (1644–1912) expanded the empire. Britain occupied Hong Kong after the **Opium War** (1839–42). In 1912 **Sun Yat-sen** established a **republic**. In 1937 the nationalist Kuomintang and communists united to fight Japanese invasion. In 1966 Mao launched the **Cultural Revolution**. From 1986 foreign investment and private enterprise were encouraged, but not political reform. In 1997 Hong Kong was returned to China as a special administrative region.

AREA 3,705,000 sq mi (9,597,000 sq km)
POPULATION 1,336,718,000
CAPITAL Beijing
GOVERNMENT Single-party Communist republic
ETHNIC GROUPS Han Chinese 92%, many others
LANGUAGES Mandarin Chinese (official)
RELIGIONS Atheist (official)
NATIONAL ANTHEM (DATE) *"Yiyonggjun Jinxingqu"* "March of the Volunteers" (1949)

Emperor Sima Yan unifies China at the end of the *"*Romance of the Three Kingdoms.*"*

COLOMBIA

Colombia's **tricolor** flag has the same colors as their neighbors Ecuador and Venezuela. It differs from Ecuador's flag only in its **ratio** – 2:3 rather than 1:2. In 1806 Venezuelan revolutionary Francisco de Miranda raised the flag in revolt against Spanish rule. In 1819 Simón Bolívar defeated the Spanish at the Battle of Boyacá and the flag became the national symbol of Greater Colombia (including Ecuador and Venezuela). After several changes, the government reverted to the original design in 1861. A popular Colombian children's song says of the national colors, "**yellow** is our gold, **blue** is our vast oceans, and **red** is the blood that gave us our freedom."

HISTORY

The pre-Colombian **Chibcha** civilization lived undisturbed in the eastern cordillera for thousands of years. In 1525 the **Spanish** established the first European settlement at Santa Marta. By 1538 conquistador Gonzalo Jiménez de Quesada conquered the Chibcha and established Bogotá. Colombia became part of the **New Kingdom of Granada**. In 1830 Ecuador and Venezuela gained independence from **Greater Colombia**. In 1885 the **Republic of Colombia** was formed. Nearly 100,000 people died in the first civil war (1899–1902). The second civil war, **La Violencia** (1949–57), was even more bloody. The **Revolutionary Armed Forces of Colombia (FARC)** have waged a guerrilla war since 1958.

Porro *is a form of Colombian dance music similar to calypso or rumba.*

AREA 440,000 sq mi (1,139,000 sq km)
POPULATION 44,726,000
CAPITAL Bogotá
GOVERNMENT Multiparty republic
ETHNIC GROUPS Mestizo 58%, White 20%, Mulatto 14%, Black 4%
LANGUAGES Spanish (official)
RELIGIONS Roman Catholic 90%
NATIONAL MOTTO *"Libertad y orden"* "Liberty and Order"
NATIONAL ANTHEM (DATE) *"Oh! Gloria inmarcesible"* "Oh! Unfading Glory" (1920)

59

COMOROS

FLAG RATIO: 3:5 **USE:** National/Civil **DATE ADOPTED:** 2002 **LAST MODIFIED:** 2002

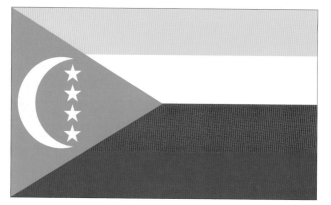

In 2002 Comoros adopted a new flag as the islands reunited as the Union of the Comoros. The flag consists of **four horizontal stripes** in **yellow, white, red** and **blue**. The **green triangle** with a **white crescent** and **four white stars** on the hoist recalls the islands' previous flag. The color green and the crescent are traditionally associated with **Islam**, the main religion of the Comoros. The four stars represent the three islands of Comoros (**Grande Comore, Anjouan, Mohéli**) and the French-administered island of **Mayotte**, over which Comoros claims sovereignty.

AREA 860 sq mi (2,200 sq km)
POPULATION 795,000
CAPITAL Moroni
GOVERNMENT Transitional
ETHNIC GROUPS Antalote, Cafre, Makoa, Oimatsaha Sakalava
LANGUAGES Arabic (official), French (official), Comoran (a blend of Swahili and Arabic)
RELIGIONS Sunni Muslim 99%, Roman Catholic 1%
NATIONAL MOTTO "*Unité, Justice, Progrès*" "Unity, Justice, Progress"
NATIONAL ANTHEM (DATE) "*Udzima wa ya Masiwa*" "The Union of the Great Islands" (1978)

HISTORY

Traders from Arabia, East Africa and **Madagascar** built settlements for the selling of slaves or food. In the late 18th century Comorians fortified the trading towns to protect them from slave raids. In 1866 the islands became a French protectorate, and plantations were established. In 1912 Comoros became a French colony governed by Madagascar. In **1975** the Comoros declared **independence**, while Mayotte chose to remain French. There were numerous **coups**, and French troops and French-backed mercenaries intervened on several occasions. In 1997 Anjouan and Mohéli declared independence. In 2001 a new constitution sought to reunify the islands but with greater autonomy. A power-sharing deal was reached in 2003, but instability continued.

Comorian *stamp displaying the old national flag and four islands in the group.*

CONGO, DEMOCRATIC REPUBLIC OF

FLAG RATIO: 3:4 **USE:** National/Civil **DATE ADOPTED:** 2006 **LAST MODIFIED:** 2006

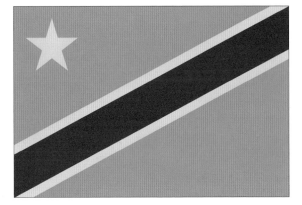

The present national flag of the Democratic Republic of Congo (DRC) is similar to the flag of 1963–71. **Sky blue** represents peace, **yellow** represents the country's wealth, the **red stripe** the blood of its martyrs, and the **star** in the upper left the country's radiant future. It was introduced as the result of the new constitution that was ratified in 2005 and came into force in 2006.

HISTORY

Large **Bantu** kingdoms emerged in the 14th century. In 1482, a Portuguese navigator became the first European to reach the mouth of the River Congo. In the 19th century, traders in slaves and ivory formed powerful states. **Henry Morton Stanley**'s explorations (1874–77) established the route of the Congo. In 1885 King **Leopold II** of **Belgium** established the **Congo Free State**. In 1908 it became the colony of **Belgian Congo**. In 1960 the Republic of the Congo gained **independence** under **Patrice Lumumba**, but **Joseph Mobutu** seized power in a military coup. In 1971 he renamed the country **Zaïre**. In 1995 millions of Hutus fled into Zäire from **Rwanda**. In 1996 **Laurent Kabila** overthrew Mobutu. Zaïre became the Democratic Republic of Congo. Between 1998 and 2001, a **civil war** killed 2.5 million people. Civil war in 1997–2003 killed and displaced millions. Despite a ceasefire, fighting continued in the north and east.

Stamp marking the 50th anniversary of the International Labor Organization (ILO).

AREA 905,000 sq mi (2,345,000 sq km)
POPULATION 71,713,000
CAPITAL Kinshasa
GOVERNMENT Single-party republic
ETHNIC GROUPS Over 200; the largest are Mongo, Luba, Kongo, Mangbetu-Azande
LANGUAGES French (official), tribal languages
RELIGIONS Roman Catholic 50%, Protestant 20%, Islam 10%, others
NATIONAL ANTHEM (DATE) *"Debout Congolais"* "Arise Congolese" (1991)

CONGO, REPUBLIC OF

FLAG RATIO: 2:3 **USE:** National/Civil **DATE ADOPTED:** 1958 **REINTRODUCED:** 1991

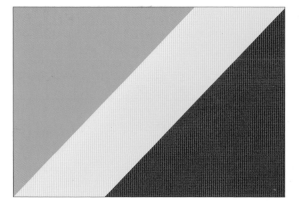

Congo adopted its present **tricolor** of **diagonal stripes** in 1958, when it became an autonomous republic within the French Community. In 1969 a new constitution established the People's Republic of Congo and adopted a Soviet-inspired flag with communist symbols. In 1991 the Congo abandoned communism and reverted to its original flag. It uses the **Pan-African** colors of **green**, **yellow**, and **red**.

HISTORY

The **Loango** and **Bakongo** kingdoms dominated the Congo when the first European arrived in 1482. The Congolese coast became a center for the slave trade. In 1880 **Pierre Savorgnan de Brazza** explored the area and it became a **French protectorate**. In 1910 **Brazzaville** became the capital of the federation of **French Equatorial Africa**. In **1960** the Republic of Congo gained **independence**. In 1964 Congo adopted **Marxism-Leninism** as the state ideology. The military, led by **Marien Ngouabi**, seized power in 1968. Ngouabi was assassinated in 1977. Colonel **Denis Sassou-Nguesso** ruled Congo from 1979 to 1992. **Pascal Lissouba** became president in 1992 multiparty elections. In 1997 Sassou-Nguesso overthrew Lissouba and the Congo plunged into **civil war**. In 2002 the Congo adopted a new constitution. Rebellion in Pool region ended in 2003.

AREA 132,000 sq mi (342,000 sq km)

POPULATION 4,244,000

CAPITAL Brazzaville

GOVERNMENT Military regime

ETHNIC GROUPS Kongo 48%, Sangha 20%, Teke 17%, M'bochi 12%

LANGUAGES French (official), many others

RELIGIONS Christianity 50%, animist 48%, Islam 2%

NATIONAL MOTTO *"Unité, Travail, Progrès"* "Unity, Work, Progress"

NATIONAL ANTHEM (DATE) *"La Congolaise"* "Song of Congo" (1962)

Traditional marriage ceremony in the Republic of Congo.

COSTA RICA

FLAG RATIO: 3:5   USE: National/Civil   DATE ADOPTED: 1848   LAST MODIFIED: 1848

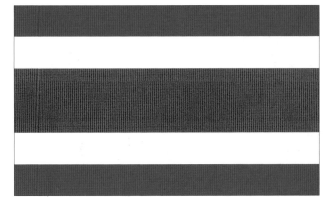

Costa Rica based its flag on the French *tricolore*. First Lady Pacífica Fernández Oreamuno designed the national flag in 1848. It consists of **five horizontal stripes** of blue, white and red. **Blue** represents the sky and opportunity. **White** stands for wisdom and peace. **Red** symbolizes the warmth of Costa Rica's people and the blood shed in the fight for freedom. In 1964 Costa Rica amended its **coat of arms**, which sometimes appears on unofficial civil flags. It shows two sailing ships on the Pacific Ocean and the Caribbean Sea, separated by three volcanos. Also included are the rising sun and seven stars, one for each province.

HISTORY

In 1502 **Christopher Columbus** sailed along the Caribbean shore and named the land Costa Rica, which is Spanish for "rich coast." The first **Spanish** colonizers arrived in 1561. Spain ruled the country until 1821, when Spain's Central American colonies broke away to join the **Mexican Empire**. In 1823 the Central American states split from Mexico to set up the **Central American Federation**. In 1838 Costa Rica achieved **independence**. It prospered on its **coffee** and **banana** exports. Costa Rica is perhaps the most stable and democratic nation in Central America, although the country was rocked by scandal in 2004 when two of its former presidents were found guilty of and imprisoned on charges of corruption.

Stamp *celebrating the International Year of the Older Persons in 1999.*

AREA 19,700 sq mi (51,100 sq km)
POPULATION 4,577,000
CAPITAL San José
GOVERNMENT Multiparty republic
ETHNIC GROUPS White (including Mestizo) 94%, Black 3%, Amerindian 1%, Chinese 1%, others
LANGUAGES Spanish (official), English
RELIGIONS Roman Catholic 76%, Evangelical 14%
NATIONAL ANTHEM (DATE) *"Himno Nacional"* "National Hymn" (1853)

63

CÔTE D'IVOIRE

FLAG RATIO: 2:3 **USE:** National/Civil **DATE ADOPTED:** 1959 **LAST MODIFIED:** 1959

Côte d'Ivoire modeled its flag on the *tricolore* of France, the former colonial power. It is a mirror image of Ireland's flag. **Orange** represents growth and the soil of the savanna on the northern and central plateaux. **White** stands for peace emerging from righteousness, as well as the rapids of the Sassandra, Bandama, and Komoé rivers. **Green** symbolizes hope for the future and the dense tropical forests in the west. Côte d'Ivoire had the largest rain forests in West Africa, until logging and plantation farming reduced the coverage of forests.

AREA 125,000 sq mi (322,000 sq km)
POPULATION 21,504,000
CAPITAL Yamoussoukro
GOVERNMENT Multiparty republic
ETHNIC GROUPS Akan 42%, Voltaiques 18%, Northern Mandes 16%, Krous 11%, Southern Mandes 10%
LANGUAGES French (official), many native dialects
RELIGIONS Islam 40%, Christianity 30%, traditional beliefs 30%
NATIONAL MOTTO *"Union, Discipline, Travail"* "Union, Discipline, Labor"
NATIONAL ANTHEM (DATE) *"L'Abidjanaise"* "Song of Abidjan" (1960)

HISTORY

The first European explorers reached Côte d'Ivoire (French, "Ivory Coast") in the 15th century and began trading in **ivory** and **slaves**. Tribal kingdoms such as the **Kong** and the **Baule** flourished inland and restricted European activity to the coastal region. In the 19th century, the French established forts, trading posts, and **coffee plantations**. In 1893 Côte d'Ivoire became a **French colony**, and in 1904 it was subsumed into the Federation of French West Africa. **Felix Houphouët-Boigny** led the country to **independence** in 1960. Civil war from 2002 led to international intervention. After elections in 2010 President **Laurent Gbagbo** refused to concede, but stood down in 2011.

***Côte d'Ivoire** celebrated 24 years of independence in 1984.*

Croatia adopted a Russian-based **red**, **white** and **blue** flag in 1848. As part of the Federation of Yugoslavia, Croatia's flag had a red star at its center. In 1990 the present **coat of arms** replaced the red star. The coat of arms consists of a **checkered shield**, dating from the 15th century, and a **crown**. The crown incorporates **four regional symbols** (from Dubrovnik, Dalmatia, Istria, and Slavonia) and the oldest-known Croatian coat of arms.

HISTORY

Croatia was one of six republics that made up the former **Yugoslavia**. An 800-year union of the Hungarian and Croatian crowns began in 1102. In 1699 all of Croatia came under **Hapsburg** rule. In 1867 the Hapsburg Empire became the **Austro-Hungarian Empire**.

After World War I, Croatia was incorporated into Yugoslavia (1929). Occupied by Germany in World War II, Croatia became a pro-Nazi state (*Ustashe*). In 1990 nationalist **Franjo Tudjman** became president. In 1991 Croatia voted for independence but Croatian Serbs took up arms in favor of staying part of Yugoslavia. War broke out between **Serbia** and Croatia, and by 1992 Croatia lost more than a third of its land. In 1993 Serbs in eastern Slavonia voted to establish the separate Republic of **Krajina**. In 1995 Croatia seized the Krajina and 150,000 Serbs fled. In 2000, after Tudjman's death, Stipe Mesic became president. Croatia's **European Union** accession treaty was signed in 2011.

Andrija Maurović *who drew this* Black Rider *is the "father of Croatian comics."*

AREA 21,800 sq mi (56,500 sq km)
POPULATION 4,484,000
CAPITAL Zagreb
GOVERNMENT Multiparty republic
ETHNIC GROUPS Croat 90%, Serb 5%, others
LANGUAGES Croatian 96%
RELIGIONS Roman Catholic 88%, Orthodox 4%, Islam 1%, others
NATIONAL ANTHEM (DATE) *"Lijepa Naša Domovino"* "Our Beautiful Homeland" (1891)

65

CUBA

FLAG RATIO: 1:2 **USE:** National/Civil **DATE ADOPTED:** 1902 **LAST MODIFIED:** 1902

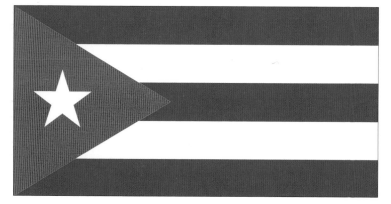

Cuba's flag was first used by Narciso Lopez, leader of a rebellion against Spanish rule in 1849. Cuba officially adopted the flag in 1902, when it gained independence from Spain. The **three blue horizontal stripes** represent the three original Cuban territories. The **red triangle** is of masonic origin and symbolizes liberty, equality, and fraternity. Red stands for the blood of the patriots. The **white star** signifies unity and the purity of revolutionary ideals. It has been suggested that the similarity between the Cuban flag and the "Stars and Stripes" of the United States indicated Cuba's desire to join the union.

AREA 42,800 sq mi (111,000 sq km)

POPULATION 11,087,000

CAPITAL Havana

GOVERNMENT Socialist republic

ETHNIC GROUPS Mulatto 51%, White 37%, Black 11%

LANGUAGES Spanish (official)

RELIGIONS Christianity

NATIONAL MOTTO *"Socialismo o muerte"* "Socialism or death"

NATIONAL ANTHEM (DATE) *"La Bayamesa"* "The Bayamo Song" (1902)

HISTORY

Christopher Columbus discovered Cuba in 1492, and Spanish settlers arrived in 1511. In 1895 **José Martí** led a war of independence. In 1898 the sinking of the US battleship *Maine* led to the **Spanish-American War**. Cuba was under **US occupation** (1898–1902) before becoming a republic. Cuba's economy flourished due to its **sugar plantations**. In 1933 **Fulgencio Batista** led a successful coup. **Fidel Castro** (supported by **Che Guevara**) launched a socialist revolution in 1956. In 1959 Castro became Premier. Castro's attempt to export revolution to the rest of Latin America ended in diplomatic alienation. He remained in power until 2008 when ill health caused him to hand power to his brother, **Raul Castro**, who introduced economic reforms.

The indigo hamlet *fish lives in the coral reefs around the island of Cuba.*

CYPRUS

FLAG RATIO: 3:5   USE: National/Civil   DATE ADOPTED: 1960   LAST MODIFIED: 1960

Adopted after gaining independence from Britain, the flag of Cyprus was designed to be a neutral symbol for the new country. The **white field** and **green olive branches** stand for peace between Turkish and Greek Cypriots. At the center is a **yellow silhouette** of the island of Cyprus. The yellow refers to the island's copper deposits. Although it is the official flag, it is used largely by Greek Cypriots (Turkish Cypriots often use a flag representing Northern Cyprus).

HISTORY

From AD 330 Cyprus formed part of the **Byzantine Empire**. In the 1570s Cyprus became part of the **Ottoman Empire**. Turkish rule continued until 1878, when Turkey leased Cyprus to **Britain**. In 1925 it became a British colony. In the 1950s Greek Cypriots, who made up *c.* 80% of the population, began a campaign for *enosis* (union) with Greece. In 1960 Cyprus gained **independence**. The new constitution provided for power-sharing between the Greek and Turkish Cypriots. The arrangement proved unworkable, and fighting broke out between the two communities. In 1983 **Turkish Cypriots** declared the northern part of the island the independent Turkish Republic of **Northern Cyprus**. Turkey is the only country to recognize it. Its **state flag** is a white field with a red crescent and star. UN talks aimed at a form of reunification took place intermittently from 2004.

Village *of Agios Dimitrios (1400–1100 BC) near Kalavasos, southern Cyprus.*

AREA 3,600 sq mi (9,300 sq km)
POPULATION 1,120,000
CAPITAL Nicosia
GOVERNMENT Multiparty republic
ETHNIC GROUPS Greek Cypriot 77%, Turkish Cypriot 18%, others
LANGUAGES Greek and Turkish (both official), English
RELIGIONS Greek Orthodox 78%, Islam 8%
NATIONAL ANTHEM (DATE) *"Ymnos eis tin Eleftherian"* "Hymn to Freedom" (1960)

CZECH REPUBLIC

FLAG RATIO: 2:3 **USE:** National/Civil **DATE ADOPTED:** 1920 **LAST MODIFIED:** 1993

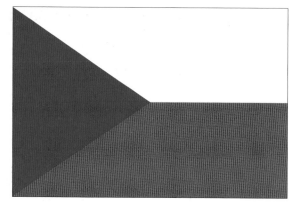

The original national flag was a red and white banner, but in 1920 Czechoslavakia adopted the **Pan-Slavic** colors of red, white and blue. The **white horizontal stripe** represents **Bohemia**, the **red horizontal stripe** represents **Moravia** and the blood shed for the freedom of the state, and the **blue triangle** on the hoist represents Slovakia. In 1993 Czechoslovakia split into two states. The Czech Republic kept the former flag. While the blue triangle no longer represents Slovakia, it does remain a symbol of impartiality and sovereignty.

HISTORY

In the 10th century Bohemia became part of the **Holy Roman Empire**. Emperor Charles IV (1316–78) made **Prague** his capital. In 1526 the Austrian **Hapsburgs** assumed control. A Czech rebellion led to the **Thirty Years' War** (1618–48). **Tomáš Masaryk** was the first president (1918–35) of an independent Czechoslovakia. In 1939 Nazi Germany occupied the country. In 1948 the communists took control. In 1968 Soviet troops crushed the **Prague Spring** reforms of **Alexander Dubček**. The peaceful "Velvet Revolution" saw the creation of a non-communist government in 1989, led by **Vaclav Havel**. In 1993 Czechoslovakia split into two countries: the Czech Republic and the **Slovak Republic**. The Czech Republic joined **NATO** in 1999 and the **European Union** in 2004.

AREA 30,500 sq mi (78,900 sq km)
POPULATION 10,190,000
CAPITAL Prague
GOVERNMENT Multiparty republic
ETHNIC GROUPS Czech 81%, Moravian 13%, Slovak 3%, Polish, German, Silesian, Gypsy, Hungarian, Ukrainian
LANGUAGES Czech (official)
RELIGIONS Atheist 40%, Roman Catholic 39%, Protestant 4%, Orthodox 3%, others
NATIONAL ANTHEM (DATE) *"Kde Domou Múj?"* "Where is my Home?" (1920)

Czech woman in national costume holding painted Easter eggs.

DENMARK

FLAG RATIO: 28:37   USE: National   DATE ADOPTED: 1696   LAST MODIFIED: 1748

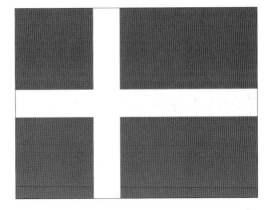

The Danish flag is called the *Dannebrog* (Danish, "flag of the Danes"). It is thought to be the oldest national flag in continuous use. In a Netherlandish book on heraldry (1370–86), a **white cross** on a **red field** appears on the coat of arms of King Valdemar IV Atterdag. According to legend, the flag fell from heaven during King Waldemar II's battle against the Estonians at Lyndanisse (June 15, 1219). It has long been associated with Christianity. The *Dannebrog* is the basis for the other Nordic flags bearing the "Scandinavian cross." A swallow-tailed version of the *Dannebrog* is the state flag and ensign.

HISTORY

Between the 9th and 11th centuries, the **Vikings** conquered much of western Europe. From 1015 to 1034 King **Canute II** ruled over England. Queen **Margrethe I** unified Denmark, **Sweden** and Norway in 1397, but Sweden broke away in 1523. In 1536 Denmark adopted Lutheranism. **Christian IV** led Denmark into the costly **Thirty Years' War** with Sweden (1618–48). It lost **Norway** to Sweden in 1814, and **Iceland** gained independence in 1918. Denmark was occupied by **Germany** in 1940, and was liberated in 1945. Queen **Margrethe II** acceded to the throne in 1972. **Poul Rasmussen** was prime minister from 1993–2009. **Greenland** gained home rule in 1979 and self-determination in 2009.

AREA 16,600 sq mi (43,100 sq km)
POPULATION 5,530,000
CAPITAL Copenhagen
GOVERNMENT Parliamentary monarchy
ETHNIC GROUPS Scandinavian, Inuit, Faeroese, German
LANGUAGES Danish (official), English, Faerose
RELIGIONS Evangelical Lutheran 95%
NATIONAL ANTHEM (DATE) *"Der er et Yndigt Land"* "There is a Lovely Land" (1844)

Viking King Harald Bluetooth founded the town of Roskilde in 998.

69

DJIBOUTI

FLAG RATIO: 2:3 **USE:** National/Civil **DATE ADOPTED:** 1977 **LAST MODIFIED:** 1977

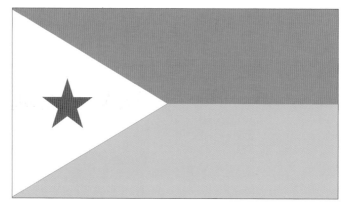

Djibouti's national flag is based on the banner of the African People's League for Independence, leaders in the struggle for liberation from France. The League adopted the flag in 1972. The **two horizontal stripes** represent the two main peoples of Djibouti. **Light blue** is the color of the Issas people, and also represents the sky and the sea. **Green** is the color of the Afars people and symbolizes the fertile earth. The **white triangle** represents peace and equality, while the **red, five-pointed star** symbolizes unity.

HISTORY

Islam arrived in the 9th century, and the conversion of the **Afars** led to conflict with Christian Ethiopians in the interior. By the 19th century, Somalian **Issas** moved into Djibouti and occupied much of the Afars' traditional grazing land. In 1888 France established the colony of **French Somaliland**. In 1917 a **railway** opened between Djibouti and Addis Ababa, capital of Ethiopia. In a 1967 referendum, 60% voted to retain links with France. The colony was renamed the **French Territory of the Afars and Issas**. In 1977 it gained **independence** as the Republic of Djibouti. **Hassan Gouled Aptidon** of the Popular Rally for Progress was elected president. In 1981 Gouled declared a one-party state. By 1992 **Afar rebels** controlled more than two-thirds of Djibouti. The first multiparty elections were in 2003 and won by Ismael Omar Guelleh; in 2005 elections he was the only candidate. In 2008 fighting broke out in the disputed Djibouti-**Eritrea** border area of **Ras Doumeira**.

AREA 9,000 sq mi (23,200 sq km)
POPULATION 757,000
CAPITAL Djibouti
GOVERNMENT Multiparty republic
ETHNIC GROUPS Somali 60%, Afar 35%
LANGUAGES Arabic and French (both official)
RELIGIONS Islam 94%, Christianity 6%
MOTTO "*Unité, Egalité, Paix*"
"Unity, Equality, Peace"
NATIONAL ANTHEM (DATE) Untitled (1977)

African nomads traditionally use carved headrests to protect elaborate hairstyles.

FLAG RATIO: 1:2 USE: National/Civil DATE ADOPTED: 1978 LAST MODIFIED: 1988

Chosen by national competition in 1978, the central emblem of the Dominican flag is the **sisserou parrot**, encircled by **ten stars** representing the ten parishes of Dominica. The sisserou parrot, an endangered species, is unique to Dominica and is the national bird. The **cross** is Christian, and the **yellow**, **black** and **white stripes** represent the Holy Trinity. The colors are also symbolic. **Yellow** represents the island's plentiful sunshine, its major agricultural crops (bananas and citrus), and the Carib people. **Black** represents the fertile soil and the African heritage of most Dominicans. **White** stands for the island's clear waters and the pure aspirations of its people. The **dark-green** field symbolizes the island's lush **forests** and vegetation.

HISTORY

Dominica is named for *dies dominica* (Latin "the Lord's day"), the day that **Christopher Columbus** sighted the island in 1493. Prior to Columbus' arrival, the **Arawak** people inhabited Dominica. The **Carib** displaced the **Arawak**. It was the last of the Caribbean islands colonized by Europeans, due mainly to the fierce resistance of the native **Caribs**. Dominica won **independence** from Britain in 1978. The republic's first prime minister was **Patrick R. John**. The economy, which is heavily dependent on tourism and banana exports, was damaged by Hurricane Dean in 2007.

AREA 290 sq mi (750 sq km)
POPULATION 73,000
CAPITAL Roseau
GOVERNMENT Multiparty republic
ETHNIC GROUPS Black 90%, Mixed 7%, Native American 2%
LANGUAGES English (official), French patois
RELIGIONS Roman Catholic 70%, Seventh-Day Adventist 5%, Pentecostal 4%
NATIONAL MOTTO "*Après Bondie, c'est la Ter*" "After God, the Earth"
NATIONAL ANTHEM (DATE) "Isle of Beauty, Isle of Splendor" (1967)

Dominican stamp marking the Year of the Elderly in 1999.

DOMINICAN REPUBLIC

FLAG RATIO: 2:3 **USE:** National **DATE ADOPTED:** 1844 **LAST MODIFIED:** 1896

Dominican Republic adopted its flag upon gaining independence in 1844. The first flag took Haiti's flag of **blue** and **red**, and superimposed a **white cross** to signify the Christian faith of the Dominican people. The colors at the fly end of the flag were later reversed. Blue represents liberty. Red stands for the blood shed in the struggle for liberation, while the white cross is a symbol of sacrifice. The national **coat of arms** appears at the center of the white cross. The coat of arms includes a Bible open at the Gospel of Saint John, a symbol of the Trinitarian movement – the Christian secret society that led the movement for independence.

HISTORY

Christopher Columbus discovered the island of **Hispaniola** in 1492. **Santo Domingo**, capital of the Dominican Republic, was the first Spanish settlement in the New World. In 1697 Spain ceded the western third of the island (now **Haiti**) to France. In 1795 France gained control of the entire island. In 1821 the Dominican Republic declared **independence** but was occupied by Haiti. In 1844 it won independence. The dictatorship of **Rafael Trujillo** lasted from 1930 to 1961. President **Joaquín Balaguer** succeeded, and was mostly in power until 1978. Recent years have seen a series of presidents and a growing service economy.

AREA 18,700 sq mi (48,500 sq km)
POPULATION 9,957,000
CAPITAL Santo Domingo
GOVERNMENT Multiparty republic
ETHNIC GROUPS Mulatto 73%, White 16%, Black 11%
LANGUAGES Spanish (official)
RELIGIONS Roman Catholic 95%
MOTTO "*Dios, Patria, Libertad*"
"God, Fatherland, Liberty"
NATIONAL ANTHEM (DATE) "*Himno Nacional*"
"National Anthem" (1883)

Casandra Damiron *is known as the "Queen of Song" in Dominican Republic.*

EAST TIMOR

FLAG RATIO: 1:2 USE: National/Civil DATE ADOPTED: 1975 REINTRODUCED: 2002

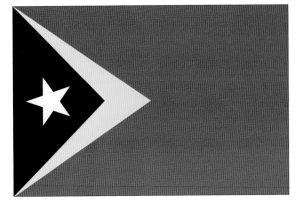

In 1975 Fretilin (*Frente Revolucionária do Timor-Leste Independente*) raised the present flag as the banner of the Democratic Republic of Timor. The republic proved short-lived as Indonesia invaded but the flag returned when independence was restored in 2002. **Yellow** represents the vestiges of East Timor's colonial past. **Black** stands for the darkness to be overcome, while **red** recalls the struggle for liberation. The **white, five-pointed star** is the guiding light of peace.

HISTORY

From *c*.1520, **Portuguese** spice traders began to settle on the island of Timor. In 1620 the **Dutch** landed and settled on the western side of Timor. **Japan** occupied Timor during World War II. In 1950 West Timor became part of **Indonesia**.

In 1975 Portugal abandoned East Timor and the colony declared independence. Nine days later, Indonesia invaded. In 1976 Indonesia **annexed** East Timor as its 27th province. The **occupation** claimed the lives of *c*.200,000 Timorese people, most notably when Indonesia's army killed *c*.270 demonstrators in the capital, **Dili**. In 1999, after a vote in favor of independence, pro-Indonesian militias sought to destabilize East Timor. A United Nations' (UN) peacekeeping force restored order, and East Timor gained full independence on May 20, 2002. Former Fretilin leader **Xanana Gusmão**, jailed from 1992 to 1999, became the first President of East Timor.

According to legend, *the island of Timor was formed out of a crocodile's back.*

AREA 5,700 sq mi (14,900 sq km)

POPULATION 1,178,000

CAPITAL Dili

GOVERNMENT Multiparty republic

ETHNIC GROUPS Austronesian (Malayo-Polynesian), Papuan

LANGUAGES Tetum, Portuguese (both official), Indonesian, English

RELIGIONS Roman Catholic 90%, Muslim 4%, Protestant 3%

NATIONAL ANTHEM (DATE) "*Pátria, Pátria*" "Motherland, Motherland" (2002)

ECUADOR

FLAG RATIO: 2:3 USE: National/Civil DATE ADOPTED: 1900 LAST MODIFIED: 1900

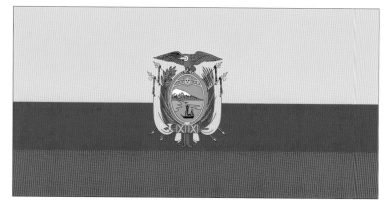

The revolutionary Francisco de Miranda created Ecuador's flag in 1806. The armies of Simon Bolívar, who liberated much of South America, fought under it. Colombia, Ecuador, and Venezuela have **tricolors** of yellow, blue and red **horizontal stripes**, based on Miranda's design. The **yellow** symbolizes the fertility of the land. The **blue** represents the sea and the sky. The **red** stands for the blood shed in the fight for liberation. At the center is the **coat of arms**, showing a **condor** soaring over Mount Chimborazo, Ecuador's highest peak at 20,561ft (6267m), and the Guayas River.

HISTORY

In 1532 **Spanish** forces, led by **Francisco Pizarro**, defeated the **Incas** at Cajamarca and established the Spanish Viceroyalty of Quito. A revolutionary war culminated in **Antonio José de Sucre**'s defeat of the Spanish at the Battle of Mount Pichincha (1822). **Simon Bolívar** negotiated the admittance of Quito to the **Federation of Gran Colombia** (Colombia, Ecuador, and Venezuela. In 1830 Ecuador seceded from the federation. In the **Treaty of Rio** (1942), Ecuador lost half its Amazonian territory to Peru. **José María Velasco Ibarro** served four terms as president (1944–47, 1952–56, 1960–61, 1968–72). In 1972 an army coup deposed Velasco. Ecuador returned to democracy in 1979. In 2006, left-leaning independent Rafael Correa became president, promising social fairness, nationalization and curbs on the role of political parties.

AREA 109,000 sq mi (284,000 sq km)
POPULATION 15,007,000
CAPITAL Quito
GOVERNMENT Multiparty republic
ETHNIC GROUPS Mestizo (mixed White/Amerindian) 65%, Amerindian 25%, White 7%, Black 3%
LANGUAGES Spanish (official), Quechua
RELIGIONS Roman Catholic 95%
NATIONAL ANTHEM (DATE) *"Salve, O Patria!"* "We Salute You, Oh Fatherland!"

***The Andean condor**, the largest bird of prey, is Ecuador's national bird.*

FLAG RATIO: 2:3 USE: National/Civil DATE ADOPTED: 1984 LAST AMENDED: 1984

The **tricolor** of red, white, and black **horizontal stripes** first appeared as Egypt's flag in 1958, when the country was part of the short-lived **United Arab Republic**. In 1972 a hawk replaced the three stars on the central band. In 1984 the **eagle of Saladin** replaced the hawk. **Red** symbolizes the struggle for liberation. **White** represents the bloodless overthrow of the monarchy. **Black** recalls the end of oppression by Britain and the monarchy.

HISTORY

The **Old Kingdom** saw the building of the Great **Pyramid** at Giza (*c.* 2500 BC). The **Middle Kingdom**'s capital at Luxor

Queen Nefertari makes an offering to the goddess Hathor.

reveal Egypt's ancient power. In 322 BC, **Alexander the Great** conquered Egypt. **Rome** gained control after the fall of **Cleopatra**. The **Umayyad** dynasty conquered Egypt in 642, introducing Arabic and **Islam**. In 1517 the **Ottomans** came to power. In 1801 **Muhammad Ali** expelled the French and founded the modern state. The completion of the **Suez Canal** (1867) encouraged **Britain** to capture Cairo in 1882. In 1922 Egypt became a monarchy under **Fuad I**. In 1953 **Gamal Abdal Nasser** overthrew King **Farouk** and led (1954–70) the new republic. **Anwar Sadat** succeeded him, but was assassinated in 1981. **Hosni Mubarak** was ousted in political unrest of 2011. Elections were held later that year, and a government formed in 2012.

AREA 387,000 sq mi (1,001,000 sq km)
POPULATION 82,080,000
CAPITAL Cairo
GOVERNMENT Transitional
ETHNIC GROUPS Egyptian/Bedouin/Berber 99%
LANGUAGES Arabic (official), French, English
RELIGIONS Islam (mainly Sunni Muslim) 94%, Christian (mainly Coptic) and others 6%
NATIONAL ANTHEM (DATE) *"Biladi, Biladi"* "My Homeland, My Homeland" (1979)

EL SALVADOR

FLAG RATIO: 189:335 USE: National/State DATE ADOPTED: 1912 LAST MODIFIED: 1972

El Salvador's tricolor flag of **blue-white-blue horizontal stripes** has its origins in the flag of the former Central American Federation (1823–39). Manuel José Arce chose the flag in 1822. The **coat of arms** consists of an equilateral triangle, symbolizing liberty, fraternity, and equality. Inside the triangle are five volcanoes, representing the five members of the federation, surrounded by the Atlantic and Pacific Oceans. Written in the sun's rays, above a Liberty cap on a pole, is "*15 De Septiembre De 1821*," the date of independence. Below the triangle is the national motto "*Dios, Union, Libertad.*" Around the triangle appears "*República De El Salvador En La America Central.*"

AREA 8,100 sq mi (21,000 sq km)
POPULATION 6,072,000
CAPITAL San Salvador
GOVERNMENT Republic
ETHNIC GROUPS Mestizo 90%, White 9%, Amerindian 1%
LANGUAGES Spanish (official)
RELIGIONS Roman Catholic 83%
NATIONAL MOTTO "*Dios, Unión, Libertad*" "God, Union, Liberty"
NATIONAL ANTHEM (DATE) "*Saludemos la Patria orgilosos*" "Salute the Proud Motherland" (1953)

HISTORY

In 1524–26 **Spanish** explorer **Pedro de Alvarado** conquered Native American tribes and the region became part of the Spanish Viceroyalty of Guatemala. In 1821 El Salvador gained **independence**. In 1825 **Manuel José Arce** became the first President of the **Central American Federation**. In the late 19th century, El Salvador developed **coffee** plantations. **General Maximiliano Hernández Martínez** led a brutal dictatorship (1931–44). A 12-year long **civil war** (1979–92) between US-backed government forces and the **Farabundo Marti National Liberation Front (FMLN)** claimed 75,000 lives. The FMLN's **Mauricio Funes** won the 2009 presidential elections.

Stamp *celebrating Inter-American Water Day in 1997.*

Equatorial Guinea's national flag consists of a **tricolor** of **horizontal stripes**, a **blue triangle** at the hoist, and the **coat of arms** at the center. The **green stripe** represents agriculture, vitally important to the national economy. The **white stripe** symbolizes peace, while the **red stripe** stands for the blood shed in the struggle for independence. **Blue** represents the Pacific Ocean. The coat of arms features the **silk-cotton tree** on a **silver shield**. King Bonkoro of Bata signed the 1843 treaty with Spain under the tree. Above the shield are **six stars** representing the mainland and five islands of Equatorial Guinea. The national motto "*Unidad, Paz, Justicia*" appears below the shield. From 1972 to 1979, under the dictator **Macías Nguema**, Equatorial Guinea had a different coat of arms.

HISTORY

In 1471 Portuguese navigator **Fernando Póo** sighted the largest island of **Bioko**. In 1778 **Portugal** ceded the islands and mainland (**Mbini**) to Spain. From 1858 to 1959 it was known as **Spanish Guinea**. In 1959 it became an overseas province of Spain. The country gained **independence** in 1968. The dictatorship of **Francisco Macías Nguema** killed over 40,000 people. In 1979 Colonel **Teodoro Obiang Nguema Mbasogo** deposed Nguema in a coup. Human-rights organizations accuse Obiang's regime of the routine arrest and torture of opponents. In 2004, a coup attempt was foiled and the leaders arrested.

AREA 10,800 sq mi (28,100 sq km)

POPULATION 668,000

CAPITAL Malabo

GOVERNMENT Unitary presidential republic

ETHNIC GROUPS Bubi (on Bioko), Fang (in Rio Muni)

LANGUAGES Spanish and French (both official)

RELIGIONS Christianity

MOTTO *"Unidad, Paz, Justicia"* "Unity, Peace, Justice"

NATIONAL ANTHEM (DATE) *"Himno Nacional"* "National Hymn" (1968)

Cocoa, harvested mainly on Bioko, is a major cash crop of Equatorial Guinea.

77

ERITREA

FLAG RATIO: 1:2 USE: National/Civil DATE ADOPTED: 1995 LAST MODIFIED: 1995

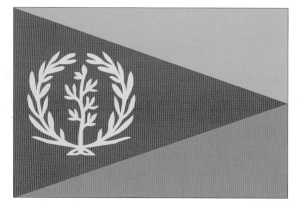

Eritrea's flag is based on the flag of the Eritrean People's Liberation Front (EPLF), leaders in the struggle for independence from Ethiopia. The **red triangle** symbolizes the blood shed in the fight for freedom. The **blue triangle** represents the resources of the Red Sea. The **green triangle** stands for agriculture. From 1952 to 1959 Eritrea flew a flag with a green wreath and olive branch in the center of a field of United Nations' blue. On the new national flag, a **golden wreath** and **olive branch** replace the yellow star of the EPLF on the hoist side of the red triangle.

HISTORY

Eritrea was a dependency of **Ethiopia** until the 16th century, when it fell to the **Ottoman Empire**. In 1890 it became an **Italian** colony. From 1941 to 1952 it was under **British** military administration. In 1952 it federated with Ethiopia, and became a province in 1962. Eritrean separatists began a 30-year campaign of **guerrilla warfare**, and 700,000 **refugees** fled to Somalia. In 1991 the Eritrean People's Liberation Front (**EPLF**) helped topple **General Mengistu**'s Ethiopian government, and won a referendum on independence. Eritrea gained **independence** in 1993. The EPLF government, led by **Isaias Afwerki**, began reconstructing a country impoverished by war and famine. A **war with Ethiopia** (1998–2000) claimed many lives – 40,000 in the Battle of Badme (1999) alone.

AREA 45,400 sq mi (118,000 sq km)

POPULATION 5,939,000

CAPITAL Asmara

GOVERNMENT Transitional government

ETHNIC GROUPS Tigrinya 50%, Tigre and Kunama 40%, Afar 4%, Saho 3% and others

LANGUAGES Afar, Arabic, Tigre and Kunama, Tigrinya

RELIGIONS Islam, Coptic Christian, Roman Catholic

NATIONAL ANTHEM (DATE) "*Ertra, Ertra, Ertra*" "Eritrea, Eritrea, Eritrea" (1993)

Eritrean stamp, issued in 1995, marking Independence Day (May 24, 1993).

ESTONIA

FLAG RATIO: 7:11   USE: National/Civil   DATE ADOPTED: 1918   REINTRODUCED: 1990

Estonia's **tricolor** flag of blue-black-white **horizontal stripes** was originally the flag of the Estonian University Student Association (first flown in 1884). The flag and colors became unofficial national symbols. In 1918 the provisional government made it the national flag. The flag was banned under Soviet rule, but continued to be used as a nationalist symbol. It was readopted in 1990. **Blue** refers to the sky and fidelity of the nation. **Black** represents the peasantry and Estonia's historical suffering. **White** symbolizes the winter snow and freedom.

HISTORY

In 1217 the German **Order of the Brothers of the Sword** conquered southern Estonia (**Livonia**). By 1346 the **Teutonic Knights** controlled the country. In 1629 **Sweden** became the dominant power. **Russia** gained all of Estonia at the end of the **Great Northern War** (1700–21). In 1918 Estonia declared **independence**. In 1940 **Soviet** forces occupied Estonia. More than 60,000 Estonians were killed or deported in the first year of Soviet occupation. In 1941 **Germany** expelled the Soviets. Soviet troops returned in 1944. Between 1945 and 1953, the Soviets deported *c*. 80,000 Estonians. Estonia became one of the 15 socialist republics of the Soviet Union. In 1990 Estonia declared **independence**, a status recognized by the Soviet Union in 1991. Estonia joined **NATO** and the **European Union** in 2004.

AREA 17,400 sq mi (45,100 sq km)
POPULATION 1,283,000
CAPITAL Tallinn
GOVERNMENT Multiparty republic
ETHNIC GROUPS Estonian 65%, Russian 28%, Ukranian 2%, Belarusian 2%, Finnish 1%
LANGUAGES Estonian (official), Russian
RELIGIONS Lutheran, Russian and Estonian Orthodox, Methodist, Baptist, Roman Catholic
NATIONAL ANTHEM (DATE) *"Mu Isamaa, mu Õnn ja Rõõm"* "My Native Land, My Joy, Delight" (1920)

Folk *costumes from Muhu, Estonia's third largest island, northeast of Saaremaa.*

79

ETHIOPIA

FLAG RATIO: 1:2 **USE:** National/Civil **DATE ADOPTED:** 1996 **LAST MODIFIED:** 1996

Emperor **Menelik II** adopted Ethiopia's **tricolor** flag of **horizontal stripes** in 1897 (in reverse order to today's flag). It changed to the present sequence in 1914. **Green** stands for the fertile land. **Yellow** represents religious freedom, while **red** symbolizes the blood shed in defending the country. The **Pan-African** movement used the colors of Ethiopia, Africa's oldest independent nation, to symbolize African unity. The central **golden pentangle** with **four radiant rays** was added in 1996. It represents equality for all Ethiopia's people. It is set against a **blue circle** to denote peace and democracy.

AREA 426,000 sq mi (1,104,000 sq km)

POPULATION 90,874,000

CAPITAL Addis Ababa

GOVERNMENT Federation of nine provinces

ETHNIC GROUPS Oromo 40%, Amhara and Tigre 32%, Sidamo 9%, Shankella 6%, Somali 6% , others

LANGUAGES Amharic (official), many others

RELIGIONS Islam 47%, Ethiopian Orthodox 40%, traditional beliefs 12%

NATIONAL ANTHEM (DATE) *"Whedefit Gesgeshi Woude Henate Ethiopia"* "March Forward, Dear Mother Ethiopia" (1992)

HISTORY

According to legend, **Menelik I**, son of King **Solomon** and the **Queen of Sheba**, founded Ethiopia in *c*.1000 BC. In AD 321, the Kingdom of **Axum** introduced **Coptic Christianity**. In 1930 **Ras Tafari Makonnen** was crowned Emperor **Haile Selassie**. In 1935 **Italy** conquered Ethiopia (Abysinnia), and it became part of **Italian East Africa**. In 1941 the Allies restored Haile Selassie. In 1962 Ethiopia annexed **Eritrea**. In 1974 Haile Selassie was killed in a coup. Major **Haile Mengistu**'s regime caused **civil war**. In 1984 **famine** led to the "Live Aid" relief effort. In 1991 Mengistu fled into exile. **Menes Zenawi** became Prime Minister of the Federal Democratic Republic of Ethiopia in 1995. **War** with Eritrea (1998–2000) claimed many lives.

Ethiopians *were the first people to cultivate coffee.*

FIJI

FLAG RATIO: 1:2 USE: National/Civil DATE ADOPTED: 1970 LAST MODIFIED: 1970

The flag is a modified version of Fiji's colonial flag. It includes the flag of the **United Kingdom**, the former colonial power, and the **shield** from the coat of arms. The flag is **light blue** to represent the Pacific Ocean that surrounds Fiji. The **cross of Saint George** quarters the shield. Each quarter features products or symbols of Fiji: a **sugar-cane** plant, a **coconut palm**, a **bunch of bananas**, and a white **dove of peace**. A **lion** holding a **cocoa pod** crowns the shield.

HISTORY

Abel Tasman discovered the islands of Fiji in 1643. In 1874 Fiji became a **British colony**. The British brought in Indians to work on the **sugar plantations**, and by the 1950s **Indians** outnumbered the native Fijian population. In 1970 Fiji gained **independence**. The election of an Indian-majority government in 1987 prompted a military coup , led by Colonel **Sitiveni Rabuka**, and the proclamation of a republic. In 1992 Rabuka became prime minister. In 1997 Fiji adopted a **multiracial** constitution. **Mahendra Chaudhry** defeated Rabuka in 1999 elections. In May 2000, **George Speight** led a coup, holding hostage the entire cabinet. The **Great Council of Chiefs** dismissed Chaudhry, and declared martial law. The **Commonwealth of Nations** suspended Fiji until 2001. Another coup in 2006 led to international isolation and the imposition of martial law.

AREA 7,100 sq mi (18,300 sq km)
POPULATION 883,000
CAPITAL Suva
GOVERNMENT Republic
ETHNIC GROUPS Fijian 50% (predominantly Melanesian with a Polynesian admixture), Indian 45%, European, other Pacific Islanders, overseas Chinese, and other 5%
LANGUAGES English (official), Fijian, Hindustani
RELIGIONS Methodist 37%, Roman Catholic 9%, Hindu 38%, Sunni Muslim 8%, Sikh 1%
NATIONAL MOTTO "*Rerevaka na Kalau ka Doka na Tui*" "Fear God and Honor the Queen"
NATIONAL ANTHEM (DATE) "*Meda Dau Doka*" "*God Bless Fiji*" (1970)

Fiji is known for its decorated pottery, such as this Saqa drinking vessel.

81

FINLAND

FLAG RATIO: 11:18   **USE:** National/Civil   **DATE ADOPTED:** 1918   **LAST MODIFIED:** 1918

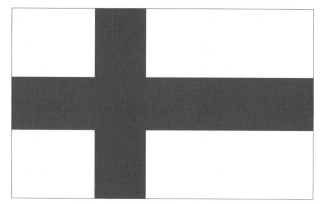

Finland's flag developed from 1861, when Czar Alexander II allowed the Nyland Yacht Club to fly a white flag with an upright blue cross to distinguish its vessels from Russian ships, which were subject to frequent attacks. In 1917 Finland provisionally adopted a lion flag, based on the coat of arms. In 1918, after the civil war, Finland acquired a flag with a **horizontal blue cross** against a **white field**. The blue represents Finland's more than 60,000 lakes. The white symbolizes the snow that blankets the land for five to seven months each year. Other Nordic countries use the "**Scandinavian cross**," but Finland's flag colors are distinct. The **state flag** has Finland's coat of arms in the center of the cross. The **coat of arms** consist of a **golden lion** holding a **sword** against a **red** background.

AREA 131,000 sq mi (338,000 sq km)
POPULATION 5,259,000
CAPITAL Helsinki
GOVERNMENT Multiparty republic
ETHNIC GROUPS Finnish 93%, Swedish 6%
LANGUAGES Finnish and Swedish (both official)
RELIGIONS Evangelical Lutheran 89%
NATIONAL ANTHEM (DATE) *"Maamme"*
"Our Land" (1848)

HISTORY

In the 8th century, Finnish-speaking settlers forced the Lapps into what is now **Lappland. Sweden** conquered Finland in the 13th century. **Lutheranism** took hold in the 16th century. **Russia** gained southeast Finland in the **Great Northern War** (1700–21). In 1809 Finland became a Grand Duchy of **Russia**. In 1917 Finland declared independence, and **Carl Mannerheim**'s forces won the resulting brutal **civil war** in 1918. More than 25,000 Finnish people died in the **Russo-Finnish War** (1939–40). In 1941 Finland allied with **Nazi Germany**. In 1944 Finland signed an armistice with the **Soviet Union**, and the country suffered greatly in the ensuing war with Germany. Finland remained **neutral** during the Cold War. **Urho Kaleva Kekkonen** led Finland from 1956 to 1981. Finland joined the **European Union** in 1995.

Finland's many lakes are a haven for birdlife. The willow ptarmigan is common.

FLAG RATIO: 2:3   USE: National/Civil   DATE ADOPTED: 1794   LAST MODIFIED: 1794

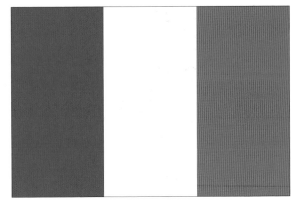

The French *tricolore* first appeared during the French Revolution of 1789. French General Marquis de Lafayette is often credited with placing the **blue** and **red** colors of the arms of **Paris** with the **white** colors of the Bourbon royal family. The *tricolore* initially symbolized the reconciliation of the King with the city, but quickly became the symbol of the revolution. It was first used only as the jack and ensign of the French navy, with the colors in reverse order to the current flag – red at the hoist. On February 15, 1794, the National Convention adopted the present flag.

HISTORY

Hugh Capet, crowned in 987, is often regarded as the first King of France. **Joan** of **Arc** helped liberate France from English rule in the **Hundred Years' War** (1337–1453). In 1589 **Henry IV** became the first **Bourbon** king. **Louis XIV's** (1638–1715) court at **Versailles** was the richest in Europe. **Louis XVI** was executed in the **French Revolution** (1789–99), and France became a republic. **Napoleon I** conquered much of Europe before defeat in 1815. France was a major battleground of **World War I** (1914–18), and Germany occupied it during **World War II** (1939–45). In 1958 **Charles de Gaulle** established the Fifth Republic. In 2012 **François Hollande** became the first socialist president for 17 years.

Henri de Toulouse-Lautrec painted Yvette Gilbert singing "Linger, Longer, Loo" (1864).

AREA 213,000 sq mi (552,000 sq km)
POPULATION 65,312,000
CAPITAL Paris
GOVERNMENT Multiparty republic
ETHNIC GROUPS Celtic, Latin, Arab, Teutonic, Slavic
LANGUAGES French (official)
RELIGIONS Roman Catholic 85%, Islam 8%, others
MOTTO *"Liberté, Egalité, Fraternité"* "Liberty, Equality, Fraternity"
NATIONAL ANTHEM (DATE) "La Marseillaise" (1795)

GABON

FLAG RATIO: 3:4 USE: National/Civil DATE ADOPTED: 1960 LAST MODIFIED: 1960

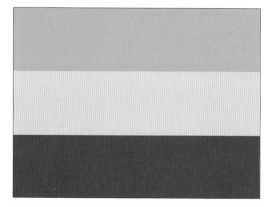

G abon's flag derives from the French *tricolore* and the colors of the **Pan-African** movement. It has **three horizontal stripes** of equal width. The **green** stripe represents the rain forests – the timber trade is very important to Gabon's economy. The **yellow** stripe stands for the sun and for the Equator which runs through Gabon. The **blue** stripe symbolizes the Atlantic Ocean. From 1958 to 1960 Gabon's flag had a French *tricolore* in the canton.

HISTORY

Portuguese explorers reached the coast in the 1470s, and the area later became a source of **slaves**. In 1839 **France** established the first European settlement. In 1849 freed slaves founded **Libreville**. Gabon became a French colony in the 1880s, and part of **French Equatorial Africa** in 1910. It achieved **independence** in 1960. **Léon Mba** was Gabon's first president (1960–67). **Omar Bongo** became president on Mba's death in 1967. In 1968 he created a one-party state. Bongo won the first multiparty presidential elections in 1993, although accusations of fraud and corruption led to riots. He remained in power until his death in 2009 and was succeeded by his son, Ali Bongo Ondimba, in an election the opposition asserted was fraudulent.

AREA 103,000 sq mi (268,000 sq km)

POPULATION 1,577,000

CAPITAL Libreville

GOVERNMENT Multiparty republic

ETHNIC GROUPS Bantu tribes: Fang, Bandjabi, Bapounou, Eshira, Myene, Nzebi, Obamba and Okande

LANGUAGES French (official), Fang, Myene, Nzebi, Bapounou/Eschira, Bandjabi

RELIGIONS Christianity 75%, animist, Islam

NATIONAL MOTTO Union, Travail, Justice"
"Union, Work, Justice"

NATIONAL ANTHEM (DATE) *"La Concorde"*
"The Concord" (1960)

Gabon's rain forests support up to 62,000 elephants – Africa's largest population.

FLAG RATIO: 2:3   **USE:** National/Civil   **DATE ADOPTED:** 1965   **LAST MODIFIED:** 1965

Gambia adopted its present flag upon gaining independence in 1965. The colors of its **horizontal stripes** represent features of the Gambian landscape. **Green** symbolizes the land and agricultural produce. **Blue** stands for the River Gambia, a vital trade route. **Red** represents the hot African sun. The two **narrow white bands** that separate the other stripes stand for peace and unity.

HISTORY

Portuguese navigators landed on the coast of Gambia in 1455, when the area was part of the **Mali Empire**. In 1664 England established a settlement. In 1765 **Britain** founded the colony **Senegambia**, which included parts of present-day Gambia and **Senegal**. The British purchased Banjul Island from a local king in 1816, and founded the town of Bathurst (now **Banjul**). In 1894 Gambia became a **British Protectorate**. It remained under British rule until it achieved **independence** in 1965. **Dawda Jawara** was Gambia's first prime minister. In 1970 Gambia became a **republic**. In July 1994 Jawara was overthrown in a military coup led by **Yahya Jammeh**. Jammeh became president in 1996 elections. In 2000 more than 12 people were shot dead during student demonstrations. Jammeh was re-elected in 2001, 2006, and 2011, amid opposition claims of vote-rigging.

AREA 4,400 sq mi (11,300 sq km)
POPULATION 1,798,000
CAPITAL Banjul
GOVERNMENT Military regime
ETHNIC GROUPS Mandinka 42%, Fula 18%, Wolof 16%, Jola 10%, Serahuli 9%, others
LANGUAGES English (official), Mandinka, Wolof, Fula
RELIGIONS Islam 90%, Christianity 9%, traditional beliefs 1%
NATIONAL MOTTO "Progress, Peace, Prosperity"
NATIONAL ANTHEM (DATE) "For The Gambia, Our Homeland" (1965)

Gambia is a popular destination for bird-watchers. The village weaver is common.

GEORGIA

FLAG RATIO: 2:3 **USE:** National/Civil **DATE ADOPTED:** 2004

Georgia adopted its flag in 2004, replacing a flag that dated back to 1918. The flag recalls Georgia's medieval past, which is regarded as the most glorious period of the country's history. The origins of the flag are disputed. The first known mention of a flag of similar design is from the 14th century. The flag may have links to the crusades.

HISTORY

From the 6th century BC, the two Black Sea kingdoms of **Iberia** and **Colchis** developed in eastern and western Georgia respectively. In 66 BC, the **Roman Empire** conquered both kingdoms. From the 4th to the 7th century, Georgia was a battleground for the **Byzantine** and **Iranian** empires. The Byzantines held Colchis, while the **Sasanians** controlled Iberia. The reign (1184–1213) of **Queen Tamar** saw Georgia build a mighty empire. The **Ottoman Turks** and **Safavid Iranians** fought for control from the mid-16th century. In 1783 Georgia accepted Russian protection, and by 1878 was part of the **Russian Empire**. After a brief era of **independence** (1918–21), Georgia joined Armenia and Azerbaijan to form the Soviet Republic of **Transcaucasia**. In 1936 Georgia became a separate republic. In 1991 it declared **independence**. The period after was characterized by spells of **unrest** and **civil war**, especially regarding the breakaway regions of **Abkhazia** and **South Ossetia**. Military conflict with **Russia** broke out briefly in 2008.

AREA 26,900 sq mi (69,700 sq km)

POPULATION 4,586,000

CAPITAL Tbilisi

GOVERNMENT Multiparty republic

ETHNIC GROUPS Georgian 70%, Armenian 8%, Russian 6%, Azeri 6%, Ossetiam 3%, Greek 2%, Abkhaz 2%, others

LANGUAGES Georgian (official), Russian

RELIGIONS Georgian Orthodox 65%, Islam 11%, Russian Orthodox 10%, Armenian Apostolic 8%

NATIONAL ANTHEM (DATE) *"Dideba zetsit kurthelus"* "Praise Be to the Heavenly Bestower" (1991)

In 1992 Georgian soldiers fighting in Abkhazia received coupons with this stamp.

GERMANY

FLAG RATIO: 3:5   **USE:** National/Civil   **DATE ADOPTED:** 1918   **REINTRODUCED:** 1949

After defeat in the Napoleonic Wars (1803–15), the **black-red-gold** tricolor became linked with the German Revival, perhaps because the colors recalled the Holy Roman Empire. After the **Revolutions of 1848**, the German League adopted the tricolor. In 1867 **Otto von Bismarck** created the North German Confederation, which used a black-white-red tricolor. In 1918 the **Weimar Republic** (1918–33) revived the 1848 flag. In 1935 **Adolf Hitler** adopted a black **swastika** on a white circle against a red field as the national flag. In 1949 the Federal Republic of (**West**) Germany returned to the 1848 flag. From 1959 to 1990 the (**East**) German Democratic Republic flag had a hammer and compass in a ring of rye on the tricolor.

HISTORY

In 962 **Otto I (the Great)** created the Holy Roman Empire, the first *Reich*. Rudolf I founded the **Hapsburg** dynasty in 1273. Charles V's reign (1519–58) saw the **Reformation**. Catholics and Protestants fought the **Thirty Years' War** (1618–48). **Frederick the Great**'s reign (1740–86) saw the growth of **Prussia**. The **Franco-Prussian War** (1870–71) created a second *Reich*. **William II** led Germany into **World War I** (1914–18). In 1933 Hitler declared a **third** *Reich*. Nazi aggression led to **World War II** (1940–45). Defeat saw the division of Germany into East and West; in 1990 it **reunified**. **Angela Merkel** became the country's first woman leader in 2005.

German composer J.S. Bach (1685–1750) was a master of Baroque counterpoint.

AREA 138,000 sq mi (357,000 sq km)
POPULATION 81,472,000
CAPITAL Berlin
GOVERNMENT Federal multiparty republic
ETHNIC GROUPS q km [137, 846sq mi]
LANGUAGES German (official)
RELIGIONS Protestant (mainly Lutheran) 34%, Roman Catholic 34%, Islam 4%, others
CURRENCY Euro = 100 cents
NATIONAL ANTHEM (DATE) *"Lied der Deutschen"* "Song of the Germans" (1922)

87

GHANA

FLAG RATIO: 2:3   USE: National/Civil   DATE ADOPTED: 1957   REINTRODUCED: 1966

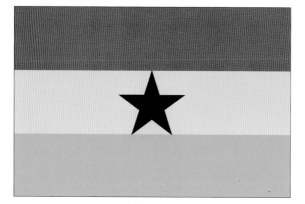

G hana was the first decolonized African nation to take the colors of **Ethiopia** and the **Pan-African movement**. It adopted the **tricolor of horizontal stripes** upon independence from Britain in 1957. From 1964 to 1966 the middle band was white. **Red** stands for the blood shed in the struggle for liberation. **Green** represents the landscape. Gold symbolizes Ghana's mineral wealth and recalls the country's former identity as the Gold Coast. The **black five-pointed star** at the center of the flag is the guiding star of African freedom.

HISTORY

Various African kingdoms existed in the region before the arrival of **Portuguese** explorers in 1471, who named it the **Gold Coast** after its precious mineral resource. In 1642 the **Dutch** gained control, and the Gold Coast became a center of the **slave trade**. In 1874 **Britain** colonized the region excluding **Ashanti**, which fell in 1901. Britain established **cacao plantations**. In 1957 Gold Coast became the first African colony to gain **independence**. **Kwame Nkrumah** was the first prime minister and the country was **renamed** Ghana after a powerful, medieval West African kingdom. In 1960 Ghana became a **republic** with Nkrumah as its president. In 1966 a military **coup** deposed Nkrumah. In 1979 **Jerry Rawlings** led a coup. In 2007 major **oil** deposits were discovered offshore. In 2009, Ghana obtained a substantial loan from the **International Monetary Fund**.

AREA 92,100 sq mi (239,000 sq km)

POPULATION 24,791,000

CAPITAL Accra

GOVERNMENT Republic

ETHNIC GROUPS Akan 44%, Moshi-Dagomba 16%, Ewe 13%, Ga 8%, Gurma 3%, Yoruba 1%

LANGUAGES English (official), Akan, Moshi-Dagomba, Ewe, Ga

RELIGIONS Christianity 63%, traditional beliefs 21%, Islam 16%

NATIONAL MOTTO "Freedom and Justice"

NATIONAL ANTHEM (DATE) "God Bless Our Homeland Ghana" (1957)

The bushbuck is the smallest spiral-horned antelope. It lives in central Africa.

GREECE

FLAG RATIO: 2:3   USE: National/State   DATE ADOPTED: 1833   LAST MODIFIED: 1978

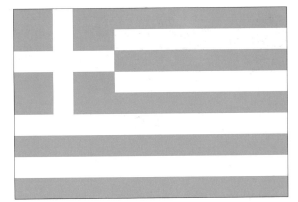

The blue and white flag of Greece has existed in various designs since the 19th century. The present flag consists of **nine horizontal stripes** in alternate lines of **blue and white**, with a **white cross** on a **blue square** in the canton. The number of stripes coincides with the syllables in the war cry of the War of Independence, "Freedom or Death." The blue and white symbolize Greece's crystal clear waters and the crests of the waves. The **Greek cross** represents the Greek Orthodox Church, the predominant faith in Greece.

HISTORY

Athens and **Sparta** led the city-states to victory in the **Persian Wars** (499–479 BC). **Corinth** and **Thebes** defeated Athens in the **Peloponnesian War** (431–404 BC). In 338 BC **Philip II of Macedon** became King of Greece. His son, **Alexander the Great**, built a world empire. In 146 BC, Greece fell to the **Romans**. From AD 330 to 1453 it formed part of the **Byzantine Empire**. In 1456 the **Ottoman Turks** conquered Greece. Greece defeated the Ottomans in the **War of Independence** (1821–29). Greece remained neutral at the start of **World War II**, but **Germany** occupied it in 1941. **Konstantinos Karamanlis** became prime minister in 1955. In 1967 a **military junta** seized power. In 1973 **the Colonels** made Greece a **republic**. In 1974 civilian rule returned. **Austerity measures** imposed in 2008 on in return for financial aid caused widespread protests. The risk of **debt default** led to political instability and economic uncertainty in the **Eurozone**.

AREA 50,900 sq mi (132,000 sq km)
POPULATION 10,760,000
CAPITAL Athens
GOVERNMENT Multiparty republic
ETHNIC GROUPS Greek 98%
LANGUAGES Greek (official)
RELIGIONS Greek Orthodox 98%
NATIONAL MOTTO *"Eleftheria i Thanatos"* "Freedom or Death"
NATIONAL ANTHEM (DATE) *"Ymnos eis tin Eleftherian"* "Hymn to Freedom" (1864)

The Greek Orthodox Church stresses the divine nature of Christ the Savior.

89

GRENADA

FLAG RATIO: 1:2 **USE:** National/Civil **DATE ADOPTED:** 1974 **LAST MODIFIED:** 1974

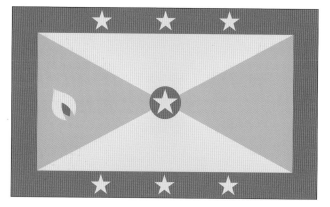

Grenada's flag consists of a **rectangle of four triangles** in alternate **yellow** and **green**, framed by a **red border**. At the center of the flag is a **yellow star** on a **red disc**, representing the borough of St. George's, the capital. On the red border are **six yellow stars**, denoting Grenada's six parishes. On the left-hand green triangle is a stylized **nutmeg**. Nutmeg is the largest export for the "Spice Isle" of Grenada. The flag uses the **Pan-African colors**. Green represents the fertile land. Yellow stands for wisdom, sunshine, and the warmth of Grenadians. Red symbolizes the people's courage and vitality.

AREA 130 sq mi (340 sq km)
POPULATION 108,000
CAPITAL St George's
GOVERNMENT Constitutional monarchy
ETHNIC GROUPS African 82% mixed race 13%, European and South Asian (East Indian) 15%, trace Arawak/Carib Amerindian
LANGUAGES English (official), French *patois*
RELIGIONS Roman Catholic 53%, Anglican 14%, other Protestant 33%
NATIONAL MOTTO "Ever Conscious of God, We Aspire, Build and Advance as One People"
NATIONAL ANTHEM (DATE) "Hail! Grenada" (1974)

HISTORY

In 1498 **Christopher Columbus** sighted the islands. The **Carib** fiercely resisted colonization. In 1650 **France** founded St. George's. In 1783 **Britain** gained control. The British brought **slaves** from Africa to work on the sugar **plantations**. In 1795 **Julian Fedon** led a slave revolt. In 1877 Grenada became a **British colony**. In 1974 it gained **independence**. **Eric M. Gairy** was the first prime minister. In 1979 Gairy was overthrown in a **coup**. In 1983, after a second coup, **United States'** troops invaded and restored democratic government. **Keith Mitchell** served as prime minister from 1995 to 2008, when Tillman Thomas won a clear victory.

The Grenada dove is an endangered species. It lives only in Grenada.

GUATEMALA

FLAG RATIO: 5:8   USE: National/Civil   DATE ADOPTED: 1871   LAST AMENDED: 1997

Like many other nations in Central America, Guatemala has a **blue and white** flag. The flag of the **Central American Federation**, of which Guatemala was a member from 1823 to 1839, had blue and white horizontal stripes. The present flag of **three vertical stripes** (two blue, one white) dates from 1871. Blue stands for justice and loyalty, and recalls the blue of the sky. White symbolizes purity and integrity. The **shield of arms** at the flag's center has two **laurel branches**, two **crossed swords**, two crossed **Remington rifles**, and a **quetzal bird** sitting atop a **scroll** inscribed with "*Libertad 15 de Septiembre de 1821*" (the date of independence).

HISTORY

Between AD 300 and 900 the Quiché **Mayas** ruled Guatemala. The ruins at **Tikal** are the tallest temple-pyramids in the Americas. In 1523–24 the **Spanish** *conquistador* **Pedro de Alvarado** defeated the native tribes. In 1821 Guatemala gained **independence**. **Rafael Carrera** dominated government until his death in 1865. The dictatorships of **Manuel Estrada Cabrera** and **Jorge Ubico** loomed over the early 20th century. From 1960 to 1996 a **civil war** claimed more than 200,000 lives. The territorial dispute with Belize over the border rumbled on into the 21st century.

Guatemala is home to more than 600 species of orchids.

AREA 42,000 sq mi (109,000 sq km)
POPULATION 13,824,000
CAPITAL Guatemala City
GOVERNMENT Republic
ETHNIC GROUPS Ladino (mixed Hispanic and Amerindian) 55%, Amerindian 43%, others 2%
LANGUAGES Spanish (official), Amerindian languages
RELIGIONS Christianity, indigenous Mayan beliefs
NATIONAL MOTTO *"Libertad!"* "Liberty!"
NATIONAL ANTHEM (DATE) *"Guatemala Feliz"* "Guatemala, Rejoice" (1896)

GUINEA

FLAG RATIO: 2:3   USE: National/Civil   ADOPTED: 1958   LAST MODIFIED: 1958

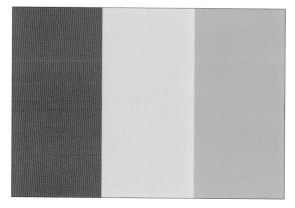

Like many former French colonies, Guinea based its flag on the French *tricolore*. Guinea's flag uses the colors of the **Pan-African** movement. It is the mirror image of Mali's flag. The colors are also symbolic of Guinea's national identity. **Red** symbolizes the blood shed in the struggle for independence and the desire for progress. **Yellow** represents the African sun, Guinean gold, and equality. **Green** stands for the lush vegetation and national prosperity. The colors also correspond to the national motto *"Travail, Justice, Solidarité."*

HISTORY

The Mali Empire dominated West Africa in the 12th century. The Songhai Empire supplanted it in the 15th century. **Portuguese** explorers arrived in the mid-15th century, and the **slave trade** began. In the 18th century, the **Fulani** embarked on a *jihad* (holy war). In 1849 France formed a protectorate on the Atlantic coast. It became the colony of **French Guinea**, and part of French West Africa in 1895. In 1958 Guinea declared independence. **Sékou Touré** was president from 1958 to 1984. In 1970 Portuguese Guinea (now **Guinea-Bissau**) launched an unsuccessful invasion of Guinea. Colonel **Lansana Conté** was president from 1984 to 2008. A military coup after his death led to sanctions. Presidential elections took place in 2010.

AREA 94,900 sq mi (246,000 sq km)
POPULATION 10,601,000
CAPITAL Conakry
GOVERNMENT Multiparty republic
ETHNIC GROUPS Peuhl 40%, Malinke 30%, Soussou 20%, others 10%
LANGUAGES French (official)
RELIGIONS Islam 85%, Christianity 8%, traditional beliefs 7%
NATIONAL MOTTO *"Travail, Justice, Solidarité"* "Work, Justice, Solidarity"
NATIONAL ANTHEM (DATE) *"Liberté"* "Liberty" (1958)

***Demidoff's** dwarf galago or bush baby is one of the smallest primates, 10 to 15 cm long.*

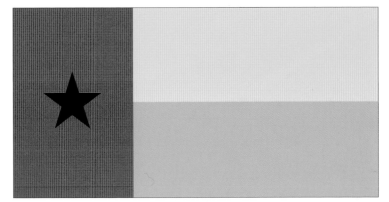

In 1973 Guinea-Bissau adopted a new flag to celebrate its independence from Portugal. Like many decolonized African nations, it took the colors of the **Pan-African** movement. The **red vertical band** symbolizes the blood shed in the liberation struggle. The **yellow horizontal stripe** stands for the hot African sun. The **green horizontal stripe** represents the fertile land and hope for the future. The **black star** on the red band represents the African continent and pays homage to the flag of **Ghana**, the first African colony to gain independence.

HISTORY

Portuguese navigators visited Guinea-Bissau in 1446. From the 17th to the early 19th century, Portugal used the coast as a **slave-trading** base. In 1836 Portugal

joined Guinea-Bissau and **Cape Verde**. Guinea-Bissau became the colony of **Portuguese Guinea** in 1879. In 1956 **Amilcar Cabral** founded the African Party for the Independence of Guinea and Cape Verde (PAIGC). In 1963 the PAIGC launched a guerrilla war. Within five years, it held more than two-thirds of Guinea-Bissau. In 1974 Guinea-Bissau gained **independence**. **Luís de Almeida Cabral**, Amilcar Cabral's brother, was the first president. Political instability is characterized by coups and attempted coups (1980, 1999, 2000, 2001, 2003, 2009), short-lived governments, riots, and assassination attempts.

AREA 13,900 sq mi (36,100 sq km)
POPULATION 1,597,000
CAPITAL Bissau
GOVERNMENT Multiparty presidential republic
ETHNIC GROUPS Balanta 30%, Fula 20%, Manjaca 14%, Mandinga 13%, Papel 7%
LANGUAGES Portuguese (official),Crioulo
RELIGIONS Traditional beliefs 50%, Islam 45%, Christianity 5%
NATIONAL MOTTO Unidade, Luta, Progresso""Unity, Struggle, Progress"
NATIONAL ANTHEM (DATE) *"Esta é a Nossa Pátria Amada"* "This is our Beloved Country" (1975)

Guinea-Bissau has many villages in the mangrove swamps along the Atlantic coast.

93

GUYANA

FLAG RATIO: 3:5   USE: National/Civil   DATE ADOPTED: 1966   LAST MODIFIED: 1966

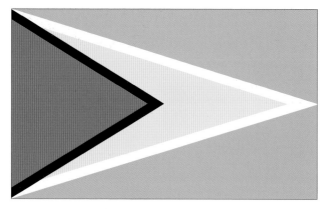

Guyana's flag is nicknamed "the Golden Arrow." It combines the colors of the **Pan-African** movement (red, yellow, green) and colors associated with **Marcus Garvey** (red, black, green). The **"golden arrow"** represents progress and Guyana's mineral wealth. The **red triangle** signifies the energy and potential of the Guyanese. The **green field** symbolizes the nation's forests and fertile land. The **white fimbriation** stands for its many rivers, and the **black fimbriation** denotes the endurance of the Guyanese.

HISTORY

In 1581 the **Dutch** built trading posts. They established **sugar plantations** in 1658, importing Africans as **slave labor**. In 1841 Britain captured the town of **Demerara**. The colony of **British Guiana** emerged in 1831. In 1834 Britain abolished slavery and began to use **indentured labor** from India and China. In 1953 **Cheddi Jagan** became prime minister. In 1961 British Guiana gained **self-rule** under Jagan. Guyana gained **independence** in 1966. **Forbes Burnham** led the country from 1964 to 1985. In 1970 Guyana became a **republic**. In 1978, 912 members of the **People's Temple cult**, led by Jim Jones, committed mass suicide. **Ethnic tensions** snapped into **riots** in 1998. In 2007 a **UN** tribunal ruled on the long-running **Guyana-Suriname** dispute over maritime territory. **Donald Ramotar** was elected president in 2011.

AREA 83,000 sq mi (215,000 sq km)

POPULATION 775,000

CAPITAL Georgetown

GOVERNMENT Multiparty republic

ETHNIC GROUPS East Indian 50%, Black 36%, Amerindian 7%, others

LANGUAGES English (official), Creole, Hindi, Urdu

RELIGIONS Christianity 50%, Hinduism 35%, Islam 10%, others

NATIONAL MOTTO "One People, One Nation, One Destiny"

NATIONAL ANTHEM (DATE) "Dear Land of Guyana, of Rivers and Plains" (1966)

Caribbean manatees *live in coastal waters and rivers. They grow to 13ft (4m) long.*

HAITI

FLAG RATIO: 3:5 USE: National DATE ADOPTED: 1986 LAST MODIFIED: 1986

Haiti's **blue-and-red flag** originates from its war of independence against France. On May 18, 1803, Haitian rebel leader Jean-Jacques Dessalines tore up the French *tricolore*, discarding the white stripe. In 1807 General Alexandre Pétion changed the orientation of the stripes from vertical to **horizontal**. The **blue stripe** represents Haitians of African and French descent. The red stripe represents the blood shed in the struggle for liberation. At the center of the flag is the **coat of arms** on a **white rectangle**. The coat of arms features a **Liberty cap** atop a **royal palm** tree and two cannons, flanked by flags. A **scroll** reads *"L'Union Fait la Force"* ("Strength in Unity"). At the 1936 Olympics, Liechtenstein noticed that it had the same flag as the civil flag (without arms) of Haiti and changed its flag.

HISTORY

Haiti and **Dominican Republic** share the island of Hispaniola. **Columbus** discovered Hispaniola in 1492. In 1697 Spain ceded Haiti to France. In 1790 **Toussaint L'Ouverture** led a slave revolt. Haiti gained **independence** in 1804. Dictators **"Papa Doc"** and **"Baby Doc" Duvalier** ruled from 1957 to 1986. In 1991 a military coup toppled **Jean-Bertrand Aristide.** He returned in 1994, but was deposed in 2004. Hurricanes in 2005 and 2008 and a massive earthquake in 2010 led to devastation and economic collapse.

AREA 10,700 sq mi (27,800 sq km)
POPULATION 9,720,000
CAPITAL Port-au-Prince
GOVERNMENT Multiparty republic
ETHNIC GROUPS Black 95%, Mulatto/White 5%
LANGUAGES French and Creole (both official)
RELIGIONS Roman Catholic 80%, Voodoo
NATIONAL MOTTO *"Liberté, Egalité, Fraternité"* "Liberty, Equality, Fraternity"
NATIONAL ANTHEM (DATE) *"La Dessalinienne"* "The Song of Dessalines" (1904)

Haiti hosted the 25th General Assembly of the Organization of American States in 1995.

95

HONDURAS

FLAG RATIO: 1:2   USE: National/Civil   DATE ADOPTED: 1866   LAST MODIFIED: 1866

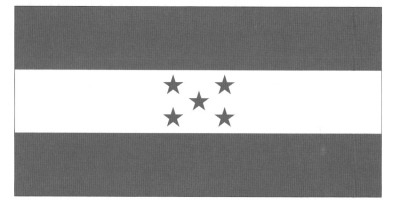

L ike many other nations in Central America, Honduras has a **blue and white** flag in homage to the Argentine Generals Belgrano and San Martín. In 1823 Honduras, Costa Rica, El Salvador, Guatemala and Nicaragua united to form the Central American Federation, which adopted a flag with **three horizontal stripes (two turquoise, one white)**. In 1839 the Federation dissolved, but Honduras retained the flag. In 1866 it added **five turquoise stars** in an X-pattern to the center of its flag. The stars represent the five former members of the Federation. The turquoise bands stand for the Caribbean Sea and Pacific Ocean.

HISTORY

Christopher Columbus sighted the coast in 1502, and Pedro de Alvarado founded the first **Spanish** settlements in 1524. In 1576 the Spanish discovered the ruins of the **Maya** civilization at Copán, western Honduras, but they became covered in dense forest and were only rediscovered in 1839. In 1821 Honduras gained **independence**, forming part of the Mexican Empire. From 1823 to 1838 Honduras was a member of the Central American Federation. Britain controlled the **Mosquito Coast**. In the 1890s the United States developed **banana plantations**. From 1963 to 1982 the military ruled Honduras. In 1969 Honduras fought the "**Soccer War**" against El Salvador. In 1998 **Hurricane Mitch** killed more than 5500 people.

AREA 43,300 sq mi (112,000 sq km)

POPULATION 8,144,000

CAPITAL Tegucigalpa

GOVERNMENT Republic

ETHNIC GROUPS Mestizo 90%, Amerindian 7%, Black (including Black Carib) 2%, White 1%

LANGUAGES Spanish (official), Amerindian dialects

RELIGIONS Roman Catholic 97%

NATIONAL ANTHEM (DATE) *"Tu Bandera"* "Your Flag" (1915)

The scarlet macaw (Ara macao) *is the national bird of Honduras.*

HUNGARY

FLAG RATIO: 2:3   USE: National   DATE ADOPTED: 1848   LAST MODIFIED: 1989

Hungary's **tricolor** of **red, white** and **green** first appeared together on the cord of a seal in 1618, in the reign of Matthias II. The present tricolor of **horizontal stripes** was adopted during the Revolution of 1848. In 1849 Austria regained control and scrapped the flag. In 1867 Austria agreed to the joint Austro-Hungarian Empire and the tricolor returned with a royal coat of arms. In 1949 Hungary became a communist republic and the tricolor acquired a Soviet-style emblem. After the Hungarian Uprising in 1956, the plain tricolor was revived as the national flag. Red symbolizes strength. White stands for fidelity, while green represents hope.

HISTORY

In *c*. 895 **Magyars**, led by **Árpád**, settled in Hungary. In 1699 Leopold I established **Hapsburg** rule. **Lajos Kossuth** declared Hungary's independence in 1848, but Emperor **Franz Joseph** regained control in 1849. Austrian defeat in the **Austro-Prussian War** (1866) led to the formation of the Austro-Hungarian Empire. In 1918 Hungary declared **independence**. In 1941 Hungary allied with **Nazi Germany**. Virulent **antisemitism** saw the murder of many Hungarian Jews. In 1948 **communists** overthrew the government of **Imre Nagy**. In 1956 a **revolt** led to the return of Nagy. The **Soviets** crushed the revolt and **János Kádár** came to power. In 1989 Kádár resigned and multiparty elections were held in 1990. Hungary joined **NATO** in 1999 and the **European Union** in 2004.

Embroidery *from Kalocsa, southern Hungary, often has beautiful floral patterns.*

AREA 35,900 sq mi (93,000 sq km)
POPULATION 9,976,000
CAPITAL Budapest
GOVERNMENT Multiparty republi
ETHNIC GROUPS Magyar 90%, Gypsy, German, Serb, Romanian, Slovak
LANGUAGES Hungarian (official
RELIGIONS Roman Catholic 68%, Calvinist 20%, Lutheran 5%, others
NATIONAL ANTHEM (DATE) *"Himnusz"*
"National Anthem of Hungary" (1844)

ICELAND

FLAG RATIO: 18:25 **USE:** National/Civil **DATE ADOPTED:** 1915 **CODIFIED:** 1944

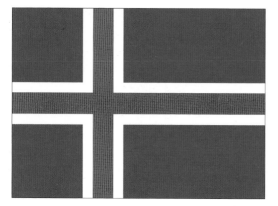

From 1380 to 1918 Iceland was under Danish rule and Denmark's flag was its national flag. In 1897 an unofficial flag appeared with a white cross on a blue field. In 1915 King Christian X of Denmark ruled that this flag was too similar to the flag of Greece, and instead approved a flag with a **red cross bordered in white** on a **blue field** for use on land and within Icelandic waters. In 1918 Iceland gained self-rule and adopted the 1915 flag. Iceland retained the flag upon becoming a republic in 1944. Blue stands for its mountains. White represents ice. Red symbolizes the fire from Iceland's volcanoes. The "**Scandinavian cross**" recalls Iceland's Nordic links.

HISTORY

In AD 874 Norwegian **Vikings** colonized Iceland, and in 930 the settlers founded the world's oldest parliament (***Althing***). In 1262 Iceland united with **Norway**. When Norway joined with **Denmark** in 1380, Iceland came under Danish rule. During the colonial period, Iceland lost much of its population due to migration, disease, and natural disaster. In 1918 it became a self-governing **kingdom**, united with Denmark. Iceland escaped Nazi German occupation during **World War II** (1940–45), largely due to the presence of United States forces. In 1944, a referendum decisively voted to sever links with Denmark, and Iceland became an independent **republic**. In 1946 it joined NATO. The extension of Iceland's fishing limits in 1958 and 1977 led to the "**Cod War**" with the United Kingdom. In 2008, Iceland's banking sector collapsed, triggering financial crisis.

AREA 39,800 sq mi (103,000 sq km)
POPULATION 311,000
CAPITAL Reykjavik
GOVERNMENT Multiparty republic
ETHNIC GROUPS Icelandic 97%, Danish 1%
LANGUAGES Icelandic (official)
RELIGIONS Evangelical Lutheran 87%, other Protestant 4%, Roman Catholic 2%, others
NATIONAL ANTHEM (DATE) *"Lofsöngur"*
"Song of Praise" (1874)

Snaefell *volcano is the highest peak in Iceland outside of the glaciated regions.*

INDIA

FLAG RATIO: 2:3   USE: National/Civil   DATE ADOPTED: 1947   LAST MODIFIED: 1947

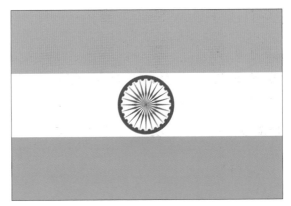

In 1931 the Indian National Congress, leaders of the struggle for independence from Britain, adopted a **horizontal tricolor** flag of **saffron, white,** and **green**. Apparently designed by Congress leader "Mahatma" Gandhi, the flag had a blue spinning wheel, a Gandhian symbol of self-sufficiency, on the white stripe. Saffron (orange) represented India's Hindu people, green stood for its Muslims, and white symbolized the peace between them. When India gained independence in 1947, the Assembly of India adopted the tricolor but replaced the spinning wheel with the *Dharma Chakra* ("Wheel of Law") on the "lion capital" of King Ashoka at Sarnath, northern India.

HISTORY

In *c.* 1500 BC **Aryans** conquered India and established **Hinduism**. **Ashoka** unified India in the 3rd century BC. In 1526 **Babur** founded the **Mogul Empire**. **Robert Clive** helped establish **British India** (1757–1947). Unrest culminated in the **Indian Mutiny** (1857–58). In the 1920s, **"Mahatma" Gandhi** began his campaign of passive resistance against British rule. On independence in 1947, the country split into **Pakistan** and India.

AREA 1,269,000 sq mi (3,287,000 sq km)
POPULATION 1,189,173,000
CAPITAL New Delhi
GOVERNMENT Multiparty federal republic
ETHNIC GROUPS Indo-Aryan (Caucasoid) 72%, Dravidian (Aboriginal) 25%, others (mainly Mongoloid) 3%
LANGUAGES Hindi, English,Telugu, Bengali, Marathi, Tamil, Urdu, Gujurati, Malayalam, Kannada, Oriya, Punjabi, Assamese, Kasmiri, Sindhi and Sanskrit (all official)
RELIGIONS Hinduism 82%, Islam 12%, Sikhism 2%, Christianity 2%, Buddhism and others
NATIONAL MOTTO *"Satyam eva jayate"* "Truth alone triumphs"
NATIONAL ANTHEM (DATE) *"Jana-Gana-Mana"* "Thou Art The Ruler Of All Minds" (1950)

Chandragupta, grandfather of Ashoka, founded the Maurya Empire (321–185 BC).

INDONESIA

FLAG RATIO: 2:3 USE: National/Civil DATE ADOPTED: 1945 LAST MODIFIED: 1945

The Indonesian flag is known as the "*Sang Saka Merah Putih*" ("Grand **bicolor** of red and white"). The flag is based on the flag of the Javanese **Majapahit Empire**, which dominated Indonesia and Malaya from the 13th century to the 16th. **Red** and **white** are sacred colors, representing the physical and the spiritual worlds. Red also symbolizes bravery and freedom. White also stands for purity and justice. In the 1920s, nationalists adopted the colors to represent their struggle against Dutch rule. On August 17, 1945, Acmad Sukarno raised the flag to proclaim independence.

HISTORY

In the 7th century the Indian **Gupta dynasty** introduced **Buddhism** and built **Borobudur**. In 1511 the Portuguese seized **Malacca**. In 1799 Indonesia became a **Dutch** colony. **Krakatoa** erupted in 1883, killing *c*. 50,000 people. In 1942 **Japan** occupied Indonesia. In 1945 Indonesia declared independence. In 1949 it became a republic. **Sukarno** was the first president. In 1965 General **Suharto** seized power. In 1975 Indonesia seized control of **East Timor**. **Megawati Sukarnoputri**, daughter of Sukarno, became president in 2001. In 2002 East Timor gained independence. In 2004, a tsunami killed some 200,000 people.

AREA 735,000 sq mi (1,905,000 sq km)
POPULATION 245,613,000
CAPITAL Jakarta
GOVERNMENT Multiparty republic
ETHNIC GROUPS Javanese 45%, Sundanese 14|%, Madurese 7%, coastal Malays 7%, *c*.300 others
LANGUAGES Bahasa Indonesian (official), many others
RELIGIONS Islam 88%, Roman Catholic 3%, Hinduism 2%, Buddhism 1%
NATIONAL MOTTO *"Bhinneka Tunggal Ika"* "Unity in Diversity"
NATIONAL ANTHEM (DATE) *"Indonesia Raya"* "Great Indonesia" (1949)

Tari gamyong is a traditional dance in Central Java province (Jawa Tengah).

The colors represent Islam (**green**), peace (**white**), and courage (**red**). They first appeared in **tricolor** form on Iran's flag in 1907. After the abdication of the Shah in 1979, the symbol at the center became **four crescents** and a **sword**, symbolize the five precepts of Islam. The **inscription** "*Allah-u Akbar*" ("God is great") is written in ancient **Kufic script** along the horizontal borders of the white stripe. It appears 22 times as to celebrate Iran's Islamic Revolution, which took place on the 22nd day of the 11th month of the Iranian calendar (February 11, 1979). The **hoist** is to the viewer's right.

HISTORY

In 550 BC, **Cyrus the Great** conquered the **Median Empire**, and established the **Achaemenid** dynasty, rulers of Iran's first Empire. The Empire survived the **Persian Wars** (492–497 BC) against the Greek city-states, but fell to **Alexander the Great** in 331 BC. In AD 224, the **Sassanids** restored Iranian rule. **Arabs** conquered Iran in 641, introducing Islam. In the 1510s, Shah **Ismail** reunified Iran and founded a **Shi'a** theocracy. In 1921, **Reza Pahlavi** seized power. In 1941 British and Soviet forces occupied Iran, and **Muhammad Pahlavi** succeeded his father as Shah. In 1979 Pahlavi fled and **Ayatollah Khomeini** established an Islamic republic. **Muhammad Khatami** became president in 1997, but was replaced by the hardliner Mahmoud Ahmadinejad in 2005.

The hawfinch (Coccothraustes coccothraustes) *is found throughout Iran.*

AREA 636,000 sq mi (1,648,000 sq km)
POPULATION 77,891,000
CAPITAL Tehran
GOVERNMENT Islamic Republic
ETHNIC GROUPS Persian 51%, Azeri 24%, Gilaki and Mazandarani 8%, Kurd 7%, Arab 3%, Lur 2%, Baluchi 2%, Turkmen 2%
LANGUAGES Persian, Turkic 26%, Kurdish
RELIGIONS Islam (Shi'ite Muslim 89%)
NATIONAL ANTHEM (DATE) Untitled (1990)

IRAQ

FLAG RATIO: 2:3 **USE:** National/Civil **DATE ADOPTED:** 1963 **LAST MODIFIED:** 2008

The **red**, **white**, and **black** colors of the Iraqi flag are based on the **Pan-Arab** colors adopted by Hussein ibn Ali. The design is similar to the design of the former United Arab Republic (UAR). The **green *takbir*** "*Allah-u Akbar*" ("God is Great"), written in Arabic script, was added during the Gulf War (1991). Three stars were removed in 2008; they had represented the members of the old United Arab Republic (Iraq, Egypt, Syria), reflecting Iraq's desire for Arab union. The **hoist** should be to the viewer's right.

HISTORY

Ancient **Mesopotamia** roughly equates to modern Iraq. **Hammurabi** founded **Babylonia** in the 18th century BC. **Nebuchadnezzar** conquered Jerusalem in 597 BC, beginning the Babylonian Captivity of the Jews. In AD 637 Arab conquest introduced **Islam**. Baghdad served as capital of the **Abbasid** caliphate (750–1258). Mesopotamia was part of the **Ottoman Empire** from 1534 to 1916. In 1921 Britain made **Faisal I** King of Iraq. In 1932 Iraq won **independence**. In 1958 Faisal was executed and a republic born. In 1963 the **Ba'ath Party** seized power. **Saddam Hussein** became president in 1979, purging the party and leading Iraq into the **Iran-Iraq War** (1980–88) and the **Gulf War** (1991). In 1991 Saddam crushed a Kurdish and Shi'a **rebellion**. In 2003, a **US-led coalition** invaded and deposed him, leading to years of insurgency, instability, and sectarian violence.

AREA 169,000 sq mi (438,000 sq km)
POPULATION 30,400,000
CAPITAL Baghdad
GOVERNMENT Republic
ETHNIC GROUPS Arab 77%, Kurdish 19%, Assyrian and others
LANGUAGES Arabic (official), Kurdish (official in Kurdish areas), Assyrian, Armenian
RELIGIONS Islam 97%, Christianity and others
NATIONAL ANTHEM (DATE) *"Ardulfurataini Watan"* "Land of Two Rivers" (1981)

Ishtar Gate*, entrance to ancient Babylon, was built (600 BC) by King Nebuchadnezzar.*

IRELAND

FLAG RATIO: 1:2 USE: National/Civil DATE ADOPTED: 1918 CODIFIED: 1937

The tricolor of **green**, **white** and **orange** was first flown as an emblem of the Young Ireland movement in 1848. It came into popular use after the Easter Rising of 1916. The colors represent aspects of Ireland's population. Green stands for the historic Gaelic and Anglo-Norman (Roman Catholic) section of society. Orange denotes the Protestant supporters of William of Orange. The white stripe symbolizes the hope for a lasting peace between the two traditions.

HISTORY

In *c*. 432 **St Patrick** introduced **Christianity**. In 1014 **Brian Boru** defeated the Viking invaders. In 1171 **Henry II** of England conquered Ireland. In 1649 **Oliver Cromwell** brutally crushed an Irish rebellion. In the 1916 **Easter Rising**, Irish nationalists declared independence. The British Army's harsh breaking of the rebellion led to a landslide victory for Sinn Féin at elections in 1918. The Anglo-Irish Treaty (1921) saw the creation of the Irish Free State and the partition of Ireland. **Arthur Griffith** became the first *taoiseach* (prime minister). **Civil war** raged in 1922–23. In 1937 a new constitution declared the nation of Éire to be the whole island of Ireland. **Eamon de Valera** served as *taoiseach* (1932–48, 1951–54, 1957–59) and president (1959–73). Ireland was badly affected by the global financial crisis and required international financial assistance.

Stamp *marking the 50th year of the organization to promote Irish traditional arts.*

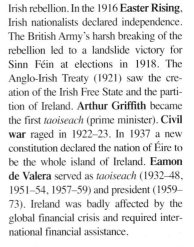

AREA 27,100 sq mi (70,300 sq km)
POPULATION 4,671,000
CAPITAL Dublin
GOVERNMENT Multiparty republic
ETHNIC GROUPS Irish 94%
LANGUAGES Irish (Gaelic) and English (both official)
RELIGIONS Roman Catholic 92%, Protestant 3%
NATIONAL MOTTO *"Cead Mile Failte"*
"One Hundred Thousand Welcomes"
NATIONAL ANTHEM (DATE) *"Amhrán Na bhFiann"*
"The Soldier's Song" (1926)

103

ISRAEL

FLAG RATIO: 8:11   **USE:** National/Civil   **DATE ADOPTED:** 1948   **LAST MODIFIED:** 1948

According to legend, the six-pointed blue star made of two triangles at the center of Israel's flag derives from the shield of **King David** (*c*. 1000 BC). Often known as the "Star of David", it also appeared on King Solomon's ring and is also called the "Seal of Solomon". In 1354 the Jewish community in Prague chose the Star of David as the symbol for their flag. In 1897 the World Zionist Organization adopted a flag with a **white field**, blue stripes and the Star of David. In 1948 Israel took the Zionist flag as its own. The **blue bands** come from the stripes of the *tallit* (Jewish prayer shawl). Blue and white are traditional Jewish colors symbolizing purity.

HISTORY

Israel forms most of the Biblical **Holy Lands**. In *c*. 2000 BC Jews moved into Palestine from Egypt. In 63 BC the **Romans** conquered Palestine. In AD 640 it fell to Muslim Arabs. From 1516 to 1918 it was part of the **Ottoman Empire**. After World War I it came under **British** control. In 1947 the United Nations agreed to partition Palestine into an Arab and a Jewish state. On May 14, 1948, the State of **Israel** was proclaimed. **David Ben-Gurion** was the first prime minister. Hundreds of thousands of Palestinians fled. Israel successfully defended itself in the **Arab-Israeli Wars**. In 1967 it occupied Sinai, Golan Height, the West Bank, and Gaza Strip. In 1982 it returned Sinai to Egypt. Conflict over the Occupied Territories continues.

AREA 8,000 sq mi (20,600 sq km)
POPULATION 7,473,000
CAPITAL Jerusalem
GOVERNMENT Multiparty republic
ETHNIC GROUPS Jewish 80%, Arab and others 20%
LANGUAGES Hebrew and Arabic (both official)
NATIONAL ANTHEM (DATE) *"Hatikva"* "The Hope" (1948)

Two dancers *on a stamp celebrating the festival of the Jewish Year 5762 (2001).*

ITALY

FLAG RATIO: 2:3   USE: National/Civil   DATE ADOPTED: 1946   LAST MODIFIED: 1946

Italy's flag was established during the Napoleonic Wars and styled after the French *tricolore*. The colors apparently derived from the uniform of the Milan civic militia. In 1796 Napoleon ordered that the military flag of the Lombard Legion bear **vertical stripes** of **green**, **white**, and **red**. In 1797 the Cispadana Republic adopted a flag with red, white, and green horizontal stripes. Later that year, Cispadana and Transpadana formed the Cisalpine Republic, which adopted the present tricolor in 1798. In 1861 the Kingdom of Italy adopted the tricolor with the Savoy coat of arms at the center. In 1946 the plain tricolor became the flag of the Republic of Italy.

HISTORY

The assassination of **Julius Caesar** led to the formation of the **Roman Empire** (27 BC) under Augustus. In 962 **Otto I** established the Holy Roman Empire. **Giuseppe Garibaldi** helped create the Kingdom of Italy under **Victor Emmanuel II** in 1861. The papacy refused to concede Rome, and **Vatican City** gained independence in 1929. Dictator **Benito Mussolini** came to power in 1922. Italy fought on the Axis side for much of World War II, but in 1943 Mussolini was dismissed and Italy surrendered. In 1948 Italy became a republic. The effects of the global financial and **Eurozone** crises led to the collapse of **Silvio Berlusconi**'s power and the installation of a government of technocrats under **Mario Monti** in 2011.

AREA 116,000 sq mi (301,000 sq km)
POPULATION 61,017,000
CAPITAL Rome
GOVERNMENT Multiparty republic
ETHNIC GROUPS Italian 94%, German, French, Albanian, Slovene, Greek
LANGUAGES Italian (official), German, French, Slovene
RELIGIONS Predominantly Roman Catholic, Judaism, Islam
NATIONAL ANTHEM (DATE) *"Inno di Mameli"* "Mameli's Hymn" (1946)

Etruscan tomb painting of a young girl from the 4th century BC.

JAMAICA

FLAG RATIO: 1:2 **USE:** National/Civil **DATE ADOPTED:** 1962 **LAST MODIFIED:** 1962

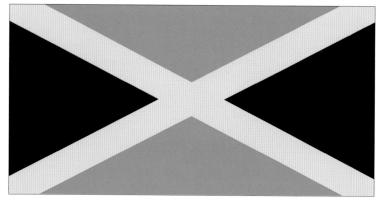

A committee of Jamaica's House of Representatives designed the national flag. "The sun shineth, the land is green, and the people are strong and creative" sums up the flag's symbolism. It features a **gold saltire** (diagonal cross), representing Jamaica's sunshine and natural resources. The **green** triangles symbolize agriculture and the hope for the future. The **black** triangles on the hoist and flag stand for the hardships creatively faced and overcome and by its people.

HISTORY

Christopher Columbus made landfall on May 5, 1494. Spanish conquerors quickly eradicated the indigenous **Arawak** population. In 1509 the first **Spanish settle-**ment appeared in the St Ann's Bay area. In 1655 **England** captured Jamaica, and the freed Spanish slaves (**Maroons**) took to the hills. **Port Royal** became a haven for buccaneers such as **Henry Morgan**. The English established **sugar plantations** using **slave labor** from Africa. The frequent slave rebellions precipitated the **abolition** of the slave trade in 1834. In 1865 Governor **Edward John Eyre** crushed the Morant Bay Rebellion. In 1872 **Kingston** became the island's capital. In 1962 Jamaica gained independence. **Sir Alexander Bustamante** was the nation's first prime minister. **Michael Manley** led Jamaica into the Caribbean Community and Common Market (CARICOM). **Portia Simpson Miller** became Jamaica's first female Prime Minister in 2006.

AREA 4,200 sq mi (11,000 sq km)
POPULATION 2,868,000
CAPITAL Kingston
GOVERNMENT Constitutional monarchy
ETHNIC GROUPS Black 91%, Mixed 7%, East Indian
LANGUAGES English (official), patois English
RELIGIONS Protestant 61%, Roman Catholic 4%
MOTTO "Out of Many, One People"
NATIONAL ANTHEM (DATE) "Jamaica, Land We Love" (1962)

The bird of paradise *or crane flower is native to South Africa.*

Japan's flag is called the *Hinomaru* ("Sun Circle"). The Japanese word for the country is *Nihon* or *Nippon* ("Land of the Rising Sun"). According to legend, the sun goddess founded the state and gave birth to the first Emperor, **Jimmu**, in the 7th century BC. The flag was officially adopted in 1870. In 1999, Japan's parliament set the proportions of the flag and the position of the **red sun disk** on the **white field**.

HISTORY

The **Yamato** clan established the state of Japanese, with **Kyoto** as its capital, in the 5th century. From the 12th to the 19th century, **shoguns** (warrior-kings) ruled Japan. European contact dates from the arrival of Portuguese navigators in 1543. Under the **Tokugawa** shogunate (1603–1867), Japan isolated itself from the rest of the world. During Emperor **Meiji**'s reign (1868–1912), Japan modernized and industrialized. Japan gained Korea in the **Russo-Japanese War** (1904–05). In 1937 Japan invaded China, starting the Second **Sino-Japanese War**. Japan allied itself with Germany and Italy during **World War II** (1939–45). In 1941 Japan attacked the US base at **Pearl Harbor**. In 1945, the US dropped **atomic bombs** on the cities of **Hiroshima** and **Nagasaki**. Emperor **Hirohito** surrendered and the US occupied Japan from 1945–52. Japan has the world's third largest economy, but was badly affected by an earthquake and tsunami in 2011.

The Gujou Odori dance festival *takes place every year in the prefecture of Gifu.*

AREA 146,000 sq mi (378,000 sq km)
POPULATION 126,476,000
CAPITAL Tokyo
GOVERNMENT Constitutional monarchy
ETHNIC GROUPS Japanese 99%, Chinese, Korean, Brazilian and others
LANGUAGES Japanese (official)
RELIGIONS Shintoism and Buddhism 84% (most Japanese consider themselves to be both Shinto and Buddhist), others
NATIONAL ANTHEM (DATE) *"Kimigayo"* "His Majesty's Reign" (2001)

JORDAN

FLAG RATIO: 1:2 USE: National/Civil DATE ADOPTED: 1921 LAST MODIFIED: 1946

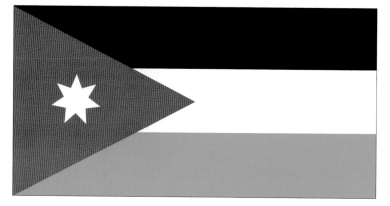

In 1916 Hussein ibn Ali raised the flag of the Great Arab Revolt against Ottoman rule in Arabia. The colors represented the **Pan-Arab** nature of the rebellion, which Lawrence of Arabia assisted. The color of the **three stripes** stood for Arab dynasties of the Early Middle Ages: **black** for the Abbasid dynasty from Baghdad, **white** for the Umayyad dynasty from Damascus, and **green** for the Fatimid dynasty from Morocco. The **crimson triangle** joining the stripes is the color of the Hashemite dynasty, rulers of Jordan. The revolt was successful but Arab unity rapidly disintegrated. In 1923 Hussein's son, Abdullah, became Emir of Transjordan. Abdullah added the **seven-pointed white star**, symbolizing both the unity of Jordan's people and the *Fatiha* – the first seven verses of the **Koran**.

HISTORY

In 1946 **Abdullah** became King of the **independent Hashemite** Kingdom of Jordan. In 1950, after the first of the **Arab-Israeli Wars**, Jordan annexed the **West Bank** and **East Jerusalem**. In 1951 Abdullah was assassinated. His son succeeded as **Hussein I** in 1953. The **Six-Day War** (1967) ended in the Israeli occupation of the West Bank and East Jerusalem. Jordan became home to more than one million **Palestinian** refugees. In 1970 Jordan fought a bloody **civil war** against the Palestinian Liberation Organization (PLO). In 1994 King Hussein signed a peace treaty with Israel. In 1999 Hussein died and was succeeded by his son as **Abdullah II**.

AREA 34,500 sq mi (89,300 sq km)
POPULATION 6,508,000
CAPITAL Amman
GOVERNMENT Constitutional monarchy
ETHNIC GROUPS Arab 98% (Palestinians 50%)
Languages Arabic (official)
LANGUAGES 42sq km [34,495sq mi]
RELIGIONS Islam (mostly Sunni) 94%,
Christianity (mostly Greek Orthodox) 6%
NATIONAL ANTHEM (DATE) *"Asha al-Maleek"*
"Long Live the King" (1946)

Madaba Mosaic *is a 6th-century map of Palestine, discovered in Jerusalem in 1897.*

KAZAKSTAN

FLAG RATIO: 1:2 USE: National/Civil DATE ADOPTED: 1992 LAST MODIFIED: 1992

Kazakstan's flag has a **sky-blue** field, a traditional color of Central Asian nomads. At the flag's center is a **golden sun**, symbolizing Kazakstan's glorious future. The sun has **32 rays**. Underneath the sun and its rays is a soaring, golden **steppe eagle** (berkut), standing for the freedom of Kazak people. At the hoist is a band of gold "national ornamentation."

HISTORY

In 1218 **Genghis Khan** conquered the area. Upon his death in 1227, present-day Kazakstan was split between the khanate of his son **Jagatai** and the Empire of the **Golden Horde**. In the early 16th century, **Kazak nomads** united to create a mighty empire under **Kasim Khan**. The empire rapidly fragmented into three khanates. In 1742, devastated by attacks from the **Dzungars**, the Kazak khanates accepted Russian protection. By 1848 the **Russian Empire** had absorbed the three khanates. Mass immigration of Russians sped the process of Russification. In 1922 Kazakstan became an autonomous republic of the **Soviet Union**. More than 1.5 million Kazaks were killed or died of starvation under the dictatorship of **Joseph Stalin**. In the 1950s, the "Virgin Lands" project sought to turn vast areas of grassland into cultivated land to feed the Soviet Union. In 1991, Kazakstan declared **independence** under President **Nursultan Nazarbayev**. In 1997 **Astana** replaced Almaty as capital. The first pipeline carrying **oil** direct from the **Caspian Sea** opened in 2001 and another to China in 2005.

***Bukhar Zhirau Kalkamanov** is a famous 18th-century Kazak poet.*

AREA 1,052,000 sq mi (2,725,000 sq km)
POPULATION 15,522,000
CAPITAL Astana
GOVERNMENT Multiparty republic
ETHNIC GROUPS Kazakh 53%, Russian 30%, Ukranian 4%, German 2%, Uzbek 2%
LANGUAGES Kazakh (official). Russian, the former official language, is widely spoken
RELIGIONS Islam 47%, Russian Orthodox 44%
NATIONAL ANTHEM (DATE) *"Mamlekettik Gemni"* "National Anthem" (1944)

KENYA

FLAG RATIO: 2:3   USE: National/Civil   DATE ADOPTED: 1963   LAST MODIFIED: 1963

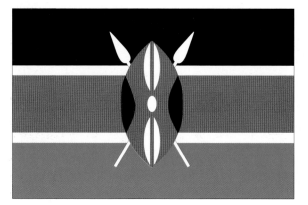

The flag of Kenya African National Union (KANU), the party that led the fight for independence, inspired the national flag. The **black** horizontal **stripe** stands for black majority rule, **red** symbolizes humanity and the struggle for liberation, and **green** represents the nation's fertile land. The thinner **white** dividing stripes, added on independence, signify peace. At the flag's center is a traditional **Masai shield** and **two crossed spears**, symbolizing the defense of freedom.

HISTORY

From the 8th century, Arab traders began to settle on the coast of **East Africa**. By the 12th century, **Mombasa** had become an **Islamic** city-state. In 1498 **Vasco da Gama** explored the coast and **Portugal** soon dominated the trade routes. In 1698 **Oman** captured Mombasa. In the 18th century, the pastoralist Masai moved into central Kenya from the north. In the 19th century, the **Kikuyu** largely displaced them. In 1895 the **British** established the **East Africa Protectorate**. In 1903 the British completed a railroad from Mombasa to **Lake Victoria**. In 1905 **Nairobi** became capital of the protectorate. After World War II (1939–45), some leaders of the Kikuyu formed a secret society, known as the **Mau Mau**, to fight for independence. In 1964 Kenya gained independence. **Jomo Kenyatta** was the first president. In 1978 **Daniel arap Moi** succeeded Kenyatta as president. Disputed elections in 2007 led to inter-ethnic violence.

AREA 224,000 sq mi (580,000 sq km)

POPULATION 41,071,000

CAPITAL Nairobi

GOVERNMENT Multiparty republic

ETHNIC GROUPS Kikuyu 22%, Luhya 14%, Luo 13%, Kalenjin 12%, Kamba 11%, other

LANGUAGES Kiswahili and English (both official)

RELIGIONS Protestant 45%, Roman Catholic 33%, traditional beliefs 10%, Islam 10%

NATIONAL MOTTO *"Harambee"* "Pull Together"

NATIONAL ANTHEM (DATE) *"Ee Mungu nguvu yetu"* "Oh God of All Creation" (1963)

Masai *nomads wear distinctive red clothing and beaded necklaces.*

Kiribati's flag was chosen by a national competition in 1979. Based on the colonial coat of arms, the College of Arms modified the design but the people of Kiribati successfully demanded a return to the original design. The **white** and **blue** wavy lines represent the Pacific Ocean. The **golden sun** rises from the waves into the **red sky**. A **frigate bird** flies over the sun, symbolizing control of the ocean.

HISTORY

Kiribati consists of 33 coral atolls divided among three island groups in the Pacific: the **Gilbert Islands** (including **Tarawa**, home to the capital Bairiki), the **Phoenix Islands**, and the **Line Islands**. Austronesian-speaking peoples settled Kiribati before the 1st century AD. In 1606 **Spanish** explorer Pedro Fernandez de Quiros sighted Butaritari, an atoll in

what later became known as the Gilbert Islands. In 1788 British naval captains **Thomas Gilbert** and **John Marshall** discovered other islands. In the 19th century, missionaries spread **Christianity**. In 1892 the Gilbert Islands and the Ellice Islands became a **British protectorate**. In 1900 **phosphate** was found on **Banaba**. In 1942 Japan occupied the Gilbert Islands. United States forces expelled the Japanese in 1943. In 1975, the mainly Polynesian Ellice Islands gained independence as **Tuvalu**. In 1979 the Gilbert Islands declared **independence** as Kiribati ("Gilberts" in the Kiribati language).

AREA 280 sq mi (730 sq km)
POPULATION 101,000
CAPITAL Tarawa
GOVERNMENT Multiparty republic
ETHNIC GROUPS Micronesian 84%, Polynesian 14%
LANGUAGES English (official), Kiribati
RELIGIONS Roman Catholic 54%, Kiribati Protestant Church 38%
NATIONAL MOTTO "*Te Mauri Te Raoi ao Te Tabomoa*" "Health, Peace and Prosperity"
NATIONAL ANTHEM (DATE) "*Teirake Kaini Kiribati*" "Stand, Kiribati" (1979)

The Moorish idol fish is native to the Pacific waters surrounding Kiribati.

111

KOREA, NORTH

FLAG RATIO: 1:2 **USE:** National/Civil **DATE ADOPTED:** 1948 **LAST MODIFIED:** 1948

The flag of the Democratic People's Republic of Korea consists of three **stripes** – blue, red, blue – separated by two narrow white lines. On the hoist of the red stripe is a **red five-pointed star** on a **white disk**. **Blue** symbolizes the desire for peace, **red** represents the blood of those who died in the socialist revolution, and **white** stands for the pure spirit of its people. The **red star** signifies the leading role of the "Great Leader" Kim Il Sung in the transition to communism.

HISTORY

The name "Korea" derives from the **Koryo dynasty**, which ruled from 918 to 1392. In 1910 **Japan** gained control. After Japan's defeat in World War II, Korea divided into two zones of occupation: Soviet forces north of the **38th Parallel**, and US troops south of this line. In 1948 North Korea established a communist government led by **Kim Il Sung**. In June 1950, North Korea invaded South Korea. The ensuing **Korean War** (1950–53) claimed *c*. 4 million lives and ended in stalemate. After the Korean War, several million Koreans fled Kim Il Sung's dictatorship, and North Korea became a secretive society. In the early 1990s, North Korea's **nuclear weapons** program gathered momentum. In 1994 Kim Il Sung died and his son **Kim Jong Il** succeeded as "Dear Leader." His policies included isolationism and rigid state control. In 2011 he was succeeded by his son **Kim Jong-un**.

AREA 46,500 sq mi (121,000 sq km)
POPULATION 24,457,000
CAPITAL Pyongyang
GOVERNMENT Single-party people's republic
ETHNIC GROUPS Korean 99%
LANGUAGES Korean (official)
RELIGIONS Buddhist and Confucian with some Christianity, but religious expression now under government control.
NATIONAL ANTHEM (DATE) *"Aegukga"*
"Patriotic Song" (1947)

The Tale of Chun Hyang is a romantic masterpiece of Korean literature.

KOREA, SOUTH

FLAG RATIO: 2:3 USE: National/Civil DATE ADOPTED: 1950 LAST MODIFIED: 1950

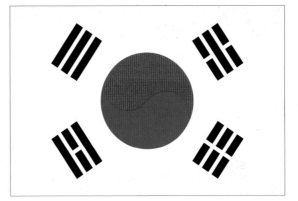

The Republic of Korea's flag is the *Taegeukgi*. The **blue lower half** of the *taegeuk* **circle** at the flag's center represents **yin** (negative cosmic forces), while the **red upper half** stands for **yang** (positive cosmic forces). Yin and yang embody the concepts of continual movement, balance and harmony. **Four barred trigrams** (*kwae*) symbolize the elements. The *kwae* of unbroken bars on the top left represents *geon* (wind), the lower left *i* (fire), the top right *gam* (water), and the bottom right *gon* (earth).

HISTORY

The name "Korea" derives from the **Koryo dynasty**, which ruled from 918 to 1392. The **Yi dynasty** succeeded the Koryo. In 1910 **Japan** gained control. After Japan's defeat in World War II, Korea divided into two zones of occupa-

tion: US forces south of the **38th Parallel**, and Soviet troops north of this line. In 1948 **Syngman Rhee** established a government in South Korea. In 1950 North Korea invaded South Korea. **The Korean War** (1950–53) claimed *c*. 4 million lives and ended in stalemate. In 1961 **General Park** overthrew Rhee in a military coup. In 1979 Park was assassinated. In 1988 Seoul hosted the Olympic Games. In 1992 **Kim Young Sam** became South Korea's first civilian president. In 1998 **Kim Dae Jung** succeeded Kim Young Sam as President. In 2000 **Kim Dae Jung** received the Nobel Peace Prize for his efforts toward peace and reunification with North Korea. Relations between the neighboring countries continued to fluctuate.

The Courtesan's Sword Dance, part of a series celebrating 5000 years of Korean art.

AREA 38,300 sq mi (99,300 sq km)
POPULATION 48,755,000
CAPITAL Seoul
GOVERNMENT Multiparty republic
ETHNIC GROUPS Korean 99%
LANGUAGES Korean (official)
RELIGIONS No affiliation 46%, Christianity 26%, Buddhism 26%, Confucianism 1%
NATIONAL ANTHEM (DATE) *"Aegukga"* "Patriotic Song" (1948)

KOSOVO

FLAG RATIO: 1:1.4 **USE:** National/Civil **DATE ADOPTED:** 2008 **DATE ADAPTED:** 2008

The flag was adopted immediately after independence from Serbia was declared in 2008. The design is adapted from an entry in an international design competition. Within the **blue field**, the **six white stars** above the **gold map** represent the six major ethnic groups in Kosovo.

HISTORY

The Republic of Kosovo was formerly part of **Serbia** and, before 2003, part of **Yugoslavia**. Most of its people are **Albanian-speakers** and **Muslims**, but there is an important Christian Serb minority. In the early 13th century, Kosovo was part of the Serbian Empire but, after the Battle of Kosovo (1389) it came under **Muslim Turkish rule**. Serbia regained control of Kosovo in 1912 and in 1918 it became part of the Kingdom of Serbia. In 1946, it joined Yugoslavia as an autonomous province within the Republic of Serbia. In 1989, Serbia curtailed Kosovo's autonomy, while **Albanian speakers** declared independence. In 1995, the Albanian speakers set up the **Kosovo Liberation Army**, which launched an uprising. In 1998, Serbia began repressive measures against Kosovo, resulting in massacres and ethnic cleansing. In 1999, NATO forces bombed Serbia and placed Kosovo under a temporary administration. The Kosovo Assembly declared **independence** in February 2008. This was recognized by the United States and major EU countries, but not by Serbia and Russia, although talks between Serbia and Kosovo over border controls were concluded in 2011.

AREA 4,200 sq mi (10,900 sq km)
POPULATION 1,826,000
CAPITAL Pristina
GOVERNMENT Republic
ETHNIC GROUPS Albanian 88%, Serb 7%, other 5%
LANGUAGES Albanian and Serbian (both official), Turkish
RELIGIONS Islam, Serbian Orthodox, Roman Catholic
NATIONAL ANTHEM (DATE) "Europe" (2008)

The Dardanian idol (c.*3500 BC*), *the earliest evidence of human settlement in the region.*

KUWAIT

FLAG RATIO: 1:2   USE: National/Civil   DATE ADOPTED: 1961   LAST MODIFIED: 1961

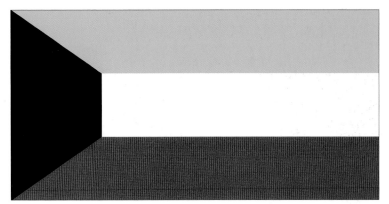

Kuwait's flag has **three horizontal stripes** and a **trapezoid** on the hoist side. Its colors are **Pan-Arab**. The colors derive from a poem by Safie Al-Deen Al-Hili. The top stripe is **green**, symbolizing Kuwaiti hospitality. The middle stripe is **white**, representing the commitment to peace. The bottom stripe is **red**, symbolizing Kuwait's determination to resist aggression. The trapezoid is **black**, signifying decisiveness.

HISTORY

The small Sheikdom of Kuwait in the **northeast of Arabia** was founded in the early 18th century. In 1756 **Sabah al-Awal** established a Sheikdom. During the 19th century, the **Ottoman** and **British Empires** fought for control of Kuwait. In 1899 it became a **British** protectorate. **Oil** was discovered in 1938, and Kuwait's huge oil reserves rapidly made it one of the richest countries in the world. In 1961 Kuwait gained **independence**. Kuwait supported **Saddam Hussein**'s Iraqi regime in the **Iran-Iraq War** (1980–88). In August 1990 **Iraq invaded** Kuwait, capturing the capital, Kuwait City, within a day. In the **Gulf War**, allied coalition troops, led by the United States, liberated Kuwait in February 1991. The cost of postwar reconstruction was c. US$100 billion. In 1992 Kuwait held its first parliamentary elections. Women were given political rights in 2005. The Amir, **Sheikh Sabah al-Sabah**, holds executive power, in the face of increasing assertiveness by parliament.

Kuwait stamp marking the sixth anniversary of Liberation Day (February 26, 1991).

AREA 6,900 sq mi (17,800 sq km)
POPULATION 2,596,000
CAPITAL Kuwait City
GOVERNMENT Constitutional monarchy
ETHNIC GROUPS Kuwaiti 45%, other Arab 35%, South Asian 9%, Iranian 4%, other 7%
LANGUAGES Arabic (official), English
RELIGIONS Islam 85%, Christianity, Hinduism
NATIONAL ANTHEM (DATE) *"Al-Nasheed Al-Watani"* "National Anthem" (1978)

KYRGYZSTAN

FLAG RATIO: 3:5 **USE:** National/Civil **DATE ADOPTED:** 1992 **LAST MODIFIED:** 1992

At the center of Kyrgyzstan's flag is a circular, stylized representation of the **roof of a yurt** (tent), the traditional home of Kyrgyz nomads. Surrounding the yurt is a **golden sun with 40 rays**, representing the 40 tribes united (according to an epic poem) by **Manas** to form Kyrgyzstan. The flag's **red field** recalls the banner of Manas.

HISTORY

The Kyrgyz, a forest-dwelling people who practiced shamanism, have inhabited the country since ancient times. In 1207 they surrendered to Genghis Khan's son **Jöchi**. Under **Mongol** rule, the Kyrgyz preserved their **nomadic** and **shamanist** culture. In the 18th century, the **Qing** (Manchu) **dynasty** of China became nominal rulers of the region. In 1830

Muhammad Ali, Khan of **Kokand**, conquered the Kyrgyz and introduced **Islam**. In 1876 Kyrgystan became part of the **Russian Empire**. Russian immigration forced many Kyrgyz into the mountains of the **Tian Shan**. In 1916 Russia crushed a native rebellion and many Kyrgyz fled into China. In 1936 Kirgizia became a republic of the **Soviet Union**. The Soviets **forcibly resettled** most of the remaining Kyrgyz population onto collective farms. In August 1991, Kyrgyzstan declared **independence**. **Askar Akayev** was the new nation's first president. He remained in power until toppled by political unrest in 2005. An uprising in 2010 led to the ousting of President Kurmanbek Bakiyev.

AREA 77,200 sq mi (200,000 sq km)
POPULATION 5,587,000
CAPITAL Bishkek
GOVERNMENT Multiparty republic
ETHNIC GROUPS Kyrgyz 65%, Russian 13%, Uzbek 13%, Ukranian 1%, others
LANGUAGES Kyrgyz and Russian (both official)
RELIGIONS Islam 75%, Russian Orthodox 20%
NATIONAL ANTHEM (DATE) *"Mamlekettik gimni"*
"National Anthem" (1992)

Kyrgyz eaglers (berkutchi) *have been hunting with golden eagles for 6000 years.*

116

LAOS

FLAG RATIO: 2:3 USE: National/Civil DATE ADOPTED: 1975 LAST MODIFIED: 1975

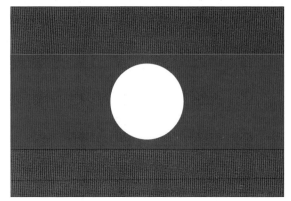

In 1975 the Republic of Laos adopted its present national flag. The flag was originally the banner of the Pathet Leo (Patriotic Front), the communist, republican movement that overthrew the royalist government. The large, horizontal central **blue stripe** is a representation of the Mekong River that flows through Laos. It also symbolizes the nation's wealth. The **red stripes** stand for the two regions of Laos that are both joined and separated by the river. It also denotes the blood shed in the struggle for independence. The **white disk** in the center signifies the full moon over the Mekong River, the country's bright future, and the unity of its people.

HISTORY

In 1533 Prince **Fa Ngum** founded the Lao kingdom of Lan Xang. **Burma** captured the kingdom in 1571. Thailand gained control in 1778. In 1893 Laos became part of **French Indochina**. **Japan** occupied Laos during World War II. **France** regained control after the war. In **1953** Laos achieved independence but plunged into civil war between royalist forces, backed by the **United States**, and republican forces supported by the **Viet Cong**. During the **Vietnam War** (1955–75), the US bombed Laos in an effort to halt supplies to the Viet Cong. In 1975 Laos became a **republic**.

Traditional wedding costumes *of the Lao Theung (midland Lao), native people of Laos.*

AREA 91,400 sq mi (237,000 sq km)
POPULATION 6,477,000
CAPITAL Vientiane
GOVERNMENT Single-party republic
ETHNIC GROUPS Lao Loum 68%, Lao Theung 22%, Lao Soung 9%
LANGUAGES Lao (official), French, English
RELIGIONS Buddhism 60%, traditional beliefs and others 40%
NATIONAL MOTTO Peace, Independence, Democracy, Unity and Prosperity
NATIONAL ANTHEM (DATE) *"Pheng Xat Lao"* "Lao National Anthem" (1947)

LATVIA

FLAG RATIO: 1:2 **USE:** National/Civil **DATE ADOPTED:** 1918 **REINTRODUCED:** 1990

Latvia has one of the oldest national flags. In 1279 Latvian tribes carried a red banner with a white stripe into battle against the Estonians. The **white stripe** represents truth, trust, righteousness, and freedom. The **red field** stands for the blood shed for the nation's independence. Latvia adopted the current design after gaining independence in 1918, and it was declared the official flag in 1921. The flag was banned after the Soviet Union invaded Latvia in 1940. In 1990 Latvia declared independence and the Soviet flag was removed. In 1991 Latvia officially adopted the flag of 1918.

HISTORY

In the 13th century, the **Livonian** Knights conquered Latvia. Russian defeat in the **Livonian War** (1558–83) left Latvia partitioned between **Poland-Lithuania** and **Sweden**. Czar **Peter the Great** gained parts of Latvia in the **Great Northern War** (1700–21) and all of Latvia fell under Russian rule after the **Partitions of Poland** (1772, 1793, 1795). In 1918 Latvia declared independence. Latvia was under Soviet and then German rule in World War II. Almost the entire Jewish population was killed in the Nazi Holocaust. In 1991 the Soviet Union recognized Latvia's **independence**. In 1993 **Guntis Ulmanlis** became the first directly elected president. The global economic crisis from 2008 led to recession and soaring unemployment.

AREA 24,900 sq mi (64,600 sq km)
POPULATION 2,205,000
CAPITAL Riga
GOVERNMENT Multiparty republic
ETHNIC GROUPS Latvian 58%, Russian 30%, Belarusian, Ukranian, Polish, Lithuanian
LANGUAGES Latvian (official), Lithuanian, Russian
RELIGIONS Lutheran, Roman Catholic, Russian Orthodox
NATIONAL ANTHEM (DATE) *"Dies Sveti Latviju"* "God Bless Latvia" (1992)

Latvian stamp of the traditional costume of peasants from Rietumvedzeme.

LEBANON

FLAG RATIO: 2:3 USE: National/Civil DATE ADOPTED: 1943 LAST MODIFIED: 1943

The green tree at the center of Lebanon's flag is the **cedar of Lebanon**. A symbol of Lebanon since Biblical times (Psalms 92:12), today precious few cedar trees survive in Lebanon. In 1918, after the collapse of Ottoman rule, Lebanon adopted a flag with a cedar tree on an entirely white field. In 1920 the flag changed to the French *tricolore* with a cedar tree in its central white band. Members of the Lebanese Parliament designed the present flag in 1943. The cedar tree is a symbol of immortality. The horizontal **red bands**, exactly half the width of the white band, represents the blood shed in the liberation struggle. The **white band** stands for peace and the snow-capped Lebanese mountains.

HISTORY

Lebanon was the heart of ancient **Phoenicia**, which became part of the **Roman** province of Syria in 64 BC. It was a major battleground of the **Crusades** (1095–1291). In 1516 the **Ottoman** Turks conquered, devolving power first to Druze dynasty of the **Maans** (1516–1697) and then to the **Shihab** dynasty (1697–1842), which converted to **Maronite** Christianity. In 1920 the League of Nations mandated Lebanon to **France**. In 1946 it gained **independence**. A civil war (1975–90) claimed *c*.130,000 lives. The assassination of former PM **Rafiq Hariri** in 2005. forced withdrawal of Syria's troops. **Israel** launched air strikes in 2006 in response to **Hezbollah's** kidnap of two soldiers.

Stamp of 13th-century painting of The Lion and Jackal *folk tale, marking Childrens' Day.*

AREA 4,000 sq mi (10,400 sq km)
POPULATION 4,143,000
CAPITAL Beirut
GOVERNMENT Multiparty republic
ETHNIC GROUPS Arab 95%, Armenian 4%, others
LANGUAGES Arabic (official), French, English
RELIGIONS Islam 70%, Christianity 30%
NATIONAL ANTHEM (DATE) *"An-Nashid Al-Watani Al-Lubnani"* "Lebanese National Anthem" (1927)

LESOTHO

FLAG RATIO: 2:3   **USE:** National/Civil   **DATE ADOPTED:** 2006   **LAST MODIFIED:** 2006

Lesotho adopted its present flag with three horizontal stripes to honor the 40th anniversary of the country's **independence**. Its colors are based on the national motto: **blue** for rain, **white** for peace, and **green** for prosperity. The **black** emblem in the central band is a **mokoroto**, a Basotho hat, which replaced the previous emblem on the white field (this consisted of an animal-skin shield, supported by an *assegai* stabbing spear, a plumed **spine**, and a **bludgeon**). In the previous flag the stripes ran diagonally from top right to bottom left. A white mokoroto appeared on the country's first flag in 1966.

HISTORY

Lesotho is an **enclave kingdom** within the Republic of **South Africa**. In 1824 **Moshoeshoe,** retreating from the terror unleashed by **Shaka**'s expansion of the **Zulu Empire**, formed a stronghold on the mountain of **Thaba Bosiu**. The settlement grew into the kingdom of Basotho. In 1871 Basutoland became part of **British Cape Colony**. In 1966 Lesotho gained **independence** under **Moshoeshoe II**. In 1970 Chief **Leabua Jonathan** seized control. In 1986 Moshoeshoe II returned to power in a coup. **Letsie III** succeeded Moshoeshoe in 1995. In 1998 South African troops restored order after an army mutiny. Many Sotho **migrate** to work in the **mines** of **South Africa**. Repeated droughts in 2001–2003 and 2007 led to states of emergency being declared. Parliamentary elections in 2002 and 2006 resulted in political instability.

AREA 11,700 sq mi (30,400 sq km)
POPULATION 1,925,000
CAPITAL Maseru
GOVERNMENT Constitutional monarchy
ETHNIC GROUPS Sotho 99%
LANGUAGES Sotho and English (both official)
RELIGIONS Christianity 80%, traditional beliefs 20%
NATIONAL MOTTO *"Khotso, Pula, Nala"* "Peace, Rain, Prosperity"
NATIONAL ANTHEM (DATE) "Lesotho Fatse La Bontata Rona" (1967)

Nkho is a traditional water pot in Lesotho. It is dug into the ground to keep water cool.

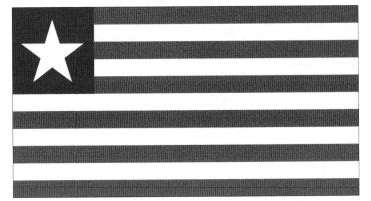

Liberia's flag is called "**Lone Star**". It is based on the flag of the **United States**. In 1822 the American Colonization Society founded Liberia as a colony for liberated slaves from the United States. Five years later, the colony adopted its own flag, similar to the present flag but with more stripes and bearing a cross, representing the Christian faith of the Society. In 1847 Liberia declared independence and adopted the current flag, designed by seven women. The **11 horizontal stripes**, six red and five white, stand for the 11 signatories to Liberia's declaration of independence. In the canton, a **white five-pointed star** against a **blue field** symbolizes the shining example of Liberia as the first independent nation in Africa.

HISTORY

In 1822 **Monrovia** was built for freed slaves. In 1847 **Joseph Roberts** became the first president of independent Liberia. In 1926 the US **Firestone Company** opened a vast rubber plantation. **William Tubman** led Liberia from 1943 to 1971. In 1980 **Samuel Doe** came to power in a **coup**. **Civil war** (1989–97), killed over 150,000. **Charles Taylor** became president in 1997. He declared a state of emergency in 2002 as fighting grew on the **Guinea border** and went into exile in 2003. Presidential elections in 2005 were won by Ellen Johnson Sirleaf.

AREA 43,000 sq mi (111,000 sq km)

POPULATION 3,787,000

CAPITAL Monrovia

GOVERNMENT Multiparty republic

ETHNIC GROUPS Indigenous African tribes 95% (including Kpelle, Bassa, Grebo, Gio, Kru, Mano)

LANGUAGES English (official), ethnic language

RELIGIONS Christianity 40%, Islam 20%, traditional beliefs and others 40%

NATIONAL MOTTO "The Love of Liberty Brought Us Here"

NATIONAL ANTHEM (DATE) "All Hail, Liberia, Hail" (1847)

Liberia has one of the largest populations of the endangered western chimpanzee.

121

LIBYA

FLAG RATIO: 1:2 USE: National/Civil DATE ADOPTED: 1951 READOPTED: 2011

In 2011, Libya readopted the 1951 flag of the kingdom of Libya, replacing Colonel Gadaffi's single field of green. It has three bands of **red**, **black**, and **green**, with a **white crescent and star** centered in the black band, which is twice as broad as the other two. Red represents the blood of the people, green freedom and independence, and the crescent and star Islam.

HISTORY

The first inhabitants were the **Berbers**. In the 7th century BC, Greeks colonized **Cyrenaica**. **Carthage** gained Phoenician settlements in **Tripolitania** in the 6th century BC. **Arabs** conquered Libya in 643, and Islam became the dominant religion. From 1551 Libya formed part of the **Ottoman Empire.** Power resided with local rulers known as **Janissaries**. During the 17th century, **Barbary** pirates attacked ships from bases on Libya's **Mediterranean** coast. In 1914 **Italy** conquered Libya. Libya was a battleground for many of the North Africa campaigns in World War II. In 1951 Libya became an **independent monarchy**, led by **King Idris**. In 1969 **Colonel Muammar al-Qaddafi** established a socialist Islamic state. In 1986, after evidence of Libya's involvement in international **terrorism**, the United States bombed **Tripoli**. In 1999 Libya sent for trial two Libyans suspected of the 1992 bombing of Pan-Am Flight 103 over **Lockerbie**, Scotland. Civil war broke out in 2011 as part of the "Arab Spring," followed by European-led NATO military strikes lasting until the overthrow and death of Qaddafi. The National Transitional Council that emerged vowed to turn Libya into a democratic, multiparty state.

AREA 679,000 sq mi (1,760,000 sq km)
POPULATION 6,598,000
CAPITAL Tripoli
GOVERNMENT Transitional
ETHNIC GROUPS Libyan Arab and Berber 97%
LANGUAGES Arabic (official), Berber
RELIGIONS Islam (Sunni Muslim) 97%
NATIONAL ANTHEM (DATE) *"Allahu Akbar"*
"God is Great" (1969)

Unity is strength *stamp. Qaddafi long championed the cause of Arab unity.*

LIECHTENSTEIN

FLAG RATIO: 3:5 USE: National/Civil DATE ADOPTED: 1937 LAST MODIFIED: 1957

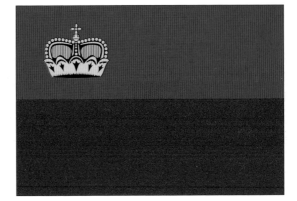

Liechtenstein's flag consists of **two** equal **horizontal stripes** of **blue** (top) and **red** with a **gold crown** on the hoist side of the top stripe. The origin of the colors is unknown, but they probably derive from the livery colors of the ruling House of Liechtenstein. Blue is the color of a radiant sky and red symbolizes the glow of the hearth at evening gatherings. At the 1936 Olympics it was noticed that Liechtenstein's flag was identical to the flag of Haiti, and a crown was added in 1937. In 1957 the design of the crown was modified. The crown represents the unity of the nation under the royal house.

HISTORY

In 1719 Emperor Charles VI merged the County of **Vaduz** and the Seigniory of **Schellenberg** to create the Principality of Liechtenstein in 1719. It remained part of the **Holy Roman Empire** until 1806, when it joined the Confederation of the Rhine. From 1815 to 1866 it formed part of the **German Confederation**. In 1866 Liechtenstein gained **independence**. In 1921 Liechtenstein entered into a currency **union** with **Switzerland** and in 1923, a customs union. Until 1990 Switzerland also handled its foreign policy. **Women** finally received the **vote** in 1984. In **1990** the country joined the **United Nations**. Liechenstein has a constitutional and hereditary monarchy. In a referendum in 2003, 64% of voters voted to hand extra powers to Prince Hans Adam II, including the right to appoint and dismiss governments.

Liechtenstein is famous for its beautifully illustrated stamps.

AREA 60 sq mi (160 sq km)
POPULATION 35,000
CAPITAL Vaduz
GOVERNMENT Constitutional monarchy
ETHNIC GROUPS Alemannic 86%
LANGUAGES German (official), Alemmannic
RELIGIONS Roman Catholic 80%, Protestant 7%
NATIONAL ANTHEM (DATE) "*Oben am jungen Rhein*" "High Above the Young Rhine" (1963)

LITHUANIA

FLAG RATIO: 1:2 **USE:** National/Civil **DATE ADOPTED:** 1918 **REINTRODUCED:** 1989

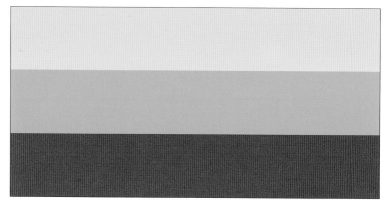

Lithuania adopted its present flag in 1989, shortly before gaining independence from the Soviet Union. The design is the same as the flag adopted in 1918, but it has the ratio 1:2 rather than 2:3. It consists of **three horizontal bands**: yellow (top), green (middle) and red (bottom). The colors are common in Lithuanian folk art and costume. **Yellow** stands for grain and wealth, **green** for forests and hope, and **red** for the blood shed in the struggle for independence. In 1953, as a republic of the Soviet Union, it adopted a **tricolor** flag of red, white, and green with a hammer and sickle on the thicker red band.

HISTORY

In 1253 Pope Innocent IV crowned **Mindaugas** as Grand Duke of Lithuania. In 1386 Lithuania united with **Poland**, and the two countries **merged** in 1569. The Battle of **Tannenberg** (1410) marked the defeat of the Teutonic Knights. **Russia** gained most of Lithuania in the Second and Third Partitions of Poland (1793, 1795). In 1918 Lithuania declared **independence**. From 1926 to 1940 it was ruled by the dictator **Antonas Smetona**. In 1941 Germany occupied Lithuania. In 1944 the **Soviet Union** occupied Lithuania. President **Vytautas Landbergis** declared independence in 1990 and Soviet troops withdrew by 2003. Lithuania joined the **European Union** in 2004.

AREA 25,200 sq mi (65,200 sq km)
POPULATION 3,536,000
CAPITAL Vilnius
GOVERNMENT Multiparty republic
ETHNIC GROUPS Lithuanian 80%, Russian 9%, Polish 7%, Belarusian 2%
LANGUAGES Lithuanian (official), Russian, Polish
RELIGIONS Mainly Roman Catholic
NATIONAL ANTHEM (DATE) "Lietuva Teyvne Musu" "Lithuania, Our Homeland" (1918)

*Aukstaiciai (Uplanders) traditional costume.
Aukstaiciai have their own dialect.*

LUXEMBOURG

FLAG RATIO: 3:5 USE: National DATE ADOPTED: 1845 LAST MODIFIED: 1972

Luxembourg's tricolor flag derives from its coat of arms, which shows a **red** lion in front of **blue** and **white** horizontal **stripes**. The first recorded use of the coat of arms is on the banner of Earl Heinrich VI in 1228. Luxembourg's flag is identical to the tricolor of the **Netherlands**, except for the flag ratio and the lighter shade of its blue band.

HISTORY

The Grand Duchy of Luxembourg has the **highest GDP per capita** in the world (US$36,400). In the 11th century, the County of Luxembourg formed one of the largest fiefs of the **Holy Roman Empire**. In 1354 Luxembourg became a Duchy. In 1482 it passed to the **Hapsburg** dynasty, and in the 16th century it became part of the **Spanish Netherlands**. In 1714 it passed to **Austria**. Occupied by **France** during the Napoleonic Wars, it became a Grand Duchy at the Congress of Vienna (1815). In 1839 **Belgium** acquired much of the Duchy. In 1867 Luxembourg gained **independence**. **Germany** occupied Luxembourg in both World Wars. In 1960 Belgium, the Netherlands and Luxembourg formed the economic union of **Benelux**. Luxembourg was a founder member of the **European Union (EU)**. In 2008 a constitutional crisis was provoked when Grand Duke Henri refused to sign a bill legalizing euthanasia. Constitutional reform reduced his role to a ceremonial one.

AREA 1,000 sq mi (2,600 sq km)
POPULATION 503,000
CAPITAL Luxembourg
GOVERNMENT Constitutional monarchy (Grand Duchy)
ETHNIC GROUPS Luxembourger 71%, Portuguese, Italian, French, Belgian, Slav
LANGUAGES Luxembourgish (official), French, German
RELIGIONS Roman Catholic 87%, others 13%
NATIONAL MOTTO *"Mir wëlle bleiwe wat mir sin"* "We want to remain what we are"
NATIONAL ANTHEM (DATE) *"Ons Hémécht"* "Our Homeland" (1895)

Grand Duke Jean *was the fifth King of the Nassau-Weilbourg dynasty.*

MACEDONIA, REPUBLIC OF

FLAG RATIO: 1:2 **USE:** National/Civil **DATE ADOPTED:** 1992 **LAST MODIFIED:** 1995

The flag of the Republic of Macedonia is **red** with a stylized **golden-yellow sun**. The sun has **eight yellow rays** emerging from its disk. The rays thicken toward the edge of the flag. In 1992 Macedonia won independence and adopted a flag with the "**Sun of Vergina**" on a red field. Vergina is the historic capital of the ancient state of Macedonia. Greece objected to use of the symbol, which they argued was an emblem of Philip II of Macedon who united Greece in the 4th century BC. In 1995 Macedonia agreed to redesign its flag.

HISTORY

Philip II's son, **Alexander the Great**, built a mighty empire that broke up after his death (323 BC). The **Romans** defeated Macedon in the Macedonian Wars. In AD 395, Macedonia became part of the **Byzantine Empire**. The region was under **Ottoman** rule from the 14th to the 19th century. The **Balkan Wars** (1912–13) saw Macedonia divided between Greece, Bulgaria, and Serbia. At the end of World War I, Serbian Macedonia joined what later became known as **Yugoslavia**. In 1946, Macedonia became a republic within Yugoslavia. In 1991 Macedonia declared **independence**. In 2001 fighting between government forces and **Albanian rebels** displaced 100,000 people. In 2011 the **International Court of Justice** ruled **Greece**'s attempt to veto Macedonia's accession to **NATO** illegal.

AREA 9,900 sq mi (25,700 sq km)

POPULATION 2,077,000

CAPITAL Skopje

GOVERNMENT Multiparty republic

ETHNIC GROUPS Macedonian 64%, Albanian 25%, Turkish 4%, Romanian 3%, Serb 2%

LANGUAGES Macedonian and Albanian (official)

RELIGIONS Macedonian Orthodox 70%, Islam 29%

NATIONAL ANTHEM (DATE) "Denes nad Makedonija" "Today over Macedonia" (1992)

Embroidery *from a Debar folk garment adorns this Macedonian stamp.*

126

MADAGASCAR

FLAG RATIO: 2:3   USE: National/Civil   DATE ADOPTED: 1958   LAST MODIFIED: 1958

Madagascar adopted its present flag in 1958, when it became a self-governing republic under French rule. The colors emphasize Madagascar's links with southeast Asia – many of Madagascar's population are ancestors of settlers from Malaysia and Indonesia *c*. 2000 years ago. In the 19th century, the Merina kingdom used a flag of red and white. **Red** and **white** stand for sovereignty and purity respectively, while **green** represents the Betsimisaraka people of the coast and symbolizes hope.

HISTORY

Madagascar is the world's **fourth-largest island**. Africans and Indonesians arrived *c*. 2000 years ago, and Muslims came in the 9th century. By the 1880s the **Merina** controlled nearly all the island. In 1896, the French defeated the Merina and **Malagasy** became a **French colony**. In 1946–48 France crushed a **rebellion**, killing *c*. 80,000 islanders. Malagasy achieved full **independence** in 1960. In 1972 the military overthrew President **Philibert Tsiranana**'s autocratic regime. In 1975 Malagasy was **renamed** Madagascar, and **Didier Ratsiraka** became president. In 1993 Ratsiraka was defeated in Madagascar's first free elections for 17 years. He returned to power in 1997. Violence followed **Marc Ravalomanana**'s victory over Ratsiraka in presidential elections in 2001. A coup in 2009 left Madagascar internationally isolated.

AREA 227,000 sq mi (587,000 sq km)

POPULATION 21,926,000

CAPITAL Antananarivo

GOVERNMENT Republic

ETHNIC GROUPS Merina, Betsimisaraka, Betsileo, Tsmihety, Sakalava and others

LANGUAGES Malagasy and French (both official)

RELIGIONS Traditional beliefs 52%, Christianity 41%, Islam 7%

NATIONAL MOTTO *"Fahafahana, Tanindrazana, Fandrosoana"* "Liberty, Fatherland, Progress"

NATIONAL ANTHEM (DATE) *"Ry Tanindrazanay Malala O"* "O, Our Beloved Fatherland" (1958)

*The bannerfish (*Heniochus acuminatus*) lives in the coral reefs of the Indian Ocean.*

127

MALAWI

FLAG RATIO: 2:3 USE: National/Civil DATE ADOPTED: 2010 LAST MODIFIED: 2010

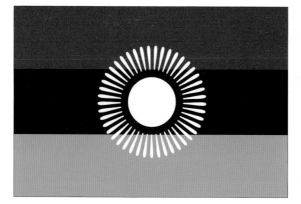

Malawi's flag derives from the Pan-African flag. It has **three horizontal bands** of red, black, and green. **Red** (top) symbolizes the blood spilled in the struggle to liberate Africa. **Black** (middle) represents Africa's people. **Green** stands for Malawi's forests and grassland. The **rising red sun** of the previous flag was replaced with a **full white sun** to symbolize the country's economic progress since independence. The change of flag was challenged in court.

HISTORY

The **Maravi** kingdom existed from the 15th to the 18th century. In the early 19th century, Malawi was a center of the **slave** trade. In 1891, it became a **British Protectorate**. Britain abolished slavery and established **coffee plantations**. In 1907 it became known as **Nyasaland**. In 1953 Nyasaland became part of the **Federation of Rhodesia**. In 1964 Nyasaland achieved **independence** as Malawi. In 1966 Malawi became a republic. **Dr Hastings Banda**'s repressive rule in Malawi lasted from 1964 to 1994. **Bakili Muluzi** of the United Democratic Front (UDF) defeated Banda and the MCP in 1994 elections. In 2002 Muluzi declared a state of national disaster with **famine** affecting 70% of the population. He remained in power until his death in 2012 and was replaced by **Joyce Banda** of the People's Party, the new name of the UDF.

AREA 45,700 sq mi (118,000 sq km)

POPULATION 15,879,000

CAPITAL Lilongwe

GOVERNMENT Multiparty republic

ETHNIC GROUPS Chewa, Nyanja, Tonga, Tumbuka, Lomwe, Yao, Ngoni and others

LANGUAGES Chichewa and English (both official)

RELIGIONS Protestant 55%, Roman Catholic 20%, Islam 20%

NATIONAL MOTTO "Unity and Freedom"

NATIONAL ANTHEM (DATE) "Oh! God, Bless Our Land of Malawi" (1964)

The bar-tailed trogon lives in the grasslands of Malawi.

MALAYSIA

FLAG RATIO: 1:2 USE: National/Civil DATE ADOPTED: 1963 LAST MODIFIED: 1967

Malaysia's flag, the *Jalur Gemilang* ("Glorious Stripes"), resembles the flag of the United States. The **14 red and white horizontal stripes** represent the members of the federation. The **dark-blue canton** stands for Malaysia's unity and its place within the **Commonwealth**. The canton contains a **yellow crescent and star**, symbols of **Islam**. The star's 14 points symbolize the unity of the 13 states with the federal government. Yellow is the color of the **Sultan** of Malaysia.

HISTORY

Britain conquered **Malacca** in 1795. In 1867 the Straits Settlement of **Penang**, Malacca and **Singapore** became a British colony. In 1888 **Sabah** and **Sarawak** became a British Protectorate. The states of **Perak, Selangor, Pahang,** and **Negeri Sembilan** federated in 1896.

In 1909 **Johor, Kedah, Kelantan, Perlis,** and **Terengganu** formed the Unfederated Malay States. **Japan** occupied Malaysia during World War II. In 1948 Britain expanded the Federation of Malaya to include the Unfederated States and Malacca and Penang. Communists launched a guerrilla war, known as the **Malayan Emergency** (1948–60), and many **Chinese** were forcibly resettled. In 1957 Malaya gained **independence**. In 1963, Singapore, Sabah, and Sarawak joined the Federation, which became known as Malaysia. In 1965 **Singapore** seceeded from Malaysia. Islam has been an increasing influence in politics.

*The starfish (*Oreaster occidentalis*) is known as* tapak sulaiman *in Malaysia.*

AREA 127,000 sq mi (330,000 sq km)
POPULATION 28,729,000
CAPITAL Kuala Lumpur/Putrajaya
GOVERNMENT Constitutional monarchy
ETHNIC GROUPS Malay and other indigenous groups 58%, Chinese 24%, Indian 8%, others
LANGUAGES Malay (official), Chinese, Englis
RELIGIONS Islam, Buddhism, Daoism, Hinduism, Christianity, Sikhism
NATIONAL MOTTO *"Bersekutu bertambah mutu"* "Unity is Strength"
NATIONAL ANTHEM (DATE) *"Negara ku"* "My Country" (1957)

129

MALDIVES

FLAG RATIO: 2:3 USE: National/Civil DATE ADOPTED: 1965 LAST MODIFIED: 1965

Like many other Islamic countries, the Maldives long used a plain red flag. By 1949, the Maldivian flag consisted of a green rectangle and white crescent on a red field with a band of black and white stripes on the hoist side. On independence the band of black and white stripes disappeared. The **green rectangle** represents the many palm trees, the life source of the islands. **Red** symbolizes the blood sacrificed in the struggle for independence. The **white crescent**, in the center of the green panel and pointing toward the fly, is a symbol of the **Islamic** faith of the Maldives.

HISTORY

The Sanskrit word "Maladiv" means "**garland of islands**," and the archipelago consists of 1196 islands in 26 atolls scattered across the Indian Ocean. In the 12th century, Arab traders introduced **Islam** to the Maldives. From the 14th century, the **ad-Din dynasty** ruled the Maldives. In 1518 the **Portuguese** claimed the islands. From 1665 to 1886 the Maldives were a dependency of **Ceylon** (now **Sri Lanka**). In 1887 they became a **British Protectorate**. In 1965, the Maldives gained **independence** under **Sultan Muhammad Farid Didi**. In 1968 the Sultan was deposed and the Maldives became a **republic**. **Maumoon Abdul Gayoom** became President in 1978. In 1982 Maldives joined the **Commonwealth of Nations**. In 2007 voters backed a proposal for a presidential system of government and elections were introduced in 2008.

AREA 120 sq mi (300 sq km)

POPULATION 395,000

CAPITAL Malé

GOVERNMENT Presidential republic

ETHNIC GROUPS Dravidian, Sinhalese, Arabs, Africans

LANGUAGES Dhivehi (official, dialect of Sinhala, script derived from Arabic), English

RELIGIONS Sunni Muslim

NATIONAL ANTHEM (DATE) *"Gaumi Salam"* "National Salute" (1972)

Yellowfin tuna is vitally important to the commercial fishing industry in the Maldives.

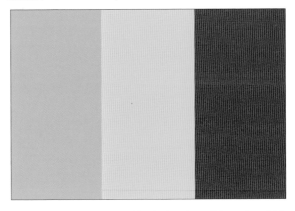

In 1959 French Sudan (now Mali) and Senegal formed the Federation of Mali. The Federation modeled its flag on the French *tricolore*. **Green**, **yellow**, and **red** are the colors both of the African Democratic Rally, the party that led the fight for independence, and the colors of the **Pan-African** movement. Green stands for the vegetation, yellow for the mineral resources, and red for the blood shed in the liberation struggle. On the central band of the federation's flag was a stylized human figure in black, known as a *kanaga*. In 1960 Senegal seceded from the federation. In 1961 Mali adopted its present flag, removing the *kanaga* figure because of the **Islamic** stricture on the representation of nature. The new flag was identical to that of **Rwanda**, which promptly altered its own flag.

HISTORY

The medieval **Empire of Mali** was one of the world's richest powers. The 14th-century reign of **Mansa Musa** saw the introduction of **Islam** and the development of **Timbuktu** as a center of learning and hub of trans-Saharan trade. In 1893 it became the colony of **French Sudan**. In 1960 Mali became a one-party state under **Modibo Keita**. In 1968 **Moussa Traoré** replaced him in a coup. Mali returned to civilian rule under Alpha Konaré in 1992.

AREA 479,000 sq mi (1,240,000 sq km)

POPULATION 14,160,000

CAPITAL Bamako

GOVERNMENT Multiparty republic

ETHNIC GROUPS Mande 50% (Bambara, Malinke, Soninke), Peul 17%, Voltaic 12%, Songhai 6%, Tuareg and Moor 10%, others

LANGUAGES French (official) and many African languages

RELIGIONS Islam 90%, Traditional beliefs 9%, Christianity 1%

NATIONAL MOTTO *"Un peuple, un but, une foi"* "One People, One Goal, One Faith"

NATIONAL ANTHEM (DATE) *"Hymne National Malien"* "National Hymn of Mali" (1962)

The Tamasheq, a group of Tuareg nomads, produce fine metalwork such as this key.

MALTA

FLAG RATIO: 2:3   USE: National/Civil   DATE ADOPTED: 1964   LAST MODIFIED: 1988

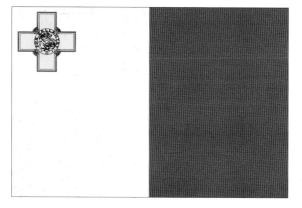

According to legend, the **white** and **red** colors of Malta's flag derive from the coat of arms of Roger I of Sicily, who conquered the islands in 1090. A red flag with a white cross was used by the **Knights of Malta** from the Middle Ages. In 1943 a **George Cross** on a blue canton was added to the flag after King George VI of Britain honored the island for its brave defense against the Axis powers in World War II. In 1964 Malta gained independence from Britain, and a thin red edging replaced the blue canton around the George Cross.

HISTORY

Malta has three inhabited islands: **Malta**, **Gozo**, and **Comino**. The Phoenicians colonized Malta in *c*.850 BC. In AD 395 Malta became part of the Byzantine Empire. An Arab invasion brought Islam in 870, but **Roger I**, Norman King of Sicily, **restored Christian rule** in 1091. In 1530 the Holy Roman Emperor gave Malta to the **Knights Hospitallers**. In 1565 the Knights held Malta against a Turkish siege. In 1814 Malta became a **British colony** and a strategic military base. Italian and German aircraft bombed the islands in World War II. In 1942, in recognition of the heroism of the Maltese resistance, **George VI** awarded the George Cross to Malta. In 1964 Malta gained **independence**, and in 1974 it became a **republic**. The last British military base closed in 1979. Malta joined the **European Union** in 2004 and adopted the **Euro** in 2008. Divorce was legalized in 2011.

AREA 120 sq mi (320 sq km)
POPULATION 408,000
CAPITAL Valletta
GOVERNMENT Multiparty republic
ETHNIC GROUPS Maltese 96%, British 2%
LANGUAGES Maltese and English (both official)
RELIGIONS Roman Catholic 98%
NATIONAL ANTHEM (DATE) *"Innu Malti"*
"Hymn of Malta" (1945)

Hoary rockrose is endangered. It grows in the holm oak forest of Wied Hazrun.

MARSHALL ISLANDS

FLAG RATIO: 1:2 USE: National/Civil DATE ADOPTED: 1979 LAST MODIFIED: 1979

The **deep-blue** background of the flag represents the Pacific Ocean. The **widening beams** symbolize the two chains of islands: **white** stands for Ratak (Sunrise) and **orange** for Ralik (Sunset). Orange represents bravery and white signifies peace. The **star** denotes the cross of Christianity, with each of its **24 points** representing a municipal district of the Marshall Islands. The **four longer points** of the star stand for the major towns of **Majuro**, **Ebeye**, **Jaluit**, and **Wotje**.

HISTORY

Inhabited by **Micronesians** for at least 2500 years, the Marshall Islands are named after British Naval **Captain William Marshall**, who sailed through the archipelago in 1788. In 1857 US explorer **Hiram Bingham, Jr.**, founded a missionary post on Ebon. In 1885 **Germany** annexed the islands. In 1914 **Japan** captured the archipelago. After World War I, the League of Nations granted a mandate to Japan. In 1944 the **Allies occupied** the Marshall Islands. From 1946 to 1956 the **United States tested nuclear weapons** on the Marshall Islands, especially on **Bikini Atoll**. In 1947 the Marshall Islands became part of the US-administered **Trust Territory of the Pacific Islands**. In 1979 the Marshalls gained **self-government**. Trusteeship ended in 1990, and the **Compact of Free Association** with the United States expired in 2003.

Marshallese *women make beautiful fans from sun-bleached coconut leaves.*

AREA 70 sq mi (180 sq km)
POPULATION 67,000
CAPITAL Majuro
GOVERNMENT Multiparty republic
ETHNIC GROUPS Marshallese
LANGUAGES Marshallese, English
RELIGIONS United Church of Christ 55%, Assembly of God 26%, Roman Catholic 8%
NATIONAL MOTTO "*Jepilpilin Ke Ejulaan*" "Accomplishment Through Joint Effort"
NATIONAL ANTHEM (DATE) "*Kej rammon Aelin Kein am*" "Forever Marshall Islands" (1991)

MAURITANIA

FLAG RATIO: 2:3 USE: National/Civil DATE ADOPTED: 1959 LAST MODIFIED: 1959

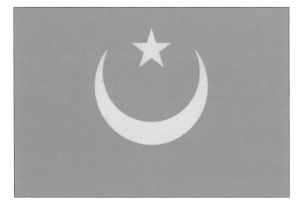

Mauritania's flag features a **crescent** and a **five-pointed star**, traditional symbols of **Islam**. **Green** and **yellow** are Islamic and **Pan-African** colors, reflecting Mauritania's position between the Arab countries of North Africa and the nations of sub-Saharan Africa.

HISTORY

Berbers migrated to the region in the first millennium AD. The **Hodh basin** lay at the heart of the ancient **Ghana Empire** (700–1200) and towns grew up along the **trans-Saharan** caravan routes. Mauritania was the cradle of the **Almoravid dynasty**, which spread Islam throughout north Africa. In the 14th and 15th century, it formed part of the ancient **Mali Empire**. In 1903 Mauritania became a **French protectorate**. In 1920 it became a colony of **French West Africa**. In 1960 Mauritania achieved full **independence**. President **Ould Daddah** established a one-party state. In 1973 Mauritania joined the **Arab League**. In 1976 Mauritania and Morocco occupied **Western Sahara**. In 1978 an army coup overthrew Ould Daddah. In 1979 Mauritania withdrew from Western Sahara. Recognition of Western Sahara's independence provoked civil unrest and **Ould Taya** came to power in 1984. Tension continues between the black African minority in southern Mauritania and Arabs and Berbers in the north.

AREA 396,000 sq mi (1,026,000 sq km)
POPULATION 3,282,000
CAPITAL Nouakchott
GOVERNMENT Multiparty Islamic republic
ETHNIC GROUPS Mixed Moor/Black 40%, Moor 30%, Black 30%
LANGUAGES Arabic and Wolof (both official), French
RELIGIONS Islam
NATIONAL MOTTO *"Honneur, Fraternité, Justice"* "Honor, Fraternity, Justice"
NATIONAL ANTHEM (DATE) Untitled (1960)

Drought (secheresse *in French) devastated livestock farming in Mauritania.*

134

MAURITIUS

FLAG RATIO: 1:2 USE: National DATE ADOPTED: 1968 LAST MODIFIED: 1968

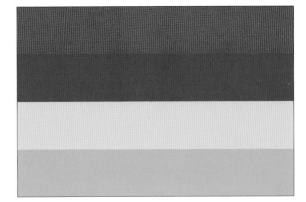

The flag of Mauritius is unique in having **four equal horizontal bands**. Designed by the British College of Arms, the colors derive from Mauritius' coat of arms awarded by King Edward VII of Britain in 1906. **Red** represents the blood shed in the liberation struggle, **blue** for the Indian Ocean, **yellow** for the bright future afforded by independence, and **green** for the islands' lush vegetation. The **civil flag** has a blue field with the national flag on its canton and the **coat of arms** on the fly. The coat of arms includes the national motto and the **dodo**, a flightless bird hunted to extinction.

HISTORY

The nation of Mauritius, *c.* 500 mi (800 km) east of Madagascar, consists of the main island of **Mauritius**, 20 nearby islets, and the dependency islands of **Rodrigues**, **Agalega**, and **Cargados Carajos**. The **Dutch** attempted to settle the islands from 1598, naming them after **Prince Maurice of Nassau**. In 1721 the **French East India Company** occupied Mauritius, which they renamed Île de France. The French established **sugarcane plantations** using **African slave labor**. In 1810 **Britain** seized Mauritius. It became a **British colony** in 1814. In 1833 slavery was abolished – **Indian indentured labor** took its place. In 1968 Mauritius achieved **independence**. Sir **Seewoosagur Ramgoolam** served as Prime Minister from 1968 to 1982. In 1992 Mauritius became a **republic**.

AREA 790 sq mi (2,000 sq km)

POPULATION 1,304,000

CAPITAL Port Louis

GOVERNMENT Multiparty republic

ETHNIC GROUPS Indo-Mauritian 68%, Creole 27%, Sino-Mauritian 3%, Franco-Mauritian 2%

LANGUAGES English (official), Creole, French, Hindi, Urdu, Hakka, Bojpoori

RELIGIONS Hindu 50%, Roman Catholic 27%, Muslim (largely Sunni) 16%, Protestant 5%

NATIONAL MOTTO *"Stella clavisque Maris Indici"* "The Star and Key of the Indian Sea"

NATIONAL ANTHEM (DATE) "Motherland" (1968)

Shipwrights (or sarpantye pirog in Creole) often work in the shade of a banyan tree.

MEXICO

FLAG RATIO: 4:7 **USE:** National/Civil **DATE ADOPTED:** 1823 **LAST MODIFIED:** 1968

In 1823, the Constituent Congress of Mexico officially adopted the **tricolor** flag. The **green** band represents hope and victory, **white** stands for the purity of Mexico's ideals, and **red** symbolizes the blood shed in the struggle for independence. At the center of the flag is the **state emblem**, which depicts an ancient Aztec legend about the founding of Mexico City. The god Huitzilopochtli guided the Aztecs to settle where an **eagle**, clutching a **snake**, landed on a **prickly-pear cactus**. In 1325 the Aztecs found the sign on an island in Lake Texcoco and named the site Tenochtitlán ("Place of the prickly-pear cactus"). On the emblem, the cactus has **red fruit**, an Aztec symbol for the heart. **Oak and laurel branches** are republican symbols.

HISTORY

The **Maya** flourished between AD 300 and 900. The **Toltecs** succeeded the Maya. In 1521 Spanish *conquistador* **Hernán Cortés** defeated **Aztec** Emperor **Montezuma**. In 1821 Mexico gained **independence** under Emperor **Augustín de Iturbide**. In 1823 it became a republic. The **Mexican War** (1846–48) saw Mexico lose half its territory to the United States. **Santa Anna** was president 1832–55 when civil war broke out. **Maximilian of Austria** was Emperor 1864–67. The dictator **Porfirio Díaz** ruled from 1876 to 1910. US troops helped defeat the peasant armies of **"Pancho" Villa** and **Emiliano Zapata** in the **Mexican Revolution** (1910–40). Modern politics are increasingly dominated by drug-related violence.

AREA 756,000 sq mi (1,958,000 sq km)

POPULATION 113,714,000

CAPITAL Mexico City

GOVERNMENT Federal republic

ETHNIC GROUPS Mestizo 60%, Amerindian 30%, White 9%

LANGUAGES Spanish (official)

RELIGIONS Roman Catholic 90%, Protestant 6%

NATIONAL MOTTO *"Arriba y adelante"* "Higher and Further"

NATIONAL ANTHEM (DATE) *"Mexicanos, al grito de guerra"* "Mexicans, to the War Cry" (1854)

In 1821 Mexico won independence. Its first flag had three diagonal stripes and stars.

MICRONESIA, FEDERATED STATES OF

FLAG RATIO: 1:2 USE: National/Civil DATE ADOPTED: 1962 LAST MODIFIED: 1979

The flag of the Federated States of Micronesia consists of **four white stars** on a **blue field**. The stars represent the four states of Micronesia (in order of population size): Chuuk, Pohnpei, Yap, and Kusrae. From 1962 to 1977 Micronesia's flag had six stars, but the Marshall Islands and the Northern Mariana Islands left the federation and the present flag was adopted on November 30, 1979.

HISTORY

The 607 islands that make up the Federated States of Micronesia stretch across more than 1700 mi (2700 km) of the **western Pacific Ocean. Spain** formally annexed the islands in 1874, but then sold them to **Germany** in 1899.

In 1914 **Japan** occupied Micronesia, and the League of Nations granted it a mandate to govern in 1920. In 1944 the **United States** occupied the islands. In 1947 the United Nations (UN) created the Trust Territory of the Pacific Islands, consisting of **Pohnpei** (including **Kusrae**), **Chuuk**, **Yap**, **Palau**, the **Marshall Islands**, and the **Northern Mariana Islands**. The United States acted as Trustee. In 1979 the Federated States of Micronesia was born. In 1986 Micronesia signed a **Compact of Free Association** with the United States. In 1991 Micronesia joined the United Nations (UN). The economy depends heavily on **aid** from the United States.

The saddled butterfly fish lives in clear waters around Micronesia's coral reefs.

AREA 270 sq mi (700 sq km)
POPULATION 107,000
CAPITAL Palikir
GOVERNMENT Federal republic
ETHNIC GROUPS Micronesian, Polynesian
LANGUAGES English (official), Chuukese, Pohnpeian, Kosraean, Yapese
RELIGIONS Protestant (largely United Church of Christ) 54%, Roman Catholic 45%
NATIONAL ANTHEM (DATE) "Patriots of Micronesia" (1980)

MOLDOVA

FLAG RATIO: 2:3 **USE:** National/Civil **DATE ADOPTED:** 1990 **LAST MODIFIED:** 1990

Moldova adopted its present flag upon proclaiming independence from the Soviet Union in 1990. The colors are the same as the **Romanian** flag, emphasising Moldova's close geographical, historical and cultural ties with Romania. On Romania's flag, the **blue** vertical **stripe** stands for the region of Transylvania, **yellow** for Wallachia, and **red** for Moldova. Moldova's flag incorporates its **coat of arms** on the central yellow band. An **eagle** holds an **Orthodox cross** in its beak and an **olive branch** and **scepter** in its claws. The eagle was a symbol of the Byzantine Empire. On the shield are a **bison's head**, a **star**, a **rose** and a **crescent** – all of which are traditional symbols of the old medieval principality of Moldavia.

HISTORY

Moldavia formed part of the Roman province of **Dacia**. In the 14th century, it became an independent principality ruled by the **Vlachs**. In 1504 the Turks conquered Moldavia, and it remained part of the **Ottoman Empire** until the 19th century. In 1859 Moldavia and **Wallachia** united to form Romania. In 1924 the Soviet republic of Moldavia formed. In 1991, after the collapse of the **Soviet Union**, Moldavia became the independent republic of Moldova. Many Moldovans wished to reunite with Romania, while Ukrainians and Russians east of the River **Dniester** declared independence as the **Transdniester Republic**.

AREA 13,100 sq mi (33,900 sq km)
POPULATION 4,314,000
CAPITA Chişinău
GOVERNMENT Multiparty republic
ETHNIC GROUPS Moldovan/Romanian 65%, Ukrainian 14%, Russian 13%, others
LANGUAGES Moldovan/Romanian, Russian (official)
RELIGIONS Eastern Orthodox 98%
NATIONAL ANTHEM (DATE) *"Limba Noastra"* "Our Tongue" (1912)

***Moldova** produces fine Romanian folk art, especially ceramics and textiles.*

MONACO

FLAG RATIO: 4:5   USE: National/Civil   DATE ADOPTED: 1881   LAST MODIFIED: 1881

The colors of Monaco's flag derive from the coat of arms of the House of Grimaldi, rulers of the small principality since 1297. The Grimaldi family's use of **red** and **white** as heraldic colors dates back to 1339. Prince Karl III officially adopted it as the national flag in 1881. Except in its ratio, it is identical to the **bicolor** flag of **Indonesia**.

HISTORY

The Principality of Monaco, an **enclave** in **southeastern France**, is the second smallest country in the world (after the Vatican). A battleground in the **Genoese** civil wars between the **Guelphs** and the **Ghibellines**, the Guelph **Rainier**

Grimaldi captured Monaco from the Ghibellines in 1297. From 1525 to 1641 it was a **protectorate** of **Spain**. In 1641 it became a **protectorate** of **France**. In 1793 France overthrew the Grimaldis and annexed the principality. In 1815 Monaco became a protectorate of the **Kingdom of Sardinia**. In 1861 Monaco regained its independence under the guardianship of France. The principality flourished after the opening of the **Monte Carlo Casino** in 1863. In 1956 Prince **Rainier III** married the US movie actress **Grace Kelly**. In 1993 Monaco joined the United Nations. Prince Albert II succeeded his father in 2005.

Monaco hosts the International Bouquet Competition (founded 1967) every April.

AREA 0.4 sq mi (1 sq km)

POPULATION 31,000

CAPITAL Monaco

GOVERNMENT Constitutional monarchy

ETHNIC GROUPS French 47%, Monégasque 16%, Italian 16%, other 21%

LANGUAGES French (official), English, Italian, Monégasque

RELIGIONS Roman Catholic 90%

NATIONAL MOTTO *"Deo Juvante"* "With God's help"

NATIONAL ANTHEM (DATE) *"Le Marche de Monaco"* "The March of Monaco" (1867)

MONGOLIA

FLAG RATIO: 1:2   **USE:** National   **DATE ADOPTED:** 1992   **LAST MODIFIED:** 1992

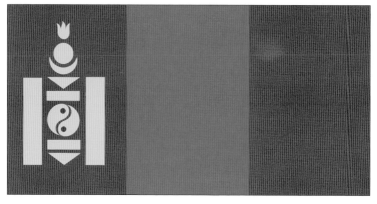

Mongolia's flag is red with a vertical blue stripe down the middle. **Red** is the color of fire, symbolizing progress and prosperity. **Blue** represents the color of the sky, and stands for peace and eternity. On the hoist band of the flag is a yellow *soyombo*, an ancient Mongolian ideogram. The three-tongued flame crowning the *soyombo* symbolizes the nation's past, present and future. The flame, together with the sun and the crescent, symbolizes the prosperity and progress of the Mongolian nation. The two downward-pointing triangles signify the defeat of the enemies of the Mongols. The horizontal rectangles symbolize honest and fair government. The yin and yang symbol signifies the unity of pairs of natural elements. The two vertical rectangles represent a fortress, indicating that the strength of the nation derives from the unity of its people.

HISTORY

Genghis Khan united Mongolia in the 13th century. His grandson, **Kublai Khan**, built up a mighty Mongol Empire. In 1650 the son of the Mongol Khan of Urga (now Ulan Bator) was named a **Living Buddha**. In the 17th century Mongolia came under **Chinese** control. In 1911 a Mongolian rising expelled China from **Outer Mongolia** and, with Soviet help, established the **independent** Mongolian People's Republic in 1924. **Inner Mongolia**, between the Gobi Desert and the Great Wall, remains part of China. The first **direct presidential elections** took place in 1993.

AREA 605,000 sq mi (1,567,000 sq km)
POPULATION 3,133,000
CAPITAL Ulan Bator
GOVERNMENT Multiparty republic
ETHNIC GROUPS Khalkha Mongol 85%, Kazakh 6%
LANGUAGES Khalkha Mongolian (official), Turkic, Russian
RELIGIONS Tibetan Buddhist Lamaism 96%
NATIONAL ANTHEM (DATE) Untitled (1950)

Living Buddhas *or* Khutuktu *governed Mongolia from 1696 to 1924.*

FLAG RATIO: 1:2 **USE:** National /Civil/State **DATE ADOPTED:** 2004 **DATE ADAPTED:** 2004

The Montenegrin flag was adopted on statehood day, July 13, 2004, and is red with the **national coat of arms** (two-thirds the height of the flag) in the center and a **golden border** (one-twentieth the width of the shorter edge of the flag). The coat of arms is a **golden double-headed eagle** holding a **scepter** and an **orb** in its talons and supporting an **escutcheon** with a **lion passant**.

HISTORY

The region was part of the **Serbian Empire** until the Turkish invasion of 1355. **Ottoman Turks** defeated Serbia in 1389, while Montenegro resisted, but by 1500, most of the territory had been captured. In 1799, Turkey recognized Montenegro's independence. In 1851, a monarchy was established, and in 1878 the state's sovereignty was formally rec-

ognized. In 1910, **Nicholas I** assumed the title of king and sought to expel the Turks. In 1914, he declared war on **Austria**, and Austro-German armies quickly overran Montenegro. He was deposed in 1918, and Montenegro united with Serbia. In 1946, Montenegro became a republic of **Yugoslavia**. In 1992 Montenegrins voted to remain part of a **Yugoslav federation** with **Serbia**. In 2006 a **referendum** was held on **independence** from Serbia, and 55% of Montenegrins voted in favor. The result was accepted by Serbia, and independence followed in June of the same year. The first parliamentary elections were held in 2006 and **Željko Šturanović** became prime minister; in 2008 he was replaced by **Milo Djukanović** and in 2010 **Igor Luksić** took over.

The double-headed eagle coat of arms was introduced by Danilo I (r. 1851–60).

AREA 5,400 sq mi (14,000 sq km)
POPULATION 662,000
CAPITAL Podgorica
GOVERNMENT Multiparty republic
ETHNIC GROUPS Montenegrin, Serbian, Bosniak, Albanian
LANGUAGES Serbian, Albanian
RELIGIONS Orthodox Christian, Muslim (18%)
NATIONAL ANTHEM (DATE) "*Oj, svijetla majska zoro*" "Oh, Bright Dawn of May" (2004)

MOROCCO

FLAG RATIO: 2:3 **USE:** National/Civil **DATE ADOPTED:** 1915 **CODIFIED:** 1956

The Alawite dynasty first adopted a red flag for Morocco in the 17th century. **Red** symbolizes the royal family's claim of descent from the prophet Muhammad. The **green pentagram** (five-pointed star), called the "Seal of Solomon," first appeared in 1915. Morocco retained the design after gaining **independence**.

HISTORY

Berbers settled *c*.3000 years ago. In *c*. AD 685, **Arab** armies invaded Morocco, introducing Islam and Arabic. In 711 Moroccan Muslims invaded Spain. In 788 Berbers and Arabs united in an independent Moroccan state. In the mid-11th century, the **Almoravids** conquered Morocco. They built a Muslim empire. The **Almohad** dynasty succeeded the Almoravids. The present ruling dynasty, the **Alawite**, came to power in 1660. In 1912 Morocco divided into **French Morocco** and the smaller protectorate of **Spanish Morocco**. **Abd al-Krim** led a revolt (1921–26) against European rule. In 1956 Morocco gained **independence**, although Spain retains Ceuta and Melilla. In 1957 Morocco became a constitutional monarchy. Sultan Sidi Muhammad changed his title to King **Muhammad V**. In 1979 Morocco assumed control of **Western Sahara**. In 2011 voters were overwhelmingly in favor of reforms proposed by King Hassan VI in response to pro-democracy protests.

AREA 172,000 sq mi (447,000 sq km)
POPULATION 31,968,000
CAPITAL Rabat
GOVERNMENT Constitutional monarchy
ETHNIC GROUPS Arab-Berber 99%
LANGUAGES Arabic (official), Berber dialects, French
RELIGIONS Islam 99%
NATIONAL MOTTO "God, Country, King"
NATIONAL ANTHEM (DATE) *"Hymne Cherifien"* "Cherifien Anthem" (1956)

A copper water jug adorns this stamp celebrating the Red Crescent organization.

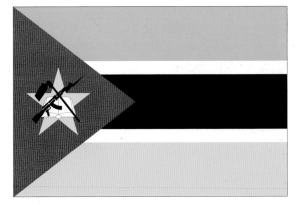

Mozambique's flag is based on the banner of the Front for the Liberation of Mozambique (Frelimo), the movement that led the struggle for self-determination. Frelimo's flag was in turn inspired by the banner of the African National Congress (ANC). The **green stripe** represents fertile land, the **white** for peace, the **black** for Africa, and the **yellow** for mineral wealth. The **red triangle** represents the blood shed in the fight for independence. Against the backdrop of a **yellow star** lie the national symbols: a **rifle**, a **hoe**, and a **book**.

HISTORY

Bantu speakers arrived in the 1st century AD. **Arab** traders settled from the 10th century. In 1498 **Vasco da Gama** was the first European to visit Mozambique, and in 1505 **Portugal** established its first settlement. In the 16th century, the Portuguese built **plantations**. In the 18th and 19th centuries, Mozambique was a center of the **slave trade**. In 1910 it became a Portuguese colony. In 1964 **Frelimo** launched a **guerrilla war** against Portuguese rule. In 1975 Mozambique gained **independence**, and **Samora Machel** became president. **Civil war** raged for 16 years, claiming many lives. In 1986 Samora Machel died and **Joachim Chissano** succeeded him. In 1995 Mozambique joined the **Commonwealth of Nations**. In 2006 the World Bank canceled almost all of Mozambique's debt.

Estrelinhas *(Portuguese for "little star") is the name for this haircut in Mozambique.*

AREA 309,000 sq mi (802,000 sq km)
POPULATION 22,949,000
CAPITAL Maputo
GOVERNMENT Multiparty republic
ETHNIC GROUPS Indigenous tribal groups (Shangaan, Chokwe, Manyika, Sena, Makua, others) 99%
LANGUAGES Portuguese (official), many others
RELIGIONS Traditional beliefs 50%, Christianity 30%, Islam 20%
NATIONAL ANTHEM (DATE) *"Patria Amada"* "Beloved Motherland" (2002)

NAMIBIA

FLAG RATIO: 2:3 **USE:** National/Civil **DATE ADOPTED:** 1990 **LAST MODIFIED:** 1990

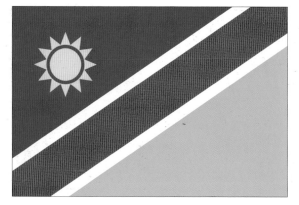

A committee chose the flag design in 1990. The colors are those of the South West Africa People's Organization (SWAPO), which led the struggle for independence, and of the Ovombo, the largest tribe in Namibia. The **red diagonal** band represents the heroism of Namibian people and their resolve for equal opportunity. The **white diagonals** stand for peace and unity. The **blue triangle** symbolizes the clear sky, the Atlantic Ocean, and Namibia's precious water resources. The **green triangle** signifies vegetation and agriculture. The **twelve-rayed golden sun** in the upper hoist represents life and energy.

HISTORY

The nomadic **San** were displaced by Bantu speakers, such as the Ovambo, Kavango and Herero. In 1884 **Germany** claimed the region as a protectorate and subsumed it into the territory of **South-West Africa**. In 1908 the discovery of **diamonds** fueled European settlement. Namibia was occupied by **South African** troops during World War I, and in 1920 South Africa gained a mandate. In 1966 SWAPO began a guerrilla war against South Africa. **Civil war** raged from 1977. SWAPO won multiparty elections in 1989, and Namibia gained **independence** in 1990. **Sam Nujoma** served as president until 2005 and was succeeded by **Hifikepunye Pohamba**.

AREA 318,000 sq mi (824,000 sq km)
POPULATION 2,148,000
CAPITAL Windhoek
GOVERNMENT Multiparty republic
ETHNIC GROUPS Ovambo 50%, Kavango 9%, Herero 7%, Damara 7%, White 6%, Nama 5%
LANGUAGES English (official), Afrikaans, German, indigenous dialects
RELIGIONS Christianity 90% (Lutheran 51%)
NATIONAL MOTTO "Unity, Liberty, Justice"
NATIONAL ANTHEM (DATE) "Namibia, Land of the Brave" (1991)

Issued *for World Post Day, the stamp shows a San man carrying water and food.*

N auru's flag is a representation of the island's geographic position. The flag shows Nauru (the **white star**) just south of the line of the Equator (the **yellow stripe**), surrounded by the **blue** of the Pacific Ocean. The **12 points** of the star represent each of the original indigenous tribes of the island. Two of these tribes are now extinct.

HISTORY

Nauru is a **coral atoll** in the western Pacific Ocean, located halfway between Australia and Hawaii. It is the world's **smallest independent republic**. In 1798 British navigator **John Fearn** explored Nauru. In 1888 the atoll was annexed to **Germany**. It later formed part of the Protectorate of the **Marshall Islands**. Nauru has rich deposits of high-grade phosphate rock which began to be mined

at the start of the 20th century by a joint British and German consortium. **Australian forces** occupied Nauru in World War I. The **Japanese** occupied Nauru from 1942 to 1945. After World War II, Australia resumed administration of the island. In 1968 the island became an **independent republic** within the **Commonwealth of Nations**. It joined the United Nations (UN) in 1999. Phosphate mining has left 80% of the island **uninhabitable**. Between 2001 and 2008, asylum seekers trying to get to Australia were held in a detention center on the island in return for aid from that country. After the demise of its offshore banking industry Nauru defaulted on its debt payments in 2004 and Australia took charge of its finances.

Common Eggfly (male) *Hypolimnas bolina*

The common eggfly butterfly lives throughout southeast Asia. The male is shown.

AREA 8 sq mi (20 sq km)
POPULATION 9,000
CAPITAL Yaren District
GOVERNMENT Multiparty republic
ETHNIC GROUPS Nauruan 58%, other Pacific Islander 26%, Chinese 8%, European 8%
LANGUAGES Nauruan (official), English
RELIGIONS Protestant 66%, Roman Catholic 33%
NATIONAL ANTHEM (DATE) *"Nauru Bwiema"* "Nauru, Our Homeland" (1968)

145

NEPAL

FLAG RATIO: 3:4 **USE:** National **DATE ADOPTED:** 1962 **LAST MODIFIED:** 1962

Nepal has the only nonrectangular flag in the world. Its unusual shape derived from two pennants representing political and royal authority. The **white crescent moon** with **eight rays** symbolized the monarchy, while the **white**, **twelve-rayed sun** stood for the Rana family, from which the Prime Ministers of Nepal were chosen from 1846 to 1951. The sun and moon now symbolize the hope that Nepal's independence is as enduring as the heavenly bodies. **White** represents the pure, everlasting eyes of god. **Crimson** is the national color and stands for energy. **Blue** denotes peace.

HISTORY

In c.563 BC, **Buddha** was born in southwest Nepal. From the 10th to the 18th century, the **Malla dynasty** ruled Nepal. In AD 1769 Nepal united under **Gurkha** rule. **Britain** defeated the Gurkhas in a war (1814–16). In 1923 Britain recognized Nepal as a sovereign state. In 1951 the Rana government was overthrown and the monarchy reestablished under **King Mahendra**. **Birendra Gyanendra**, succeeded his brother Birendra in 2001. From the 1990s until 2006, when direct rule ended, a **Maoist revolt** claimed more than 12,000 lives. In elections in 2008, the Maoists emerged as the largest party; the monarchy was abolished.

AREA 56,800 sq mi (147,000 sq km)
POPULATION 29,392,000
CAPITAL Katmandu
GOVERNMENT Federal republic
ETHNIC GROUPS Rahman, Chetri, Newar, Gurung, Magar, Tamang, Sherpa and others
LANGUAGES Nepali (official), local languages
RELIGIONS Hinduism 86%, Buddhism 8%, Islam 4%
NATIONAL MOTTO "The Motherland is Worth More than the Kingdom of Heaven"
NATIONAL ANTHEM (DATE) "Sayaun Thunga Phool Ka" "Made of Hundreds of Flowers" (2007)

The Rana Tharu are hunter-gatherers of the Himalayan foothills of western Nepal.

NETHERLANDS

FLAG RATIO: 2:3   USE: National/Civil   DATE ADOPTED: 1937   LAST MODIFIED: 1937

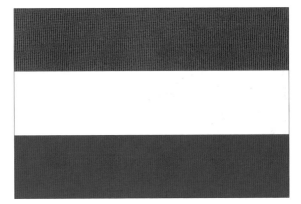

The Dutch **tricolor** of **horizontal red, white, and blue stripes** derives from the orange, white, and blue "*Prinsenvlag*" ("Prince's flag") of Prince William I of Orange, leader of the Revolt of the Netherlands (1567–79) against Spain. The orange stripe evolved into a deep red, perhaps because the orange was not bold enough for recognition at sea. Orange remains the national color. The Dutch flag is almost identical to the flag of **Luxembourg**.

HISTORY

Philip II of Spain's attempt to impose Catholicism led to the **Revolt of the Netherlands**. The Union of Utrecht (1579) established the **United Provinces of the Netherlands**. The **Dutch East India Company** was founded in 1602, and the **Dutch Empire** strengthened in two **wars with Britain** (1652–54,

1665–67). In 1689 Prince William III became King **William III** of England. In 1815 the former United Provinces, Belgium, and Luxembourg united to form the **Kingdom of the Netherlands** under William I. Belgium left in 1830, and Luxembourg seceded in 1890. **Queen Wilhelmina** reigned from 1890 to 1948. The Netherlands was **neutral** in World War I. Most Dutch Jews were murdered under **Nazi occupation** during World War II. New Guinea and Suriname gained independence in 1962 and 1975. In 1980 **Queen Juliana** abdicated in favor of her daughter **Beatrix**. The Netherlands was a founder member of the European Union.

AREA 16,000 sq mi (41,500 sq km)
POPULATION 16,847,000
CAPITAL Amsterdam/The Hague
GOVERNMENT Constitutional monarchy
ETHNIC GROUPS Dutch 83%, Indonesian, Turkish, Moroccan and others
LANGUAGES Dutch (official), Frisian
RELIGIONS Roman Catholic 31%, Protestant 21%, Islam 4%, others
NATIONAL MOTTO *"Je Maintiendrai"* *"I Will Maintain"*
NATIONAL ANTHEM (DATE) *"Wilhelmus van Nassouwe"* "William of Nassau" (1932)

Friesland, a province in northern Netherlands, unified in 1498.

147

NEW ZEALAND

FLAG RATIO: 1:2 USE: National/Civil DATE ADOPTED: 1902 LAST MODIFIED: 1902

New Zealand's **red**, **white** and **blue** flag recalls its historic links with Britain. Many former British colonies incorporate the **"Union Jack"** on the hoist of their flag. Like other countries in the southern hemisphere, New Zealand's flag features the stars of the **Southern Cross** constellation. The **blue field** represents the sky and the Pacific Ocean.

HISTORY

Maori settled in New Zealand more than 1000 years ago. The first European discovery was by the Dutch navigator **Abel Tasman** in 1642. British explorer **James Cook** landed in 1769. In 1840 the **British** built a settlement at **Wellington**. The Treaty of **Waitangi** (1840) promised to honor Maori land rights in return for recognition of British sovereignty. In 1841 New Zealand became a separate **colony**. Increasing colonization led to the first **Maori War** (1843–48). British seizure of land led to the protracted **Maori Wars** (1860–72). In 1893 New Zealand became the first country to give **women** the vote. In 1907 New Zealand became a **self-governing** Dominion. **William Massey** was Prime Minister from 1912 to 1925. More than 16,000 New Zealand soldiers died in **World War I**. Labor Party leaders **Michael Savage** and **Peter Fraser** guided government during World II. In 1951 New Zealand joined the **Anzus Pact**. It joined the South East Asia Treaty Organization (**SEATO**) in 1954. The rights of **Maoris** and the preservation of their culture are major political issues.

AREA 104,000 sq mi (271,000 sq km)
POPULATION 4,290,000
CAPITAL Wellington
GOVERNMENT Constitutional monarchy
ETHNIC GROUPS New Zealand European 74%, New Zealand Maori 10%, Polynesian 4%
LANGUAGES English and Maori (both official)
RELIGIONS Anglican 24%, Presbyterian 18%, Roman Catholic 15%, others
NATIONAL ANTHEM (DATE) "God Defend New Zealand" (1940)

The kiwi, the national bird, is one of three flightless birds found only in New Zealand.

148

NICARAGUA

FLAG RATIO: 3:5   USE: National/Civil   DATE ADOPTED: 1908   LAST MODIFIED: 1971

Like many other nations in Central America, Nicaragua has a **blue and white** flag in homage to Argentina. In 1823 Nicaragua, Honduras, Costa Rica, El Salvador and Guatemala united to establish the **Central American Federation**, which adopted a flag with **three horizontal stripes**. In 1839 the Federation dissolved, but Nicaragua retained the flag. The arrangement of colors show Central America (**white stripe**) between the Atlantic and Pacific Oceans (**blue stripes**). The oceans also feature in the **triangular coat of arms**. Other symbols on the arms are **five volcanoes** (representing the members of the former federation), a **rainbow** (standing for hope), and a **red Liberty cap** (denoting freedom).

HISTORY

Christopher Columbus reached Nicaragua in 1502. **Spanish** colonization claimed the lives of *c*. 100,000 **Native Americans**. In the 17th century, Britain seized control of the **Mosquito Coast**. In 1821 Nicaragua gained **independence**. In 1934 **US marines** helped **Anastasio Somoza García** to defeat **Augusto Sandino**. The Somozas ruled Nicaragua until 1980, when the **Sandinistas** seized power from **Anastasio Somoza**. The United States aided the **Contra** rebels in a 10-year civil war against **Daniel Ortega**'s Sandinista socialist government. **Violeta Chamorro** defeated Ortega in 1990 elections. In 2004 the World Bank wrote off most of the country's debt. Ortega returned to power in 2006.

Footprints of Acahualinca *in Managua are more than 6000 years old.*

AREA 50,200 sq mi (130,000 sq km)
POPULATION 5,666,000
CAPITAL Managua
GOVERNMENT Multiparty republic
ETHNIC GROUPS Mestizo 69%, White 17%, Black 9%, Amerindian 5%
LANGUAGES Spanish (official)
RELIGIONS Roman Catholic 85%, Protestant
NATIONAL ANTHEM (DATE) *"Salve a ti, Nicaragua"* "Hail to You, Nicaragua" (1939)

149

NIGER

FLAG RATIO: 2:3 USE: National/Civil DATE ADOPTED: 1959 LAST MODIFIED: 1959

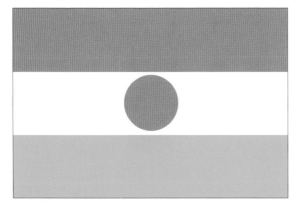

Modeled on the French *tricolore*, the three horizontal stripes represent the three main geographic regions of Niger. **Orange** denotes the desert land in the north, **white** represents the central savanna, and **green** stands for the grassy plains in the south. The **orange disk** in the center represents the hot sun shining over Niger. Niger's flag is very similar to the flag of **Côte d'Ivoire**, symbolic of the historical ties between the two nations.

HISTORY

The **Hausa** states ruled southern Niger from the 10th century to 1804, when **Usman dan Fodio** established the Fulani sultanate of **Sokoto**. In the 14th century, the **Tuareg** kingdom of **Takedda** developed west of the **Aïr Mountains**, flourishing on the trans-Saharan trade in copper. The **Sultanate of Agadez** succeeded Takedda. In the medieval period, the **Kanem-Bornu Empire** dominated eastern Niger, while the **Songhai Empire** commanded western Niger. Scottish explorer **Mungo Park** was probably the first European to reach Niger (1795). A **French** expedition arrived in 1891, but the Tuareg resisted French rule until 1922, when Niger became a **French colony**. In 1960 Niger gained **independence**. **Hamani Diori** was Niger's first president. In 1975 **Colonel Seyni Kountché** overthrew Diori and founded a dictatorship that lasted until his death in 1987. From 1990–95 and 2007–8 Tuaregs waged a **civil war** for a separate state. A military coup in 2010, prompted by the president's attempt to extend his power, was followed by 2011 elections.

AREA 489,000 sq mi (1,267,000 sq km)

POPULATION 16,469,000

CAPITAL Niamey

GOVERNMENT Multiparty republic

ETHNIC GROUPS Hausa 56%, Djerma 22%, Tuareg 8%, Fula 8%, others

LANGUAGES French (official), Hausa, Djerma

RELIGIONS Islam 80%, indigenous beliefs, Christianity

NATIONAL ANTHEM (DATE) *"La Nigerienne"* "Song of Niger" (1961)

African ring-necked parakeet, *a long-tailed parrot, lives in much of West Africa.*

NIGERIA

FLAG RATIO: 1:2   USE: National/Civil   DATE ADOPTED: 1960   LAST MODIFIED: 1960

Nigeria's flag was the winning entry in a national competition held in 1959. The **green-white-green vertical stripes** are a stylized depiction of the River Niger (**white** stripe) flowing through the fertile fields of Nigeria (**two green stripes**). Green also symbolizes agriculture, the main source of income in Nigeria, and white stands for peace and unity. Nigeria adopted the flag upon independence from Britain in 1960.

HISTORY

The kingdom of **Kanem** arose in the 9th century, and in the 14th century merged into the kingdom of **Bornu**. In the 16th century, the Empire of Kanem-Bornu controlled the **Hausa states**. The **Yoruba** kingdom of **Ife** influenced **Benin** and **Oyo**. The **Songhai Empire** dominated northern Nigeria in the early 16th century. In 1804 **Usman dan Fodio** created the **Fulani** sultanate of **Sokoto**. Nigeria was a center of the **slave trade**. In 1861 **Britain** seized **Lagos**, ostensibly to stop this. By 1906 Britain conquered all of Nigeria. In 1960 Nigeria gained **independence** under **Sir Abubakar Tafawa Balewa**. In 1963 it became a republic, led by **Tafawa Balewa**. In 1967 the **Ibo** declared the independence of **Biafra**. Civil war raged for three years before Biafra capitulated. Between 1960 and 1998 Nigeria enjoyed only nine years of civilian government. Separatism, sectarian violence and attacks on foreign-owned oil infrastructure grew in the early 21st century.

Ibo from southeast Nigeria perform the acrobatic Nkpokiti dance.

AREA 357,000 sq mi (924,000 sq km)
POPULATION 155,216,000
CAPITAL Abuja
GOVERNMENT Federal multiparty republic
ETHNIC GROUPS Hausa and Fulani 29%, Yoruba 21%, Ibo (or Igbo) 18%, Ijaw 10%, Kanuri 4%
LANGUAGES English (official), Hausa, Yoruba, Ibo
RELIGIONS Islam 50%, Christianity 40%, traditional beliefs
NATIONAL ANTHEM (DATE) "Arise, O Compatriots!" (1978)

151

NORWAY

FLAG RATIO: 8:11 **USE:** National/Civil **DATE ADOPTED:** 1821 **CODIFIED:** 1898

Frederik Meltzer, the member of Parliament from Bergen, designed Norway's flag in 1821. It was officially adopted as the national flag in 1898. The design combined the red-and-white *Dannebrog*, the flag of Denmark, with the blue of Sweden's flag. Its **red**, **white** and **blue** colors also recall the French *tricolore*, a symbol of liberty. The "**Scandinavian cross**" appears in blue.

HISTORY

From the 9th to the 11th century, **Vikings** raided western Europe. King **Olaf II**, patron saint of Norway, introduced **Christianity** in the early 11th century. **Lutheranism** became the state religion in the mid-16th century. In 1397 Norway, Sweden, and Denmark united in the **Kalmar Union**. Denmark ruled Norway from 1442 to 1814, when **Sweden** gained control. Norway declared independence, but Swedish troops forced Norway to accept union under the Swedish crown. In 1905 Norway became an **independent monarchy**. Norway remained neutral during World War I. In April 1940, **Germany** invaded. In 1942 the Nazis set up a puppet government under **Vidkun Quisling**. More than 50% of Norway's merchant fleet was destroyed during World War II. Liberation finally came in May 1945. Norway joined NATO in 1949, and was a cofounder (1960) of the European Free Trade Association (EFTA). It voted against joining the European Union (EU) in 1971 and 1994. In 1991 **King Olav V** was succeeded by his son **Harald V**. In 2011 more than 70 people, mostly at a summer youth camp, were murdered by a right-wing extremist as an attack on the ruling Labor Party.

AREA 125,000 sq mi (324,000 sq km)
POPULATION 4,692,000
CAPITAL Oslo
GOVERNMENT Constitutional monarchy
ETHNIC GROUPS Norwegian 97%
LANGUAGES Norwegian (official)
RELIGIONS Evangelical Lutheran 86%
NATIONAL ANTHEM (DATE) "*Ja, Vi Elsker Dette Landet*" "Yes, We Love This Land" (1864)

Bunad *making is a Norwegian handicraft. Bunads are folk costumes.*

OMAN

FLAG RATIO: 1:2 USE: National/Civil DATE ADOPTED: 1970 LAST MODIFIED: 1995

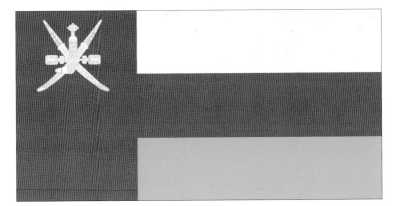

Oman's flag was monochrome **red** until 1970, when **white** and **green** bands were added. White symbolizes peace. Green is a traditional **Islamic** color, but also stands for the fertility of the land. Red represents the blood shed in the struggle for liberation. The Sultanate's **white coat of arms** on the upper hoist consists of two **crossed swords**, a *khnajar* (dagger), and **belt**. In 1995 the flag was altered by making the white and green bands of equal width.

HISTORY

In ancient times, Oman was an important trading area on the main trading route between the Arabian (Persian) Gulf and the Indian Ocean. In 1507 the Portuguese captured several ports in Oman, including Muscat. **Portugal** con-trolled maritime trade until it was expelled by the **Ottomans** in 1659. The **al-Said** family has ruled Oman since 1741. During the 20th century, the Sultanate was often in conflict with religious leaders (*imams*) of the **Ibahdi** sect, who sought to create a more theocratic society. British colonial interference and economic inequality led to popular rebellions in the 1950s and 1960s. In 1970 Sultan **Sa'id bin Taimur** was deposed by his son, **Qaboos bin Sa'id**. In 2003 the first election to the consultative council in which all citizens over the age of 21 could vote took place. Widespread popular protests in 2011 led to the promise of reform.

AREA 119,000 sq mi (310,000 sq km)
POPULATION 3,028,000
CAPITAL Muscat
GOVERNMENT Monarchy with consultative council
ETHNIC GROUPS Arab, Baluchi, Indian, Pakistani
LANGUAGES Arabic (official), Baluchi, English
RELIGIONS Islam (mainly Ibadhi), Hinduism
NATIONAL ANTHEM (DATE) *"Nshid as-Salaam as-Sultani"* "The Sultan's Anthem" (1970)

Bahla, in northern Oman, is the center for traditional Omani pottery.

153

PAKISTAN

FLAG RATIO: 2:3 USE: National DATE ADOPTED: 1947 LAST MODIFIED: 1947

The **white** and **dark green** flag of Pakistan represents the country's religious minorities (white) and Muslim majority (green). The **crescent moon** and **five-pointed star** are traditional motifs of **Islam**. The crescent also stands for progress. The star symbolizes light and knowledge.

HISTORY

In 712 **Arabs** conquered **Sind**, and introduced **Islam**. The **Delhi Sultanate** ruled from 1211 to 1526, when the **Mughal Empire** supplanted it. In the early 19th century, **Ranjit Singh** made **Punjab** the center of **Sikhism**. The **British** conquered Sind (1843), Punjab (1849), and much of **Baluchistan** in the 1850s. **British India** won independence in 1947, and split into India and Pakistan (Urdu, "Land of the Pure"). **Muhammad Ali Jinnah** was Pakistan's first leader. In 1947 the long dispute with India over **Kashmir** began. **Muhammad Ayub Khan** was president from 1958 to 1969. In 1971 East Pakistan declared independence as **Bangladesh** and a bloody civil war ensued. **Zulfikar Ali Bhutto** was prime minister from 1973 to 1977. His daughter, **Benazir Bhutto**, was Pakistan's first woman prime minister. The presence of militants, particularly the **Taliban**, in the northwest frontier provinces is problematic. US special forces killed **Osama bin Laden** in Abbottabad in 2011 without forewarning the Pakistani government.

AREA 307,000 sq mi (796,000 sq km)
POPULATION 187,343,000
CAPITAL Islamabad
GOVERNMENT Federal republic
ETHNIC GROUPS Punjabi, Sindhi, Pashtun (Pathan), Baluchi, Muhajir
LANGUAGES Urdu (official), many others
RELIGIONS Islam 97%, Christianity, Hinduism
NATIONAL MOTTO "Faith, Unity, Discipline"
NATIONAL ANTHEM (DATE) *"Qaumi Tarana"* "National Anthem" (1954)

Terracotta jar (c.*2600 BC*) *from the Harappan site of Nausharo, Baluchistan.*

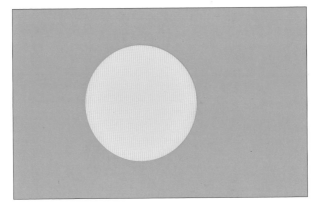

The flag was officially adopted in 1981 when the archipelago became self-governing. The **blue field** represents the geographic position of the islands in the northern Pacific Ocean. Blue also symbolizes independence. The **yellow disc** stands for the full moon and productivity – an ancient belief holds that the full moon is the best time for fishing and harvesting. Currently, eight of Palau's 16 states have their own **state flag**.

HISTORY

Ten of Palau's states and its capital, Korot, are on the largest island of **Babeldaob**. Settled by migrants from Southeast Asia *c*.3000 years ago, the **Spanish** arrived in 1710. In 1898 Spain sold the islands to **Germany**. In 1914 **Japan** occupied the archipelago. At the end of World War II, control passed to the **United States**, which administered Palau as part of the **US Trust Territory of the Pacific Islands**. In 1981 the islands gained self-government. In 1994 Palau became an **independent republic** in free association with the United States, which is responsible for its defence. **Migrant workers**, mainly from the **Philippines**, account for 30% of Palau's population.

The bai, *a meeting place for village chiefs, is a distinctive Microneisan architectural form.*

AREA 180 sq mi (460 sq km)
POPULATION 21,000
CAPITAL Melekeok
GOVERNMENT Federal multiparty republic
ETHNIC GROUPS Palauan (Micronesian) 70%, Asian (mainly Filipinos) 28%, white 2%
LANGUAGES English and Palauan (official) – except on Sonsoral (Sonsoralese, English), Tobi (Tobi, English), and Angaur (Angaur, Japanese, English)
RELIGIONS Roman Catholic 40%, Modekngei 33% (indigenous), Evangelical Church 10%, Mormon 2%, Jehovah's Witness 2%, Baha'i 2%
NATIONAL ANTHEM (DATE) Untitled (1980)

155

PANAMA

FLAG RATIO: 2:3 USE: National/Civil DATE ADOPTED: 1903 RATIFIED: 1941

Panama's flag is a **rectangle** divided into **four quarters**. The lower left quarter is **blue** and stands for the Conservative Party. The top right quarter is **red** and represents the Liberal Party. Other quarters are **white**, symbolizing peace between the parties. The **blue star** in the top left quarter stands for purity and honesty. The **red star** in the bottom right quarter denotes government and law.

HISTORY

In 1502 **Christopher Columbus** landed in Panama. The indigenous population was soon wiped out and **Spain** asserted control. In 1821 Panama became a province of **Greater Colombia**. After a revolt in 1903, Panama declared **independence** from Colombia. The **Hay-Bunau-Varilla Treaty** (1903) gave the United States control of the proposed **Panama Canal**. The trans-isthmian canal opened in 1914. In 1977 a treaty confirmed Panama's sovereignty over the Canal, while providing for US bases in the Canal Zone. General **Manuel Noriega** came to power in 1983. In 1989 Noriega made himself president and declared war on the United States. The United States invaded and overthrew Noriega, who received a 40-year prison sentence. **Pérez Balladares** became president in 1994 elections. In 1999 Panama was given control of the canal by the United States. In 2005 voters supported a plan to upgrade the canal.

AREA 29,200 sq mi (75,500 sq km)
POPULATION 3,460,000
CAPITAL Panamá
GOVERNMENT Multiparty republic
ETHNIC GROUPS Mestizo 70%, Black and Mulatto 14%, White 10%, Amerindian 6%
LANGUAGES Spanish (official), English
RELIGIONS Roman Catholic 85%, Protestant 15%
NATIONAL MOTTO "*Pro Mundi Beneficio*" "For the Benefit of the World"
NATIONAL ANTHEM (DATE) Untitled (1980)

The full and flowing pollera dress is Panama's national costume for women.

156

PAPUA NEW GUINEA

FLAG RATIO: 3:4 USE: National/Civil DATE ADOPTED: 1971 LAST MODIFIED: 1971

Papua New Guinea's flag consists of two right-angled triangles. A yellow *kumul* bird of paradise is on the **upper red triangle**. It symbolizes Papua New Guinea's emergence as an independent nation. The plumes of the *kumul* are often used as ceremonial decoration in Papua New Guinea. The **white five-pointed stars** on the **lower black triangle** represent the constellation of the **Southern Cross**. The Southern Cross is a common motif of countries in the southern hemisphere. Black, red, and yellow are the national colors of Papua New Guinea.

HISTORY

In 1526 the Portuguese became the first Europeans to sight New Guinea. In 1828 the **Dutch** took western New Guinea (now Irian Jaya, **Indonesia**). In 1884 Germany captured northeast New Guinea, which became **German New Guinea**, while Britain created **British New Guinea** in the southeast. In 1906 British New Guinea passed to **Australia** as the **Territory of Papua**. In 1921 the League of Nations mandated German New Guinea to Australia as the **Territory of New Guinea**. In 1949 Papua and New Guinea combined to form the Territory of Papua and New Guinea. In 1973 it achieved self-government as a prelude to **independence** as Papua New Guinea in 1975. In the 1990s the government fought against separatists on **Bougainville**, but a peace deal in 2001 led to the election of an autonomous government in 2005.

AREA 179,000 sq mi (463,000 sq km)
POPULATION 6,188,000
CAPITAL Port Moresby
GOVERNMENT Constitutional monarchy
ETHNIC GROUPS Papuan, Melanesian, Micronesian
LANGUAGES English (official), Melanesian Pidgin, more than 700 other indigenous languages
RELIGIONS Traditional beliefs 34%, Roman Catholic 22%, Lutheran 16%, others
NATIONAL ANTHEM (DATE) "O Arise, All You Sons" (1975)

Telefomin shield-carriers from West Sepik, Papua New Guinea, were unarmed.

157

PARAGUAY

FLAG RATIO: 3:5   **USE:** National/Civil   **DATE ADOPTED:** 1842   **LAST MODIFIED:** 1988

In 1812 Paraguay adopted a **red, white and blue tricolor** as its national flag. It derived the design from the French *tricolore*, a popular symbol of liberty in the early 19th century. In 1842 it adopted the present flag with two different sides. The **obverse** of the flag displays the concentric circles of the **national shield**. At the center of the shield is a yellow "Star of May" on a **blue disk**, recalling the date of independence (May 14, 1811). **Laurel branches**, a traditional symbol of peace, surround the disk. The **reverse** of the flag shows the **seal** of the Paraguayan National Treasury, consisting of the national motto and a **lion** guarding a **red Liberty cap** on a pole.

HISTORY

The earliest known inhabitants were the **Guaraní**. In 1537 the **Spanish** built a fort at Asunción, which became the capital of its South American colonies. In 1811 Paraguay won **independence. José Francia** was dictator from 1811 to 1840. Paraguay lost more than half of its population and much territory in the **War of the Triple Alliance** (1865–70) against Brazil, Argentina, and Uruguay. Paraguay regained some land in the **Chaco War** (1932–35) against Bolivia. General **Alfredo Stroessner**'s dictatorship lasted from 1954 to 1989. In 1993 elections **Juan Carlos Wasmosy** became the first civilian president for almost 40 years. The election of Fernando Lugo in 2008 ended 61 years of rule by conservative factions.

AREA 157,000 sq mi (407,000 sq km)
POPULATION 6,459,000
CAPITAL Asunción
GOVERNMENT Multiparty republic
ETHNIC GROUPS Mestizo 95%
LANGUAGES Spanish and Guarani (both official)
RELIGIONS Roman Catholic 90%, Protestant
NATIONAL MOTTO *"Paz y Justice"*
"Peace and Justice"
NATIONAL ANTHEM (DATE) *"Himno Nacional"*
"National Anthem" (1846)

The agouti paca, a tailless rodent, lives in the tropical forests of Paraguay.

PERU

FLAG RATIO: 2:3 USE: National/Civil DATE ADOPTED: 1825 LAST MODIFIED: 1825

In legend, Peru's **red and white striped** flag was inspired by a flock of flamingos that General José de San Martín spotted flying over his army when liberating Peru from Spain in 1820. Seeing this as a good omen, San Martín declared red and white to be the colors of liberty. Red also stands for the blood shed in the struggle for independence. White symbolizes peace. At the center of the flag is the **coat of arms**. The tripartite shield, framed and topped by **green wreaths**, has a pile of **gold coins**, a **vicuña**, and a **keno tree**. Simon Bolívar defined the flag in 1825.

HISTORY

In 1500 the **Inca Empire** extended from Ecuador to Chile. Spanish conquistador **Francisco Pizarro** captured Inca King **Atahualpa** in 1532. By 1533 **Spain** ruled most of Peru. Spanish rule saw many native revolts, most notably that of **Tupac Amaru**. In 1821 Peru declared **independence**. Spain still held much of the interior, and **Simon Bolívar** completed Peru's liberation in 1826. Peru lost some of its land to Bolivia in the **War of the Pacific** (1879–84). **Civil war** between the government and rebels (such as **Shining Path** and Tupac Amaru) claimed more than 30,000 lives in the 1980s. In 2000, after a decade as president, **Alberto Fujimori** faced bribery charges and fled into exile. In 2009 he was convicted of human rights abuses.

***Cuzco**, southern Peru, hosts the annual* Inti Raymi *(June 24), Inca Festival of the Sun.*

AREA 496,000 sq mi (1,285,000 sq km)
POPULATION 29,249,000
CAPITAL Lima
GOVERNMENT Constitutional republic
ETHNIC GROUPS Mestizo (Spanish-Indian) 44%, Creole (mainly African American) 30%, Mayan Indian 11%, Garifuna (Black-Carib Indian) 7%, others 8%
LANGUAGES English (official), Creole, Spanish
RELIGIONS Roman Catholic 62%, Protestant 30%
NATIONAL ANTHEM (DATE) *"Marcha Nacional"* "National March" (1822)

PHILIPPINES

FLAG RATIO: 1:2 **USE:** National/Civil **DATE ADOPTED:** 1898 **RATIFIED:** 1946

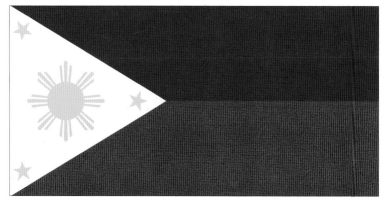

General Emilio Aguinaldo, leader of the revolt against Spain, designed Philippines' flag. The **equilateral triangle** at the hoist denotes equality. Its **white** color symbolizes purity. The **yellow sun** stands for the giant steps made by Filipinos in building a nation. The sun's **eight rays** represent the first eight Filipino provinces to rebel against Spain. The **three yellow stars** represent the main geographical regions – Mindanao, Luzon, and Visayas. The **blue stripe** stands for the unity and noble aspirations of Filipinos. The **red stripe** symbolizes the blood shed in the fight for independence.

HISTORY

In 1565 **Spain** began its conquest of the islands, naming them *Filipinas* after King Philip II. In 1896 Filipinos revolted against Spanish rule. The **United States** gained the islands after victory in the Spanish-American War (1898). From 1899 to 1902, Filipinos vainly fought against US occupation. In 1935 **Manuel Luis Quezon** became the first president of the Commonwealth of the Philippines. **Japan** occupied the islands from 1941 to 1944; the US liberated the country. Philippines won **independence** in 1946. Dictator **Ferdinand Marcos** ruled from 1965 to 1986. Conflict with rebels wanting an Islamic state on Mindanao has claimed more than 120,000 lives.

AREA 116,000 sq mi (300,000 sq km)
POPULATION 101,834,000
CAPITAL Manila
GOVERNMENT Multiparty republic
ETHNIC GROUPS Christian Malay 92%, Muslim Malay 4%, Chinese and others
LANGUAGES Filipino (Tagalog) and English (both official), Spanish and many others
RELIGIONS Roman Catholic 83%, Protestant 9%, Islam 5%
NATIONAL MOTTO *"Maka-diyos, maka-tao, makakalikasan at makabansa"* "We are religious, we are friendly, we are rich, and we love our country"
NATIONAL ANTHEM (DATE) *"Lupang Hinirang"* "Beloved Land" (1898)

Golden Tara *of Agusan (c.1400) is the earliest Indian artifact found in the Philippines.*

POLAND

FLAG RATIO: 3:8   USE: National   DATE ADOPTED: 1919   LAST MODIFIED: 1919

Poland's flag of **horizontal white and red stripes** dates back to the red banner with white eagle of Vladislav Jagiello at the Battle of Tannenberg (1410). Polish kings used various combinations of white and red in the 17th century. In 1831 the *Sejm* (Polish assembly) adopted white and red as national colors in the uprising against Russian rule. In 1919 Poland adopted its present flag. The **state flag** has the coat of arms, a **white eagle** with a **golden crown** on a **red shield**, on the white band.

HISTORY
Mieszko I founded a Polish state in the 10th century. In 1386 Poland unified with **Lithuania**. In 1717 **Russia** conquered Poland. The **War of the Polish Succession** (1733–35) involved most of Europe. The **Partitions of Poland** (1772, 1793, 1795) erased Poland from the map. **Tadeusz Kosciuszko** led resistance. In 1918 Poland regained **independence** from Russia. In 1921 it became a republic. In 1939 **Germany** invaded Poland, prompting **World War II**. The **Nazis** established concentration camps in which more than 6 million Poles (mainly Jews) perished. Poland regained **independence** in 1945. In 1952 it adopted a Soviet-style constitution. In 1990 the trade union **Solidarity** toppled **General Jaruzelski**'s communist regime and **Lech Walesa** became president. Poland joined NATO in 1999 and the **EU** in 2004.

Krakowiak *is a fast dance performed by several couples. Chopin wrote one in 1828.*

AREA 125,000 sq mi (323,000 sq km)
POPULATION 38,442,000
CAPITAL Warsaw
GOVERNMENT Multiparty republic
ETHNIC GROUPS Polish 97%, Belarusian, Ukranian, German
LANGUAGES Polish (official)
RELIGIONS Roman Catholic 95%, Eastern Orthodox
NATIONAL ANTHEM (DATE) *"Mazurek Dabrowskiego"* "Dabrowski's Mazurka" (1927)

PORTUGAL

FLAG RATIO: 2:3 **USE:** National/Civil **DATE ADOPTED:** 1911 **LAST MODIFIED:** 1911

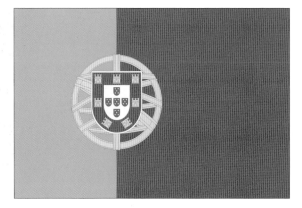

Portugal's national flag divides into two **vertical bands** of **green** and **red** representing hope and revolution respectively. The national **coat of arms** sits at the center of an **armillary sphere** – an early navigational instrument and symbol of Portugal's leading role in early global exploration. The coat of arms includes important aspects of the nation's history and Christian beliefs. The **five blue shields** recall King Alfonso I's victory over five Moorish princes in 1139. The five **white dots** on each shield are symbolic of the wounds of Christ at the crucifixion. The **seven gold castles** stand for the fortified cities captured from the Moors.

HISTORY

In 711 **Moors** captured the entire country, except for the northern County of Portugal. **Alfonso I** drove out the Moors, and Spain recognized Portuguese **independence** in 1143. The reconquest ended with the Moors' retreat from the **Algarve** in 1249. In 1385 **John I** founded the **Aviz dynasty**. The reign of **Manuel I** (1495–1521) was Portugal's "golden age" when explorers such as **Vasco da Gama** built a vast **Portuguese Empire**. In 1500 **Pedro Cabral** conquered Brazil. The fall of the dynasty brought **Philip II** of Spain to the throne in 1580 for the next 60 years. In 1640 **John IV** founded the **Braganza dynasty** which reigned until 1910, when Portugal became a **republic**. **António Salazar**'s dictatorship lasted from 1932 to 1968. In 1974 a military coup toppled **Marcelo Caetano**. The global financial crisis and the constraints of membership of the **Euro** left Portugal needing financial assistance in 2011.

AREA 34,300 sq mi (88,800 sq km)
POPULATION 10,760,000
CAPITAL Lisbon
GOVERNMENT Multiparty republic
ETHNIC GROUPS Portuguese 99%
LANGUAGES Portuguese (official)
RELIGIONS Roman Catholic 94%
NATIONAL ANTHEM (DATE) *"A Portugesa"*
"The Portuguese" (1910)

An amolador *(knife-grinder) was a familiar figure in the streets of 19th-century Lisbon.*

Qatar's national flag is very similar to the flag of **Bahrain**, a reflection of their close historical links. Until *c.*1860 the flag was monotone red. Qatar added a **vertical, serrated white stripe** at the request of the British, who sought to prevent piracy in the Arabian Gulf by including a white stripe for friendly Arab States. The **nine-point serrated** line indicates that Qatar is the ninth member of the "reconciled Emirates" of the Arabian Gulf after the treaty with Britain in 1916. The **ratio** of the flag is different to that of Bahrain (11:28 rather than 3:5). In 1949 Qatar changed the color of the right-hand band to **maroon** to differentiate it further from Bahrain. White also symbolizes peace, and maroon represents the blood shed in the 19th-century wars.

HISTORY

In the 1780s the **al-Khalifa** family gained control of Bahrain and Qatar. From 1872 to 1913 Qatar was part of the **Ottoman Empire**. In 1916 Qatar became a **British Protectorate**. **Oil** was first discovered in 1939. In 1971 Qatar gained **independence**. Sheikh **Khalifa bin Hamad Al-Thani** became Emir after a coup in 1972. Qatar was a founder member of the Gulf Cooperation Council (GCC) in 1981. Qatar allowed Allied coalition forces to use its territory to expel Iraqi forces from Kuwait in the **Gulf War** (1991). In 1995 Sheikh **Hamad bin Khalifa Al-Thani** became Emir. In 2011, the Emir announced the first national legislative elections, scheduled to take place in 2013.

Qatar is a liberal Islamic society where women can choose to cover their heads.

AREA 4,200 sq mi (11,000 sq km)
POPULATION 848,000
CAPITAL Doha
GOVERNMENT Absolute monarchy
ETHNIC GROUPS Arab 40%, Pakistani 18%, Indian 18%, Iranian 10%
LANGUAGES Arabic (official), English
RELIGIONS Islam 95%
NATIONAL ANTHEM (DATE) *"As Salam al Amiri"* "Salute to the Emir" (1996)

163

ROMANIA

FLAG RATIO: 2:3 **USE:** National/Civil **DATE ADOPTED:** 1861 **REINTRODUCED:** 1989

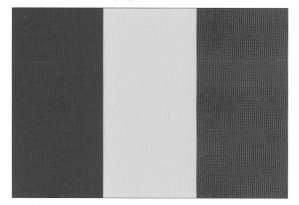

In some accounts, Romania's **tricolor** of **blue**, **yellow** and **red vertical stripes** dates back to Michael the Brave, Prince of Wallachia (1593–1601). In 1834 Sultan Mahmud II allowed Wallachia to fly an ensign of red, blue and yellow horizontal stripes. After the Revolution of 1848, Wallachia adopted first a horizontal then a vertical tricolor of blue, yellow, and red. In 1861 Wallachia and Moldavia united to form Romania. The new nation adopted Wallachia's flag. In 1948 Romania's communist government introduced a separate state flag with a coat of arms. In 1989 the communist regime collapsed and the flag was scrapped.

AREA 92,000 sq mi (238,000 sq km)

POPULATION 21,905,000

CAPITAL Bucharest

GOVERNMENT Multiparty republic

ETHNIC GROUPS Romanian 89%, Hungarian 7%, Roma 2%, Ukranian

LANGUAGES Romanian (official), Hungarian, German

RELIGIONS Eastern Orthodox 87%, Protestant 7%, Roman Catholic 5%

NATIONAL ANTHEM (DATE) *"Desteaptate, Romane"* "Awake, Romanians" (1990)

HISTORY

Romania roughly corresponds to ancient **Dacia**, which the **Romans** conquered in AD 106. The principalities of **Wallachia** and **Moldavia** emerged in the 14th century. They formed part of the **Ottoman Empire** from the 15th to the 19th century. Russia gained control after the **Russo-Turkish War** (1828–29). In 1861 Wallachia and Moldavia merged to create Romania. In 1940 **Ion Antonescu** became dictator. Romania joined the German invasion of the Soviet Union in June 1941. More than 50% of Romanian Jews were killed during World War II. In 1944 **Soviet** troops occupied Romania. **Gheorghe Gheorghiu-Dej** replaced Antonescu. In 1965 the dictator **Nicolae Ceausescu** assumed power; in 1989 he and his wife were executed. In 2007 Romania joined the **European Union**.

Traditional Romanian *Easter eggs are hand painted in geometric designs.*

RUSSIA

FLAG RATIO: 2:3   USE: National/Civil   DATE ADOPTED: 1991   LAST MODIFIED: 1993

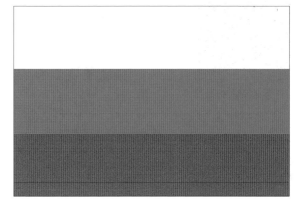

In 1991 Russia adopted a **tricolor** of **white**, **blue** and **red horizontal stripes**. In 1993 it changed the **ratio** from 1:2 to 2:3. White, blue and red are **Pan-Slavic** colors. A triband flag with these colors has been in use since the reign (1682–1721) of Czar Peter the Great. In 1799 Czar Alexander I adopted it as the civil ensign, and from 1883 it served as an alternative to the black-gold-white civil flag. In 1918 the Bolsheviks introduced a monochrome red flag with yellow Cyrillic letters. From 1954 the flag of the Soviet republic of Russia featured a red field with a blue stripe and a hammer and sickle on the hoist. According to tradition, white represents nobility, blue stands for honesty, and red represents courage.

HISTORY

The **Romanov** Czarist dynasty ruled Russia from 1613 to 1917. **Peter the Great** founded **St. Petersburg** in 1712. Czarina **Catherine the Great** made Russia the greatest European power. In 1917, the **Bolsheviks,** led by **Lenin,** overthrew Czar **Nicholas** II and Russia became part of the **Soviet Union**. In 1924 **Joseph Stalin** succeeded Lenin. In 1941 **Germany** invaded Russia. About 25 million Soviet people died in **World War II**. In December 1991, the Soviet Union collapsed. From 2000, under **Vladimir Putin**, Russia has adopted a more assertive foreign policy, especially in areas that it regards as within its sphere.

***In 1997 Vologda**, northwest Russia, marked its 850th anniversary.*

AREA 6,593,000 sq mi (17,075,000 sq km)
POPULATION 138,740,000
CAPITAL Moscow
GOVERNMENT Federal multiparty republic
ETHNIC GROUPS Russian 82%, Tatar 4%, Ukrainian 3%, Chuvash 1%, more than 100 others
LANGUAGES Russian (official), many others
RELIGIONS Russian Orthodox, Islam Judaism
NATIONAL ANTHEM (DATE) *"Gosudarstvenny Gimn Rossiyskaya Federatsiya"* "State Anthem of the Russian Federation" (2001)

RWANDA

FLAG RATIO: 2:3   USE: National   DATE ADOPTED: 2002   LAST MODIFIED: 2002

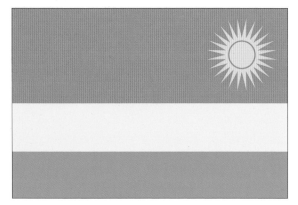

In 2002 Rwanda adopted a **tricolor** flag of **blue, yellow and green horizontal stripes**. The flag was part of an effort to forge a new national identity after the genocide of the 1990s. The flag recalls Rwanda's landscape of lush forests and desert under the African sun. Green symbolizes hope for prosperity. Yellow represents work, and blue stands for peace and happiness. The **sun** denotes unity and the fight against ignorance.

HISTORY

In the 15th century, **Tutsi** cattle herders moved into the area and soon dominated the **Hutus**. By the late 18th century, Rwanda and Burundi formed a single state, ruled by a Tutsi king (*mwami*). In 1890 it became part of **German East Africa**. In 1919 **Belgium** gained control. In 1959 the *mwami* died and a civil war claimed more than 150,000 lives. Hutu victory led to a mass exodus of Tutsis. In 1962 Rwanda won **independence**. In 1973 Juvénal **Habyarimana** ousted President **Grégoire Kayibanda**. In 1994 Habyarimana and President Ntaryamira of Burundi died in a rocket attack. The Hutu army began a war of **genocide** against the Tutsi minority, killing more than 800,000 people. In 1994 the Tutsis toppled the regime, creating 2 million Hutu refugees. A government of national unity emerged and prosecutions of those involved in the genocide began.

AREA 10,200 sq mi (26,300 sq km)
POPULATION 11,370,000
CAPITAL Kigali
GOVERNMENT Republic
ETHNIC GROUPS Hutu 84%, Tutsi 15%, Twa 1%
LANGUAGES French, English and Kinyarwanda (all official)
RELIGIONS Roman Catholic 57%, Protestant 26%, Adventist 11%, Islam 5%
NATIONAL ANTHEM (DATE) *"Rwanda nziza"*
"Beautiful Rwanda" (2001)

Rwanda has many traditional instruments. The lulunga is an eight-stringed harp.

SAINT KITTS AND NEVIS

FLAG RATIO: 2:3 USE: National/Civil DATE ADOPTED: 1983 LAST MODIFIED: 1983

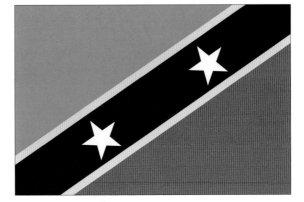

Saint Kitts and Nevis' flag has **green** and **red right-angled triangles**, separated by **three diagonal stripes** (two **yellow** and one **black**). The black stripe has **two white stars**. Yellow represents the nation's abundant sunshine. Green stands for its fertile lands. Red represents the struggle for freedom from colonialism and slavery. Black symbolizes its African heritage, and the two white stars denote the freedom of the two islands.

HISTORY

Saint Kitts is a shortened form of its official name, Saint Christopher, given to it by **Christopher Columbus** when he discovered the island in 1493. In 1623 Saint Kitts became the first **English** colony in the West Indies. The French arrived in 1624. Europeans massacred the indigenous **Caribs**. In 1698 colonists settled on the neighboring island of **Nevis** (Spanish, "snow"). The Treaty of Paris (1783) confirmed British possession of the islands, which prospered through imported African **slave labor** on **sugar plantations**. Nevis became known as the "Queen of the Caribees" because of its productive sugar industry. In 1918 Britain joined Saint Kitts and Nevis with Anguilla and the Virgin Islands. The islands gained self-government in 1967, and full **independence** in 1983. In 1998 Nevis held a referendum on independence, but there was not a sufficient majority in favor of separation. In 2005 the loss-making sugar industry closed down.

Pirates plundered many pieces-of-eight from Spanish ships around Saint Kitts-Nevis.

AREA 100 sq mi (260 sq km)
POPULATION 50,000
CAPITAL Basseterre
GOVERNMENT Constitutional monarchy
ETHNIC GROUPS Black African 96%
LANGUAGES English (official)
RELIGIONS Anglican 50%, Methodist 25%, Roman Catholic 10%, Jehovah's Witness 1%
NATIONAL MOTTO "Country Above Self"
NATIONAL ANTHEM (DATE) "Oh Land of Beauty" (1983)

SAINT LUCIA

FLAG RATIO: 1:2 **USE:** National/Civil **DATE ADOPTED:** 1967 **LAST MODIFIED:** 1979

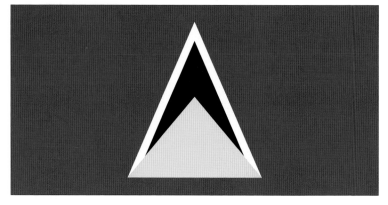

Dunstan St. Omer, a local artist, designed Saint Lucia's flag in 1967. At the center of a **blue field** are **three triangles** (**gold**, **black**, and **white**) superimposed on each other. Blue represents fidelity, the tropical sky, and the surrounding waters of the Caribbean Sea and Atlantic Ocean. Gold stands for the sunshine and prosperity. Black and white symbolize Saint Lucia's two cultures working together in unity. The superimposition of the triangles reflects the dominance of Saint Lucia's black African culture. The triangles also recall Saint Lucia's famous twin volcanic peaks of the Pitons.

AREA 210 sq mi (540 sq km)
POPULATION 162,000
CAPITAL Castries
GOVERNMENT Constitutional monarchy
ETHNIC GROUPS Black African 90%, mixed race 6%, European and East Indian 4%
LANGUAGES English (official), French patois
RELIGIONS Roman Catholic 80%, Seventh-Day Adventist 7%, Anglican 3%, Hindu 1%
NATIONAL MOTTO "The Land, the People, the Light"
NATIONAL ANTHEM (DATE) "Sons and Daughters of Saint Lucia" (1967)

HISTORY

Europeans discovered the island around 1500. In 1605 and 1638 the **Caribs** successfully resisted English attempts at colonization. In 1660 **France** signed a treaty with the Carib. The French built the first town, **Soufriere**, in 1746. The **British** attempted to capture the island at the **Battle of Cul de Sac** (1778). The British and French established **sugar plantations** using **slave labor** from Africa. After a series of conflicts, Britain gained Saint Lucia by the Treaty of Paris (1814). Saint Lucia achieved **self-government** in 1967, and full **independence** in 1979. **John Compton** spent three periods as Prime Minister: 1964–79, 1982–96, and 2006–07. In 2003 the constitution was amended to replace the oath of allegiance to the British monarch with a pledge of loyalty to Saint Lucians.

The banded butterfly fish lives on the coral reefs surrounding Saint Lucia.

SAINT VINCENT AND THE GRENADINES

FLAG RATIO: 2:3 USE: National/Civil DATE ADOPTED: 1985 LAST MODIFIED: 1985

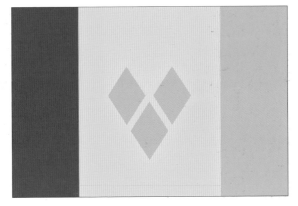

Saint Vincent and the Grenadines has a **tricolor** of **vertical stripes** of **blue**, **yellow**, and **green**. At the center of the flag are **three green diamonds** in the shape of a letter "V" for Vincent. The diamonds define the islands as "the gems of the Antilles." Blue represents the tropical sky and crystal clear waters around the nation. Yellow stands for the golden sands of the Grenadines, and green recalls the islands' lush vegetation. From 1979 to 1985 the flag had the coat of arms on a breadfruit leaf in the center.

HISTORY

The nation consists of the volcanic island of **Saint Vincent** and the five islands of the **Grenadine** group, the best known of which is **Mustique**. Saint Vincent was probably visited and named by **Christopher Columbus** in 1498. The native **Carib** fiercely resisted settlement until the **British** established a colony in 1762. After a revolt in 1795, the British deported most of the Carib and imported **slave labor** from Africa. Saint Vincent and the Grenadines formed part of the British colony of the **Windward Islands** from 1833 to 1958 and of the **West Indies Federation** from 1958 to 1962. It gained self-government in 1969, and **independence** in 1979. In 2009 voters decided to keep the British monarch as head of state.

Forestry logo *of Saint Vincent and the Grenadines. Forest covers 30% of St. Vincent.*

AREA 150 sq mi (390 sq km)
POPULATION 104,000
CAPITAL Kingstown
GOVERNMENT Constitutional monarchy
ETHNIC GROUPS Black African 66%, mixed race 19%, East Indian 6%, Carib 2%
LANGUAGES English, French patois
RELIGIONS Methodist 20%, Roman Catholic 10%, Seventh-Day Adventist 7%
NATIONAL MOTTO *"Pax et Justitia"* "Peace and Justice"
NATIONAL ANTHEM (DATE) "St. Vincent! Land so Beautiful" (1969)

SAMOA

FLAG RATIO: 1:2 USE: National/Civil DATE ADOPTED: 1948 LAST MODIFIED: 1949

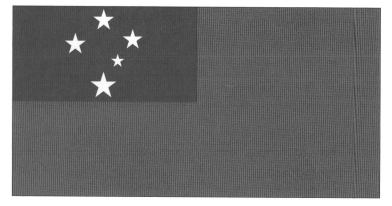

Samoa's national flag has a **red field** and a **blue canton** with **five white stars**. It adopted the national flag in 1948, but with four stars instead of five. A fifth was added in 1949 as a representation of the **Southern Cross**. It is common for countries in the southern hemisphere to use the constellation as a motif. The three colors stand for courage (red), purity (white), and freedom (blue).

HISTORY

First settled in *c*.1000, the islands are the cradle of **Polynesian** culture. Dutch navigator **Jacob Roggeveen** sighted the island in 1722, and **Louis Antoine de Bougainville** claimed them for France in 1768. European colonialism brought conflict and disease. British missionaries arrived in the 1830s, and soon converted the native population to **Christianity**. In 1899 **Western Samoa** became a **German Protectorate**, and the **United States** annexed Eastern Samoa (now **American Samoa**). In 1914 **New Zealand** seized Western Samoa, and the League of Nations mandated it to New Zealand in 1920. In 1929 New Zealand troops killed 11 members of the **Mau**, a passive resistance movement. In 1946 Western Samoa became a trust territory of New Zealand. In 1962 Western Samoa became the first Polynesian nation to gain **independence**. In 1997 it changed its name to **Samoa**.

AREA 1,100 sq mi (2,800 sq km)

POPULATION 193,000

CAPITAL Apia

GOVERNMENT Constitutional monarchy

ETHNIC GROUPS Samoan 93%, Euronesians (mixed European and Polynesian) 7%

LANGUAGES Samoan (Polynesian), English

RELIGIONS Congregational 43%, Roman Catholic 21%, Methodist 17%, Latter-Day Saints 10%, Seventh-Day Adventist 3%

NATIONAL ANTHEM (DATE) "The Banner of Freedom" (1962)

The many-colored fruit dove is a rare bird, found only in Polynesia.

SAN MARINO

FLAG RATIO: 3:4 USE: National DATE ADOPTED: 1862 LAST MODIFIED: 1862

San Marino officially adopted its bicolor flag of **blue** and **white horizontal stripes** in 1862. It was first mentioned in 1797, after Napoleon's invasion of Italy. The colors originate from earlier versions of the state's coat of arms, which lies at the center of the flag. The **coat of arms** features the **three peaks** and castle towers of Monte Titano, San Marino's highest mountain. An **ostrich feather** tops each tower. The upper white stripe symbolizes the snow covered peaks of Titano. The blue stripe represents the sky. San Marino also flies a **civil flag** without the coat of arms.

HISTORY

San Marino is the **world's second smallest republic** (after Nauru) and perhaps Europes oldest state. According to legend, it was founded in the early 4th century AD, when a Christian stonemason named **Marinus the Dalmatian** fled there to escape the Roman Emperor Diocletian. Saint Marinus established a small Christian community on **Monte Titano**. The area became an independent commune in the 13th century. Until the 15th century, the state consisted solely of Mount Titano when **Pope Pius II** gave San Marino the towns of Fiorentino, Montegiardino, Serravalle, and Faetano. While San Marino has its own currency and stamps, Italian and Vatican equivalents are widely used. It possesses its own legislative assembly, the Great and General Council, which elects Captains Regent as heads of state.

The towers of the three fortresses on Monte Titano are the symbol of San Marino.

AREA 20 sq mi (60 sq km)
POPULATION 32,000
CAPITAL San Marino
GOVERNMENT Republic
ETHNIC GROUPS San Marinese, Italian
LANGUAGES Italian (official)
RELIGIONS Roman Catholic
NATIONAL MOTTO *"Libertas"* "Liberty"
NATIONAL ANTHEM (DATE) *"Inno Nazionale"* "National Anthem" (1894)

171

SÃO TOMÉ AND PRÍNCIPE

FLAG RATIO: 1:2 **USE:** National/Civil **DATE ADOPTED:** 1975 **LAST MODIFIED:** 1975

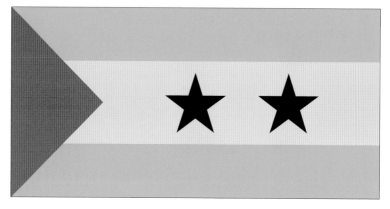

São Tomé and Príncipe's national flag derives from the banner of the *Movimento de Liberacion de São Tomé and Príncipe* (MLSP), which led the struggle for liberation. The flag uses the **Pan-African** colors of **green**, **red**, and **yellow**. The **two five-pointed black stars** represent the islands of São Tomé and Príncipe.

HISTORY

In *c.* 1470 **Portugal** discovered the small (uninhabited) islands, and they built a settlement on **São Tomé** (Portuguese, "Saint Thomas") in 1485. In 1522 the islands became a Portuguese colony. The **Dutch** controlled the islands from 1641 to 1740, but Portugal regained control and brought **slaves** from the African mainland to work on the **sugar plantations**. After the collapse of the sugar market, **Príncipe** (Portuguese, "Prince") served as Portugal's staging post in the **slave trade** to Brazil. In 1822 Portugal introduced **cacao**, and São Tomé soon became a leading world producer. In 1975 a military coup forced Portugal to grant **independence** to the islands. President **Manuel Pinto da Costa**, who ruled from 1975 to 1991, pursued a broadly communist agenda. In 1991 **Miguel Trovada** won the nation's first democratic elections. In 1995 Príncipe received **autonomy**. In 2007 the International Monetary Fund wrote off about 90% of the country's debt.

AREA 370 sq mi (960 sq km)
POPULATION 180,000
CAPITAL São Tomé
GOVERNMENT Multiparty republic
ETHNIC GROUPS *Mestico, Angolares* (both Angolan slave descendants), *Forros* (freed slave descendants), *Servicais* (contract laborers), *Tongas* (*Servicais* descendants)
LANGUAGES Portuguese (official)
RELIGIONS Roman Catholic 83%, Protestant 15%, traditional African beliefs 1%
NATIONAL MOTTO "*Unidade, Disciplina, Trabalho*" "Unity, Discipline, Work"
NATIONAL ANTHEM (DATE) "*Independência Total*" "Total Independence" (1975)

In 2000 São Tomé celebrated the third anniversary of cooperation with China.

FLAG RATIO: 2:3 **USE:** National/Civil **DATE ADOPTED:** 1973 **LAST MODIFIED:** 1973

Saudi Arabia's flag consists of a **green field** with **Arabic script** and a **sword** pointing toward the hoist. The Arabic writing is the *shahada*, the profession of Muslim faith: "There is no God but Allah, and Muhammad is his Prophet." **Green** is a traditional color of **Islam** and the Wahhabi sect. The *shahada* on a green field derives from the late 18th-century flag of the Wahhabi movement. In 1902 Ibn Saud became King of the Nejd, and added a sword to the flag. In 1973 the Saudi constitution defined the flag.

HISTORY

In 570 the Prophet **Muhammad** was born in **Mecca**, western Saudi Arabia. In the 18th century, the **Wahhabi** (a strict Islamic sect) won the support of the **Saud** family, who formed a state in **Nejd**. In 1810 **Turkey** conquered the region. In 1902 **Ibn Saud** captured **Riyadh**, and by 1906 he ruled the entire Nejd. In 1913 **Al Hasa** province fell. In 1920 Ibn Saud seized the **Asir**, and by 1925 he gained the whole of the **Hejaz**. In 1932 Ibn Saud formed the **Kingdom of Saudi Arabia**, ruling in line with the *sharia* of Wahhabi Islam. Saudi Arabia supported Iraq in the **Iran-Iraq War** (1980–88), but backed the Allied coalition against Iraq in the **First Gulf War** (1991). In the **Second Gulf War**, Saudi Arabia refused to allow its facilities to be used to attack **Iraq**. Terrorist attacks occur sporadically. In 2011 King **Abdullah** announced increased rights for women, including the right to Vote.

AREA 830,000 sq mi (2,150,000 sq km)
POPULATION 26,132,000
CAPITAL Riyadh
GOVERNMENT Absolute monarchy
ETHNIC GROUPS Arab 90%, Afro-Asian 10%
LANGUAGES Arabic (official)
RELIGIONS Islam 100%
NATIONAL ANTHEM (DATE) *"Aash Al Maleek"*
"Long Live our Beloved King" (1950)

Stamp *marking the Muslim victory at the Battle of Badr (624), near Medina.*

SENEGAL

FLAG RATIO: 2:3 **USE:** National/Civil **DATE ADOPTED:** 1960 **LAST MODIFIED:** 1960

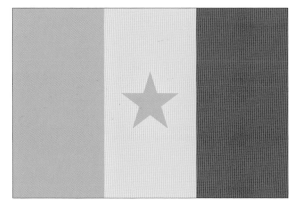

Based on the French *tricolore*, the Senegalese flag consists of **three equal, horizontal stripes**. At the center of the flag is a **green star**. It uses the **Pan-African** tricolor of **green**, **gold**, and **red**. Green is a traditional color of **Islam**, but also stands for fertility and hope. Gold represents prosperity and the hard work of the Senegalese people. Red symbolizes the blood shed in the struggle for independence. The **five-pointed** star represents Senegal's place among the nations of the five continents.

AREA 76,000 sq mi (197,000 sq km)
POPULATION 12,644,000
CAPITAL Dakar
GOVERNMENT Multiparty republic
ETHNIC GROUPS Wolof 44%, Pular 24%, Serer 15%
LANGUAGES French (official), tribal languages
RELIGIONS Islam 94%, Christianity (mainly Roman Catholic) 5%, traditional beliefs 1%
NATIONAL MOTTO *"Un Peuple, Un But, Une Foi"* "One People, One Target, One Faith"
NATIONAL ANTHEM (DATE) *"Pincez Tous vos Koras, Frappez les Balafons"* "Pluck Your Koras, Strike the Balafons" (1960)

HISTORY

From the 6th to 10th century, Senegal formed part of the **Empire of Ghana**. The **Tukulor** state of **Tekrur** dominated the Senegal valley from the 11th to the 14th century. The **Almoravid** dynasty of Berbers introduced **Islam**. In 1444 **Portuguese** sailors reached Cape Verde. In 1658 **France** built the port of **St. Louis**. In 1765 Senegal became part of the **British** colony of **Senegambia**. France regained control in 1783, and Senegal joined **French West Africa** in 1895. In 1959 Senegal united with French Sudan (now **Mali**) to form the Federation of Mali. In 1960 Senegal withdrew from the union and became an **independent** republic. **Léopold Senghor** was president from 1960 to 1980. In 2001 elections, **Abdoulaye Wade** defeated **Abdou Diouf**, ending 40 years of socialist rule.

Senegalese women often wear beautiful traditional cotton dresses and headscarves.

Serbia's **horizontal tricolor** uses the **Pan-Slavic colors** of red, blue, and white with its lesser **coat of arms** centered vertically and shifted toward the hoist by one-seventh of the width of the flag. The **colors** derive from the 19th-century flag of Russia. It replaced the similar 2004 flag. Before then the Serbian state flag bore no arms. After Montenegro left the Union of Serbia and Montenegro in 2006, Serbia phased out the use of the Union's flag.

HISTORY

In 1918 the **Kingdom of Serbs, Croats, and Slovenes** formed under Peter I of Serbia. Alexander I succeeded as King in 1921. In 1929 he renamed the country **Yugoslavia**. From 1941 **Josep Broz Tito**'s communist partisans and Royalist chetniks resisted Nazi occupation. In 1945 Tito formed a socialist republic in Yugoslavia. In 1991 **Slovenia and Croatia seceded** from the federation. In 1992 **Bosnia-Herzegovina** declared independence. Serbia helped Bosnian Serbs in the civil war. In 1992 a new Yugoslav federation emerged. In 1999, after the expulsion of Albanians from the Serbian province of **Kosovo**, NATO launched air strikes against Yugoslavia, and Kosovo came under international protection. Yugoslavia was renamed **Serbia and Montenegro** in 2003, but this changed to **Serbia** in 2006 when **Montenegro** formed a separate state. Kosovo's declaration of independence in 2008 was not recognized by Serbia.

Traditional *dress of the Bunjevci from Bačka, Vojvodina, in northern Serbia.*

AREA 29,900 sq mi (77,500 sq km)
POPULATION 7,311,000
CAPITAL Belgrade
GOVERNMENT Federal republic
ETHNIC GROUPS Serb 83%, Hungarian 4%, others
LANGUAGES Serbian (official), Hungarian
RELIGIONS Serbian Orthodox, Roman Catholic, Islam, Protestant
NATIONAL ANTHEM (DATE) *"Hej Slaveni"* "O Slavs" (1945)

175

SEYCHELLES

FLAG RATIO: 1:2 **USE:** National/Civil **DATE ADOPTED:** 1996 **LAST MODIFIED:** 1996

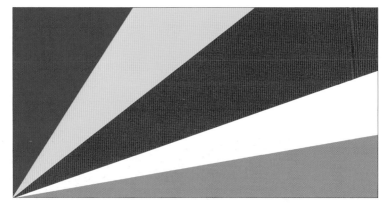

The Seychelles' flag consists of **five oblique bands** of **blue, yellow, red, white**, and **green**. Blue represents the sea and sky around and above the Seychelles. Yellow stands for the islands' abundant sunshine. Red denotes the Seychellois and their united determination to achieve future prosperity. White symbolizes justice and harmony. Green represents the land. From 1976 to 1977 the Seychelles' flag had a white saltire dividing triangles of blue (top and bottom) and red (hoist and fly). From 1977 to 1996 the flag had red, green, and white horizontal wavy bands.

HISTORY

In 1502 **Vasco da Gama** explored the islands and named them the "Seven Sisters." **France** colonized the islands in 1756, establishing **spice plantations** worked by slaves from Mauritius. The **British** captured the archipelago (1794) during the Napoleonic Wars and, in 1814, it became a dependency of **Mauritius**. In 1903 the Seychelles became a separate Crown Colony. In 1976 the islands gained **independence** from Britain. In 1977 a coup established **Albert René** as President. In 1981 South African mercenaries attempted to overthrow the government. Continued civil unrest and another failed coup (1987) led to the first **multiparty elections** in 1991. Widespread damage was caused by the **Boxing Day tsunami** in 2004.

AREA 180 sq mi (460 sq km)

POPULATION 89,000

CAPITAL Victoria

GOVERNMENT Multiparty republic

ETHNIC GROUPS Seychellois Creole (European, Asian, and African) 96%

LANGUAGES English (official), French (official), Creole (official)

RELIGIONS Roman Catholic 90%, Anglican 8%, Hindu 1%

NATIONAL ANTHEM (DATE) *"Koste Seselwa"* "Come Together All Seychellois" (1996)

The male Seychelles sunbird *has a curved beak, blue throat, and yellow pectoral tufts.*

SIERRA LEONE

FLAG RATIO: 2:3   USE: National/Civil   DATE ADOPTED: 1961   LAST MODIFIED: 1961

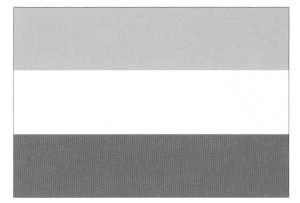

Sierra Leone has a **tricolor** flag of **green**, **white** and **blue** horizontal stripes. Green represents the nation's agriculture and its lush mountain slopes. Blue stands for the waters of the Adriatic that lap Sierra Leone's coast. White symbolizes the desire for peace, justice and unity.

HISTORY

In 1460 **Portuguese** sailors reached the coast. In the 16th century Sierra Leone was a source for **slaves**. In 1787 the British Anti-Slavery Society founded **Freetown** as a settlement for freed slaves. In 1808 the settlement became a **British Crown Colony**. Britain made the interior a **Protectorate** in 1896. In 1951 the Protectorate and Colony united. In 1961 Sierra Leone gained **independence**. Sir

Milton Margai was the nation's first prime minister. In 1971 Sierra Leone became a **republic**. From 1992 to 1999 **civil war** between the government and the Revolutionary United Front (RUF) claimed *c*.10,000 lives. Ahmed Kabbah became President in 1996 elections, but was deposed in a coup in 1997. He returned to power in 1999. In 2000 rebels, led by **Foday Sankoh** and backed by Liberia, abducted UN troops and renewed the war. British soldiers arrived to support the UN and captured Sankoh. The rebels mostly disarmed in 2002. Despite rebel raids from Liberia in 2003, stability was gradually restored and, in 2005, the last UN troops left the country.

AREA 27,700 sq mi (71,700 sq km)
POPULATION 5,364,000
CAPITAL Freetown
GOVERNMENT Single-party republic
ETHNIC GROUPS Native African tribes 90%
LANGUAGES English (official), Mende, Temne, Krio
RELIGIONS Islam 60%, traditional beliefs 30%, Christianity 10%
NATIONAL MOTTO Unity, Freedom, Justice"
NATIONAL ANTHEM (DATE) "High We Exalt Thee, Realm of the Free" (1961)

Sierra Leone   Le 1500

Jentink's Duiker *Cephalophus Jentinki*

Jentink's duiker is an endangered small antelope found in Sierra Leone.

SINGAPORE

FLAG RATIO: 2:3 USE: National/State DATE ADOPTED: 1959 LAST MODIFIED: 1959

S ingapore first hoisted its **bicolor** flag in 1959, and retained it when breaking away from the Federation of Malaysia in 1963. It consists of a **red horizontal stripe**, symbolizing brotherhood and equality, and a **white horizontal stripe**, representing purity and virtue. The **crescent moon** denotes the emergence of the new nation, while the **five stars** stand for the five ideals of democracy, peace, justice, progress, and equality.

HISTORY

According to legend, Singapore was founded in 1299. It was first called Temasak (Sea Town), but was renamed **Singapura** (City of the Lion). In 1819 Sir **Thomas Stamford Raffles** of the **British East India Company** leased the island from **Johor**, and the Company founded the city of Singapore. In 1826 Singapore, Pinang, and Malacca formed the **Straits Settlement**. **Japan** seized the island in 1942, but British rule returned in 1945. In 1946 the Straits Settlement dissolved and Singapore became a separate colony. In 1959 Singapore won **self-government**. In 1963 it became part of the **Federation of Malaysia**, but separated to become an **independent republic** in 1965. **The People's Action Party (PAP)** has ruled Singapore since 1959. **Lee Kuan Yew** was Prime Minister from 1959 to 1990. His son, **Lee Hsien Loong** followed in the role from 2004.

AREA 260 sq mi (680 sq km)

POPULATION 4,741,000

CAPITAL Singapore City

GOVERNMENT Multiparty republic

ETHNIC GROUPS Chinese 77%, Malay 14%, Indian 8%

LANGUAGES Chinese, Malay, Tamil and English (all official)

RELIGIONS Buddhism, Islam, Hinduism, Christianity

NATIONAL MOTTO *"Majulah Singapura"* "May Singapore Prosper"

NATIONAL ANTHEM (DATE) *"Majulah Singapura"* "May Singapore Prosper" (1959)

The trishaw is a traditional form of transportation in Singapore.

SLOVAK REPUBLIC

FLAG RATIO: 2:3 USE: National/Civil DATE ADOPTED: 1992 LAST MODIFIED: 1992

The Slovak Republic has a **tricolor** flag of **white**, **blue**, and **red** horizontal stripes. It first adopted a white, blue, and red flag in 1848, and the present order of colors first appeared in 1868. As part of Czechoslovakia from 1919 to 1991, the Slovak Republic used the flag currently flown by the **Czech Republic**. In 1992, after the breakup of Czechoslovakia, the present flag was officially adopted. The **coat of arms**, set slightly toward the hoist, was added to distinguish the flag from that of Russia. The coat of arms is taken from part of the Hungarian arms, and shows a **double cross** set on **three hills** to commemorate the arrival of Christianity to the Carpathian region in the 9th century. Red, white, and blue are **Pan-Slavic** colors.

HISTORY

Slavic peoples settled in the region in the 5th and 6th centuries AD. Conquered by the **Magyars** in the 10th century, **Hungary** dominated the region for about 900 years. The **Austro-Hungarian Empire** emerged in 1867. After the defeat of Austria-Hungary in World War I, Slovakia became an autonomous region of **Czechoslovakia**. The Czechs dominated the union, and many Slovaks became dissatisfied. In 1939 Slovakia gained nominal independence as a protectorate of **Nazi Germany**. In 1945 it returned to Czechoslovakia. In 1993, after elections in which **independence** was a principal issue, the federation dissolved. The Slovak Republic joined both **NATO** and the **European Union** in 2004.

***Folk clothing from Detva**, central Slovakia, includes wide linen trousers and a fur cloak.*

AREA 18,900 sq mi (49,000 sq km)
POPULATION 5,477,000
CAPITAL Bratislava
GOVERNMENT Multiparty republic
ETHNIC GROUPS Slovak 86%, Hungarian 11%
LANGUAGES Slovak (official), Hungarian
RELIGIONS Roman Catholic 60%, Protestant 8%, Orthodox 4%, others
NATIONAL ANTHEM (DATE) *"Nad Tatrou sa Blyská"* "Storm above the Tatras" (1993)

179

SLOVENIA

FLAG RATIO: 1:2 USE: National/Civil DATE ADOPTED: 1991 LAST AMENDED: 1991

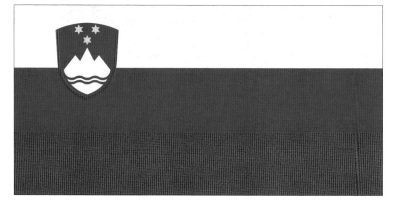

Slovenia's **tricolor** flag derives from the historical flag of the Duchy of Carniola (1848–1918). Blue, white, and red are **Pan-Slavic** colors. On the upper hoist of the flag is the **coat of arms**, designed in 1991. The arms is a **shield** featuring a stylized depiction of the **three peaks** of Mount Triglav in **white** on a **blue background**. The **two wavy blue lines** below Triglav symbolize the Adriatic Sea. Above Triglav are **three six-pointed gold stars** in the pattern of a triangle. The stars derive from the coat of arms of the County of Celje, which united much of Slovenia in the Middle Ages.

HISTORY

The Slovenes, the western branch of the **South Slavs**, established a king-dom in the 7th century. From the 10th century they were enserfed by German lords. From the 13th century until 1918, the **Austrian Hapsburgs** ruled Slovenia. In 1918 Slovenia became part of the **Kingdom of the Serbs, Croats, and Slovenes**, renamed **Yugoslavia** in 1929. During World War II, Slovenia was invaded and par-titioned between Italy, Germany, and Hungary. After the war, Slovenia returned to Yugoslavia. In 1990 **Milan Kucan** led a noncommunist govern-ment. In 1991 Slovenia declared **inde-pendence**, which led to brief fighting between the Slovenes and the Federal Yugoslav Army before agreement was reached. In 2004 Slovenia joined the **European Union** and **NATO**.

AREA 7,800 sq mi (20,300 sq km)
POPULATION 2,003,000
CAPITAL Ljubljana
GOVERNMENT Multiparty republic
ETHNIC GROUPS Slovene 92%, Croat 1%, Serb, Hungarian, Bosniak
LANGUAGES Slovenian (official), Serbo-Croatian
RELIGIONS Mainly Roman Catholic
NATIONAL ANTHEM (DATE) *"Zdravljica"* "A Toast" (1990)

Decorated honey-cake ("loški" *or* "mali kruhek") *is a traditional gift for Epiphany.*

SOLOMON ISLANDS

FLAG RATIO: 1:2 **USE:** National/Civil **DATE ADOPTED:** 1977 **LAST MODIFIED:** 1977

Solomon Islands' flag consists of a blue **right-angled triangle** and a **green right-angled triangle**, separated by a **yellow diagonal stripe**. On the hoist are **five white five-pointed stars**. Blue represents the Pacific Ocean around the islands. Green stands for the islands' lush vegetation. Yellow denotes the abundant sunshine of Melanesia. The five stars represent the five districts of the Solomon Islands at the time of the flag's adoption.

HISTORY

The Solomon Islands extend across more than 900 mi (1400 km) of the **Pacific Ocean**. **Spain** discovered the islands in 1568. The indigenous **Melanesians** resisted colonization until the late 19th century. In 1893 the southern islands became a **British Protectorate**. **Germany** controlled the northern islands from 1895. In 1900 Germany ceded its territory to Britain. During World War I, **Australian** troops occupied Bougainville and Buka (now part of **Papua New Guinea**), and the League of Nations mandated them to Australia in 1920. In 1942 the **Japanese** occupied the southern islands. In 1944, after heavy fighting, particularly on **Guadalcanal**, US troops liberated the islands. In 1976 the Solomon Islands achieved **self-government**, as a prelude to full **independence** in 1978. A military coup in 2000 provoked civil war. An Australian peacekeeping force arrived in 2003.

AREA 11,200 sq mi (28,900 sq km)
POPULATION 572,000
CAPITAL Honiara
GOVERNMENT Constitutional monarchy
ETHNIC GROUPS Melanesian 93%, Polynesian 4%, Micronesian 2%, European 1%
LANGUAGES English (official), 90 vernaculars (including Solomon Islands pidgin)
RELIGIONS Anglican 35%, Roman Catholic 19%, South Sea Evangelical 17%, United Church (Methodist) 11%, Seventh-Day Adventist 10%
NATIONAL MOTTO "To Lead is to Serve"
NATIONAL ANTHEM (DATE) "God Save Our Solomon Islands" (1978)

Solomon Islanders use kastom *or custom dances to tell stories about the past.*

SOMALIA

FLAG RATIO: 2:3 USE: National/Civil DATE ADOPTED: 1954 LAST MODIFIED: 1954

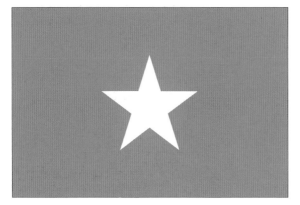

In 1954 Italian Somaliland adopted the current flag. The **blue** derived from the color of the United Nations' (UN) flag – Italian Somaliland was a UN Trust Territory from 1950 to 1960. The **white five-pointed star** represents the five regions inhabited by Somali people (north and south Somalia, Djibouti, southern Ethiopia, and northern Kenya). White symbolizes peace and prosperity.

HISTORY

In the 7th century, Arab traders established coastal settlements and introduced **Islam**. The interest of European imperial powers increased after the opening of the **Suez Canal** in 1869. In 1887 **Britain** established a **Protectorate** in northern Somalia. By 1905, **Italy** controlled central and southern Somalia. In 1936 Italian Somaliland united with the Somali regions of **Ethiopia** to form **Italian East Africa**. In 1950 Italian Somaliland became a United Nations' (UN) Trust Territory, administered by Italy. In 1960 it united with British Somaliland to form an **independent** Somalia. In 1969 **Siad Barre** led a military coup, and Somalia became an Islamic republic. In 1991 Barre was overthrown, and Somalia fell into civil war between rival clans. UN forces failed to restore peace but provided **famine** relief. By 2011 militant group Al Shabah controlled much of the centre and south. Lawlessness, most notably piracy, and drought continue to be problems.

AREA 246,000 sq mi (638,000 sq km)
POPULATION 9,926,000
CAPITAL Mogadishu
GOVERNMENT Transitional, parliamentary federal government
ETHNIC GROUPS Somali 85%, Bantu, Arab, others
LANGUAGES Somali (official), Arabic, English, Italian
RELIGIONS Islam (Sunni Muslim)
NATIONAL ANTHEM (DATE) *"Soomaaliyeey Toosoo"* "Somalia Awake" (2000)

Somalia's *coat of arms, shown on this stamp, is two leopards holding a shield.*

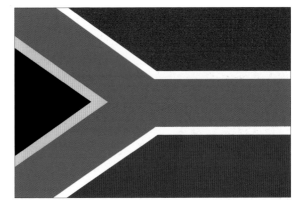

South Africa adopted a new flag after the **African National Congress** (ANC) won the country's first multiracial elections in 1994. The flag combines the **black**, **green**, and **yellow** of the ANC with the **red**, **white**, and **blue** of the old colonial powers, the **Netherlands** and **Britain**. The **Y-shape** on the flag symbolizes convergence and a united future.

HISTORY

The indigenous people are the **San**. In 1652 the **Dutch East India Company** founded a colony at Table Bay. Dutch **Afrikaners** (or **Boers**) established farms, employing slaves. In the early 19th century, **Britain** gained control of the Cape region. In 1833 the Boers embarked on the **Great Trek**. Britain defeated the **Zulu** in the **Zulu War** (1879) and the Boers in the **South African Wars** (1880–81, 1899–1902). In 1910 the **Union of South Africa** was formed, and won **independence** in 1931. In 1948 the Nationalist government adopted its racist policy of **apartheid**. The **African National Congress (ANC)** resisted and many of its prominent members were jailed. **Nelson Mandela** was in prison from 1964 to 1990, and in 1994 he became president of a multiracial democracy. **Thabo Mbeki** succeeded him in 1999, followed by **Jacob Zuma** in 2009.

Thabo Mbeki replaced Nelson Mandela as President of South Africa in 1999.

AREA 471,000 sq mi (1,221,000 sq km)
POPULATION 49,004,000
CAPITAL Cape Town/Pretoria
GOVERNMENT Multiparty republic
ETHNIC GROUPS Black 76%, White 13%, Coloured 9%, Asian 2%
LANGUAGES Afrikaans, English, Ndebele, Pedi, Sotho, Swazi, Tsonga, Tswana, Venda, Xhosa and Zulu (all official)
RELIGIONS Christianity 68%, Islam 2%, Hinduism 1%
NATIONAL ANTHEM (DATE) "The National Anthem of South Africa" (1995)

183

SOUTH SUDAN

FLAG RATIO: 1:2 **USE:** National/Civil **DATE ADOPTED:** 2005 **DATE ADAPTED:** 2005

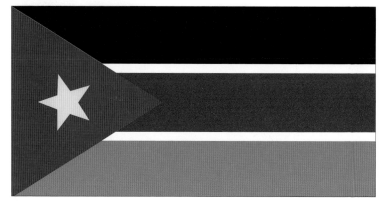

South Sudan's flag, adopted in 2005, before **independence**, is a **horizontal tricolor** of the **Pan-African colors** separated by **white**, with a **blue chevron** holding a **gold star** on the **hoist** side. It is the flag of the **Sudan People's Liberation Movement**. **Black** represents the South Sudanese people; **white**, peace; **red**, blood shed for freedom; **green**, the land; **blue**, the waters of the Nile; and the **Star of Bethlehem** represents the unity of the country's states.

HISTORY

South Sudan's population of *c.* 200 ethnic groups migrated to the region from farther south more than 1000 years ago. The south's deep cultural and religious differences with the north, and accusations that agreements made on independence from **Britain** in 1952 had been broken, led to a civil war from 1964–72 and some degree of autonomy for the south. **Civil war** broke out again from 1983–2005 when autonomy was rescinded by the north. Fighting ceased when South Sudan was again granted some autonomy. **Salva Kiir Mayardiit** was elected president in 2005, and again in multiparty elections in 2010. In January 2011, a referendum was held in which the majority of the people in the south voted for independence, which came about in July. After independence, ties with Sudan were strained over the border region of **Abyei** and in the **Nuba Mountains,** and over oil revenues.

AREA 239,000 sq mi (620,000 sq km)
POPULATION 8,260,000
CAPITAL Juba
GOVERNMENT Federal democratic presidential republic
ETHNIC GROUPS Dinka, Nuer, others
LANGUAGES English (official), local languages
RELIGIONS Traditional beliefs, Christian
NATIONAL MOTTO "Justice, Liberty, Prosperity"
NATIONAL ANTHEM (DATE) *"South Sudan Oyee!"*
"South Sudan Hooray!" (2011)

The first stamps of South Sudan *showed the new flag of the new nation.*

SPAIN

FLAG RATIO: 2:3 **USE:** National/Civil **DATE ADOPTED:** 1936 **LAST MODIFIED:** 1981

Spain has a **bicolor** flag of **horizontal stripes** (**two red, one yellow**). The colors probably derive from its historic kingdoms. In 1785 King Charles III adopted the bicolor flag as the war ensign. In 1843 it became the state flag. From 1931 to 1939, Spain had a tricolor of red, yellow and purple. The **coat of arms** to the left of center of the flag last changed in 1981. The **shield**, topped by a crown and flanked by **pillars**, features the **arms** of the regions of **Castile, León, Navarre,** and **Granada**. Wrapped around the pillars is a banner with the national motto.

HISTORY

Iberians and **Basques** were Spain's early inhabitants. In 1483 **Ferdinand V** and **Isabella I** launched the **Inquisition**. In 1492 the **reconquest** of Granada ended **Moorish** rule in Spain. **Christopher Columbus'** discovery of America (1492) helped Spain become the leading imperial power. The accession of **Bourbon** King **Philip V** provoked the War of the **Spanish Succession** (1700–14). In 1923 **Primo de Rivera** formed a dictatorship. **General Franco**'s victory in the **Spanish Civil War** (1936–39) crushed the **second republic**. His dictatorship lasted until his death in 1975, when a constitutional monarchy emerged. In 1977 the Basque Country *(Pais Vasco)*, Catalonia and Galicia gained limited autonomy. The world financial crisis of 2008 sparked a deep, prolonged recession.

***Paper maché giants** parade at the September festival of La Mercé, Barcelona.*

AREA 192,000 sq mi (498,000 sq km)
POPULATION 46,755,000
CAPITAL Madrid
GOVERNMENT Constitutional monarchy
ETHNIC GROUPS Mediterranean and Nordic types
LANGUAGES Castillian Spanish (official) 74%, Catalan 17%, Galician 7%, Basque 2%
RELIGIONS Roman Catholic 94%, others
NATIONAL MOTTO *"Plus Ultra"* "More Beyond"
NATIONAL ANTHEM (DATE) *"Marcha Real"* "Royal March" (1942)

185

SRI LANKA

FLAG RATIO: 1:2 USE: National/Civil DATE ADOPTED: 1951 LAST MODIFIED: 1978

In legend, Sri Lanka's "Lion Flag" dates back to around 486 BC, when Prince Vijaya arrived on the shores of Sri Lanka. The last king to use the flag was Sri Vikrama Rajasinghe, whose reign ended in 1815. The **yellow border** represents the *Maha Singha*, chief advisers to the king. The **yellow lion holding a sword** in its right paw denotes justice and righteousness. The **crimson field** symbolizes immortality. The **four bo leaves** represent the four **Brahma** *Viharana*, standards for Buddhist living: *metta, karuna, muditha, upeksha* (compassion, kindness, joy in others' prosperity, equanimity). The **vertical stripes** of **green** and **saffron** stand for the minority communities of Muslims and Tamils respectively.

AREA 25,300 sq mi (65,600 sq km)
POPULATION 21,284,000
CAPITAL Colombo
GOVERNMENT Multiparty republic
ETHNIC GROUPS Sinhalese 74%, Tamil 18%, Moor 7%
LANGUAGES Sinhala and Tamil (both official)
RELIGIONS Buddhism 70%, Hinduism 15%, Christianity 8%, Islam 7%
NATIONAL ANTHEM (DATE) *"Sri Lanka Matha"* "Mother Sri Lanka" (1952)

HISTORY

Sinhalese settlers made the island a center of **Theravada Buddhism**. In the 14th century **Tamils** formed a **Hindu** kingdom in the northeast. The **Portuguese** landed in 1505. In 1658 Portuguese lands passed to the **Dutch East India Company**. In 1815 Britain captured the kingdom of **Kandy**, completing its control of the island. In 1948 Ceylon gained independence. **Don Senanayake** was the first prime minister. In 1959 Prime Minister **Solomon Bandaranaike** was assassinated and his widow, **Sirimavo**, became the world's first woman prime minister. Their daughter, **Chandrika Kumaratunga**, became president in 1993. In 1972 Ceylon became the republic of Sri Lanka ("Resplendent Island"). Between 1983 and 2009 **civil war** with the **Tamil Tigers** claimed more than 70,000 lives.

Galle, *southwest Sri Lanka, is a center of lacemaking, a craft introduced by the Dutch.*

Sudan's flag uses the red, white, black and green colors of the **Pan-Arab** movement. The **red stripe** symbolizes the blood shed in the struggle for freedom. The **white stripe** represents Islam, Sudan's dominant religion. The **black stripe** stands for the Mahdist revolution that briefly freed Sudan from colonial rule in the late 19th century. The **green triangle** at the hoist denotes prosperity. The **presidential flag** has the **coat of arms** in the middle of the white stripe. The arms feature a **secretary bird** with a **shield** on its breast. Above the bird is a **scroll** bearing the **national motto**.

HISTORY

From the 11th century BC to *c*.AD 350, it formed part of the Kingdom of **Kush**. **Christianity** arrived in the 6th century. In the 13th century, northern Sudan came under Muslim control. In 1821 **Muhammed Ali**'s Egyptian forces occupied the north. In 1881 **Muhammad Ahmad** declared himself Mahdi and led a rising against colonial rule. In 1898 British **General Kitchener** defeated the Mahdists at **Omdurman**. The colony of **Anglo-Egyptian Sudan** emerged in 1899. In 1956 Sudan gained **independence**. Civil war broke out between the government, dominated by northern Muslims, and the mainly Christian south. **Gaafar Nimeiri** ruled from 1969 to 1985. Since 2003, conflict and ethnic cleansing in **Darfur** in the west has claimed more than 200,000 lives. The south **seceded** in 2011 to become **South Sudan**.

AREA 728,000 sq mi (1,886,000 sq km)
POPULATION 35,680,000
CAPITAL Khartoum
GOVERNMENT Federal presidential democratic republic
ETHNIC GROUPS Arab, Beja, black, others
LANGUAGES Arabic (official), Nubian, Beja, others
RELIGIONS Islam
NATIONAL MOTTO *"Al Nadr Nila"* "Victory is Ours"
NATIONAL ANTHEM *"Nahnu Djundullah"* "We Are God's Army"

Sudan *belongs to the Common Market for Eastern and Southern Africa (COMESA).*

187

SURINAME

FLAG RATIO: 2:3 USE: National/Civil LAST MODIFIED: 1975 COAT OF ARMS: 1975

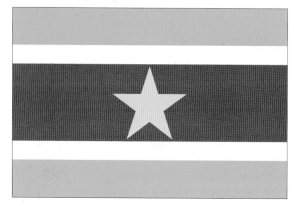

Suriname's flag consists of **five colored bands** and a **yellow, five-pointed star** at the center of the middle band. The star symbolizes national unity – each point represents one of Suriname's five main ethnic groups. **Yellow** denotes Suriname's golden future. The **red stripe** stands for progress and the struggle for a better life. The **two green stripes** signify hope and fertility. The **two white stripes** symbolize freedom and justice. The presidential flag replaces the star with the **coat of arms** and **national motto**.

HISTORY

In 1499 Spanish explorer Alfonso de Ojeda reached Suriname's coast, but the **British** founded the first colony in 1651. In 1667 Britain ceded it to **Holland** in exchange for New Amsterdam (now New York City). It became known as **Dutch Guiana**. Most of the population are either descendants from **African slaves** brought over in the 17th and 18th centuries, or descendants of **Indian** and **Indonesian indentured laborers** who arrived in the 19th century. Suriname became autonomous in 1954, and gained full **independence** in 1975. In 1980 the **army** seized control and Suriname plunged into **civil war**. Civilian rule returned in 1991. In 2007, the **UN** settled a long-standing dispute with **Guyana** over the position of the border.

AREA 63,000 sq mi (163,000 sq km)

POPULATION 492,000

CAPITAL Paramaribo

GOVERNMENT Multiparty republic

ETHNIC GROUPS Hindustani/East Indian 37%, Creole (mixed White and Black) 31%, Javanese 15%, Black 10%, Amerindian 2%, Chinese 2%, others

LANGUAGES Dutch (official), Sranang Tonga

RELIGIONS Hinduism 27%, Protestant 25%, Roman Catholic 23%, Islam 20%

NATIONAL MOTTO *"Justitia, Pietas, Fides"* "Justice, Faith, Loyalty"

NATIONAL ANTHEM (DATE) *"God zij met ons Suriname"* "God Bless Our Suriname" (1959)

In 2000 *Suriname issued this stamp to mark 25 years of independence.*

FLAG RATIO: 2:3 **USE:** National/Civil **DATE ADOPTED:** 1968 **LAST MODIFIED:** 1968

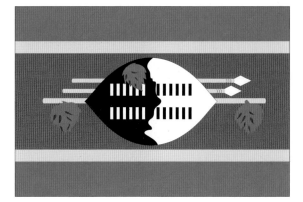

In 1941 King Sobhuza II gave a flag to the Emasotsha Regiment, a Swazi pioneer corps that fought in World War II. Swaziland's present flag is identical to that flag, except for the absence of a lion. It consists of **five horizontal stripes** and a central stylized depiction of a native oxhide **shield** with **two spears** and a **fighting staff**. From the staff and the shield hang tassels, symbols of the Swazi monarchy. The shield, staff and spear represent the defense of Swaziland. The **black and white** shield symbolizes racial harmony. The **blue stripes** denote peace. The **yellow stripes** stand for the nation's mineral wealth. The **red stripe** symbolizes the blood shed in past struggles.

HISTORY

In the 1840s, under attack from the **Zulu**, the Swazi sought **British** protection. In 1894 the British and **Boers** put Swaziland under the authority of the **Transvaal**. Britain took control at the end of the second **South African War** (1899–1902). In 1968 Swaziland gained **independence** with **King Sobhuza II** as head of state. In 1973 Sobhuza II assumed supreme power. He banned all political parties in 1978. In 1982 Sobhuza II died. His son, Makhosetive, became **King Mswati III** in 1986. In 2006 a new **constitution** strengthened his powers.

Ligcebesha *is a traditional Swazi costume worn by men.*

AREA 6,700 sq mi (17,400 sq km)
POPULATION 1,370,000
CAPITAL Mbabane
GOVERNMENT Monarchy
ETHNIC GROUPS African 97%, European 3%
LANGUAGES Siswati and English (both official)
RELIGIONS Zionist (a mixture of Christianity nd traditional beliefs) 40%, Roman Catholic 20%, Islam 10%
NATIONAL MOTTO *"Siyinquaba"* "We are a Fortress"
NATIONAL ANTHEM (DATE) "Oh God, Bestower of the Blessings of the Swazi" (1968)

189

SWEDEN

FLAG RATIO: 5:8   USE: National/Civil   DATE ADOPTED: 1906   LAST MODIFIED: 1906

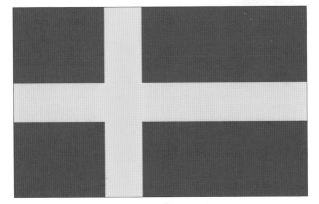

The exact age of the Swedish flag is unknown, but records date back to the reign (1523–60) of **Gustaf I**. Its "**Scandinavian cross**" design probably derives from the Danish flag, while the **blue** and **gold** might come from Sweden's Lesser **coat of arms**. Sweden has two coat of arms: the Greater (*c*.1440) and the Lesser (*c*.1336). The Lesser is **blue** with three **gold crowns**. In the 17th century Sweden flew a **triple-tailed flag**. Today, the royal family use this flag. The king and queen's flag has the greater coat of arms in the center of the cross.

HISTORY

Swedes were probably among the **Vikings** who plundered Europe between the 9th and 11th centuries. In 1319 **Magnus VII** joined Sweden and Norway.

AREA 174,000 sq mi (450,000 sq km)

POPULATION 9,089,000

CAPITAL Stockholm

GOVERNMENT Constitutional monarchy

ETHNIC GROUPS Swedish 91%, Finnish, Sami

LANGUAGES Swedish (official), Finnish, Sami

RELIGIONS Lutheran 87%, Roman Catholic, Orthodox

NATIONAL ANTHEM (DATE) *"Du gamla, du fria"* "Thou ancient, thou freeborn" (1880s)

Sweden united with Denmark and Norway under Danish leadership in the **Kalmar Union** of 1389. In 1520 **Gustaf Vasa** led a rebellion and later was crowned King **Gustaf I** of independent Sweden. Gustaf made **Lutheranism** the state religion. **Gustaf II** swept through central **Germany** in the **Thirty Years' War** (1618–48). **Karl X**'s efforts to capture the **Baltic** led to the **First Northern War** (1655–60). **Karl XII** lost the **Great Northern War** (1700–21) with **Russia**. In 1809 Sweden lost **Finland** to Russia, but acquired Norway from Denmark in 1814. In 1905 the union with Norway dissolved. Sweden was **neutral** in both World Wars. **Tage Fritiof Erlander** was prime minister from 1946 to 1969. **Karl XVI Gustaf** succeeded **Gustaf VI Adolf** as King in 1973. In 1995 Sweden joined the **European Union**, but the people voted against adopting the **Euro**.

Face of King Karl XII's watch. Karl XII ruled Sweden from 1697 to 1718.

SWITZERLAND

FLAG RATIO: 1:1 **USE:** National/Civil **DATE ADOPTED:** 1848 **LAST MODIFIED:** 1889

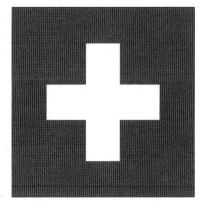

The Swiss flag derives from Christian iconography, symbolizing the blood shed by Christian martyrs. The flag of the Holy Roman Empire was a **white cross** extending to the edges of a **red field**, and represented the Emperor's role as the protector of Christianity. In the 14th century, all the cantons of the Swiss Confederation placed a white cross on their battle flags. In 1815 the Confederation designed a state seal with a short white cross on a red field. In 1817 General Henri-Guillaume Dufour proposed a federal flag consisting of a stocky white cross made of five equal sized squares on a red field. In 1848 the Swiss Federation officially adopted this flag. In 1889 the Federal Assembly amended the flag, making the arms of the cross one-sixth longer than they were wide. The flag of the **International Red Cross**, based in Geneva, is the reverse of the Swiss flag: a red cross on white field.

HISTORY

In the 11th century, Switzerland unified as part of the **Holy Roman Empire**. In 1291 the **cantons** of **Schwyz**, **Uri**, and **Unterwalden** formed a league, which defeated the **Hapsburgs** in 1315. In the mid-14th century, **Lucerne**, **Bern** and **Zürich** joined the **Swiss Confederation**. In 1815 the Confederation reestablished. In 1848, after the **Sonderbund War**, Switzerland became a federal state. In 2002 Switzerland voted to join the UN.

AREA 15,900 sq mi (41,300 sq km)
POPULATION 7,640,000
CAPITAL Bern
GOVERNMENT Federal republic
ETHNIC GROUPS German 65%, French 18%, Italian 10%, Romansch 1%, others
LANGUAGES French, German, Italian, Romansch (all official)
RELIGIONS Roman Catholic 46%, Protestant 40%
MOTTO "*Honor et Fidelitas*" "Honor and Fidelity"
NATIONAL ANTHEM (DATE) "*Schweizer Psalm*" (German) "*Cantique Suisse*" (French) "*Salmo Svizzero*" (Italian) "*Psalm Svizzer*" (Romansch) "The Swiss Anthem" (1961)

HELVETIA 180

Reutigen, Bern, with the Niesen and Eiger, Monch and Jungfrau mountains behind.

SYRIA

FLAG RATIO: 2:3 USE: National/Civil DATE ADOPTED: 1958 REINTRODUCED: 1980

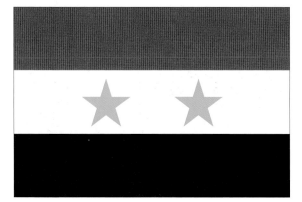

Like many other Arab nations, Syria's flag derives from the banner raised by Hussein ibn Ali during the Arab Revolt (1916) against Ottoman rule. Red, white, black and green are **Pan-Arab** colors. **Black** represented the Abbasid dynasty of Baghdad. **White** stood for the Umayyad dynasty of Damascus. **Green** denoted the Fatimid dynasty of Morocco, and **red** was the color of the Hashemite dynasty. In 1932 Syria adopted a green-white-black tricolor with three red five-pointed stars, representing Damascus, Aleppo, and Dayr az-Zawr. In 1958 Syria and Egypt formed the United Arab Republic (UAR), adopting a **red-white-black horizontal tricolor** with **two green stars**. In 1961 Syria reverted to the 1946 flag. In 1963 the Ba'ath Party seized power, and added a green star to the flag. In 1972 Syria, Egypt, and Libya united to form the Federation of Arab Republics, replacing the stars with the hawk of Quraish. In 1980 Syria reverted to the UAR flag.

HISTORY

In 637 **Arabs** conquered Syria, introducing **Islam**. From 661 to 750 **Damascus** was the capital of the **Umayyad dynasty**. In 1516 Syria became part of the **Ottoman Empire.** In 1920 it was mandated to **France**. In 1941 Syria gained **independence**. **Union** with other Arab nations failed in 1961 and 1972. In 1967 Syria lost the **Golan Heights** to Israel. **Hafez al-Assad** seized power in 1970. In 2000 he died and was succeeded by his son, **Bashar al-Assad**. Crackdowns on protests that began in 2011 were violent and escalated into civil war.

AREA 71,500 sq mi (185,000 sq km)
POPULATION 22,518,000
CAPITAL Damascus
GOVERNMENT Multiparty republic
ETHNIC GROUPS Arab 90%, Kurdish, Armenian, others
LANGUAGES Arabic (official), Kurdish, Armenian
RELIGIONS Sunni Muslim 74%, other Islam 16%
NATIONAL ANTHEM (DATE) *"Homat el Diyar"*
"Guardians of the Homeland" (1936)

Altusi (1201–74) was a great Islamic astronomer and pioneer of trigonometry.

TAIWAN

FLAG RATIO: 1:2 **USE:** National/Civil **DATE ADOPTED:** 1928 **LAST MODIFIED:** 1928

In 1895 Lu Hao-Tung designed the "white sun in a **blue sky**" on the **canton** of Taiwan's national flag as the emblem of the Hsing-chung Hui (Society for Regenerating China), founded by Sun Yat Sen. Just before the overthrow of the Qing dynasty in 1911, the Society added a **crimson field** to its flag. In 1912 the Society was renamed the Kuomintang. In 1928 its flag became that of the Republic of China. The flag's colors represent Sun's "Three Principles of the People": crimson stands for nationalism, blue for democracy, and white for prosperity. The 12 points of the sun represent the two 12-hour periods of the day, symbolizing unceasing progress. In 1949 Chinese communists defeated the Kuomintang, which founded a government-in-exile on the island of Taiwan. The Kuomintang flag became the national flag of Taiwan.

HISTORY

In 1590 the Portuguese landed on the island, which they named **Formosa** ("Beautiful"). The **Dutch** established the first European settlements in 1625. In 1685 the **Qing** dynasty of **China** captured Taiwan. **Japan** governed Taiwan from 1895 to 1945. In 1949 China became a communist republic and **Chiang Kai-shek**, leader of the Kuomintang, fled to Taiwan, where he formed the **Republic of China**. In 1975 Chiang-shek's son, **Chiang Ching-kuo** became president. In 2000 **Chen Shui-ban** led the first non-Kuomintang government for 50 years, before losing elections in 2008.

Spirit Way, *a stone ramp between two staircases, is a feature of Taiwan's architecture.*

AREA 13,900 sq mi (36,000 sq km)
POPULATION 23,072,000
CAPITAL Taipei
GOVERNMENT Unitary multiparty republic
ETHNIC GROUPS Taiwanese 84%, mainland Chinese 14%
LANGUAGES Mandarin Chinese (official), Min, Hakka
RELIGIONS Buddhism, Taoism, Confucianism
NATIONAL ANTHEM (DATE) "*San Min Chu I*" "The Rights of the People" (1930)

193

TAJIKISTAN

FLAG RATIO: 1:2 **USE:** National/Civil **DATE ADOPTED:** 1992 **LAST MODIFIED:** 1992

In 1992 Tajikistan adopted a **tricolor** flag of red, white and green **horizontal stripes** to celebrate its newly won independence. Iran's flag has the same colors, indicating the strong historical links between the two nations. **Red** stands for the land and also recalls Tajikistan's communist past. **White** symbolizes cotton, Tajikistan's main agricultural export. **Green** represents agriculture, the nation's chief economic activity. At the center of the flag is a **gold crown** under an arc of **seven gold stars**. From 1953 to 1992, under Soviet rule, the Tajik flag had four horizontal bands (red, white, green, red) and the hammer and sickle on the hoist.

HISTORY

Tajiks are descendants of **Iranians**, who settled in the area *c*.2500 years ago. In the 4th century BC, **Alexander the Great** conquered the region. Arabs captured Tajikistan in the 7th century AD, introducing **Islam**. The Tajik cities of **Bukhara** and **Samarkand** were vital centers of trade and Muslim learning. In the 9th century, Tajikistan fell to the **Iranian Empire**. **Tamerlane** made Samarkand his capital in the 14th century. From the 16th century to the 19th, Uzbeks ruled the area as the **Khanate of Bukhara**. **Russia** conquered it in 1868. After the Russian Revolution of 1917, Tajikistan was part of the **Soviet Union**. In 1991 Tajikistan gained **independence**. **Civil war** ensued, lasting five years and killing an estimated 100,000 people. **Emomali Rakhmonov** (**Rakhmon**) became President in 1992 elections, and retained power in 1999 and 2006; all three elections were internationally criticized.

AREA 55,300 sq mi (143,000 sq km)
POPULATION 7,627,000
CAPITAL Dushanbe
GOVERNMENT Republic
ETHNIC GROUPS Tajik 65%, Uzbek 25%, Russian
LANGUAGES Tajik (official), Russian
RELIGIONS Islam (Sunni Muslim 85%)
NATIONAL ANTHEM (DATE) *"Surudi Milli"*
"National Anthem" (1991)

***Tajikistan** is famous for its fine geometric carpets, such as this 19th-century example.*

194

FLAG RATIO: 2:3   USE: National/Civil   DATE ADOPTED: 1964   LAST MODIFIED: 1964

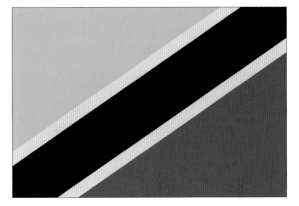

Tanzania's flag combines elements from the flags of the once separate lands of Tanganyika and Zanzibar. The **green triangle** came from the flag of Tanganyika. It symbolizes **agriculture**, the main economic activity. The **blue triangle** came from the flag of Zanzibar and represents the Indian Ocean. The **gold diagonal stripes** stand for the nation's mineral resources, principally diamonds. The central **black diagonal stripe** denotes Tanzania's people.

HISTORY

In 1498 **Vasco da Gama** became the first European to reach Tanzania. For the next 200 years, **Portugal** controlled coastal trade. In the 18th century, the island of **Zanzibar** was the main center of the East African **ivory** and **slave trade**. In 1887 mainland Tanganyika became part of **German East Africa**. Zanzibar became a **British Protectorate** in 1890. In 1919 the League of Nations mandated Tanganyika to Britain. In 1961 Tanganyika won **independence. Julius Nyerere** was the first President. Zanzibar gained independence in 1963. In 1964 Tanganyika and Zanzibar **unified** to form Tanzania. Nyerere issued the **Arusha Declaration** (1964). Tanzania helped Ugandan rebels topple Idi Amin in 1979. In 1985 **Ali Hassan Mwinyi** succeeded Nyerere as President. **Benjamin Mkapa** was president from 1995 to 2005, when he was replaced by Jakawa Kikwete.

AREA 365,000 sq mi (945,000 sq km)

POPULATION 42,747,000

CAPITAL Dodoma

GOVERNMENT Multiparty republic

ETHNIC GROUPS Native African 99% (Bantu 95%)

LANGUAGES Swahili (Kiswahili) and English (both official)

RELIGIONS Islam 35% (99% in Zanzibar), traditional beliefs 35%, Christianity 30%

MOTTO "*Uhuru na Umoja*" "Peace and Unity"

NATIONAL ANTHEM (DATE) "*Mungu ibariki Afrika*" "God Bless Africa" (1961)

Vanilla *is a climbing orchid. It flourishes on the "spice island" of Zanzibar.*

THAILAND

FLAG RATIO: 2:3   **USE:** National/Civil   **DATE ADOPTED:** 1917   **LAST MODIFIED:** 1917

Thailand's flag of **horizontal red, white** and **blue stripes** is called the *trairanga* (**tricolor**). From the mid-17th century, Thailand's flag was a plain red banner. During the reign (1851–68) of Rama IV, a white elephant was placed at the center of the flag. In 1916 white stripes were introduced at the top and bottom of the flag. King Rama VI designed the current flag in 1917. The elephant was replaced by a central **blue band**, a symbol of solidarity with the Allies in World War 1. The colors represent the three pillars of the nation. The outer red stripes represent the land. Blue stands for the monarchy, and white symbolizes the purity of Buddhism, the national religion.

HISTORY

In *c.*1238 **Bang Klang Hao** overthrew **Khmer** rule and established the Thai Kingdom of **Sukhothai**. In 1350 **Ramathibodi** made **Ayutthaya** the capital of **Siam**. In 1767 **Burma** sacked Ayutthaya. In 1782 General Chakri became King **Rama I**, founding the **Chakri dynasty** that has ruled ever since. Rama I founded a new capital at **Bangkok**. Thailand was the only Southeast Asian nation to escape European colonization. In 1931 Siam became a constitutional monarchy. Premier **Phibun Songkhram** changed the country's name to Thailand in 1939. Political instability has not prevented economic progress.

AREA 198,000 sq mi (513,000 sq km)
POPULATION 66,720,000
CAPITAL Bangkok
GOVERNMENT Constitutional monarchy
ETHNIC GROUPS Thai 75%, Chinese 14%, other
LANGUAGES Thai (official), English, ethnic and regional dialects
RELIGIONS Buddhism 95%, Islam, Christianity
NATIONAL ANTHEM (DATE) *"Phleng Chat"* "National Anthem" (1939)

Thotsakan, King of the Demons, guards Wat Arun (Temple of Dawn), Bangkok.

TOGO

FLAG RATIO: 3:5 USE: National/Civil DATE ADOPTED: 1960 LAST MODIFIED: 1960

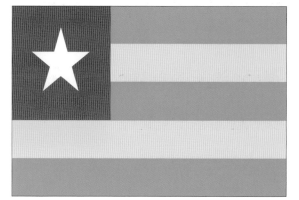

Togo adopted its present flag on independence. It has **five horizontal stripes** (three green and two yellow) and a **white five-pointed star** on a **red canton**. The **five** stripes represent action and the five regions of Togo. The **alternate** colors stand for unity in diversity. **Red** represents blood shed in the struggle for independence. The **star** symbolizes life, liberty, and labor. **Green** represents hope and agriculture, the major economic activity, and **yellow** Togo's mineral wealth.

HISTORY

The historic region of **Togoland** comprised what is now the Republic of Togo and western **Ghana**. From the 17th to the 19th century, the **Ashanti** raided Togoland, seizing the inhabitants, the **Ewe**, and selling them to Europeans as **slaves**. In 1884 Togoland became a **German** protectorate. The Germans built the capital, **Lomé**. In 1914 Britain and France captured Togoland from Germany. In 1922 the League of Nations created the mandated territories of **British Togoland** and **French Togoland**. In 1957 British Togoland became part of Ghana. In 1960 French Togoland gained **independence** as the Republic of Togo. **Sylvanus Olympio** was the first premier. In 1963 Olympio was assassinated and **Nicolas Grunitzky** became premier. In 1967 **Gnassingbe Eyadema** overthrew Grunitzky. After his death in 2005, his son Faure Gnassingbe won disputed elections.

AREA 250 sq mi (650 sq km)
POPULATION 106,000
CAPITAL Nuku'alofa
GOVERNMENT Multiparty republic
ETHNIC GROUPS Ewe-Adja 43%, Tem-Kabre 26%, Gurma 16%
LANGUAGES French (official), Ewe, Kabiye
RELIGIONS Traditional beliefs 50%, Christianity 35%, Islam 15%
MOTTO *"Travail, Liberté, Patrie"* "Work, Liberty, Motherland"
NATIONAL ANTHEM (DATE) *"Terre de nos aïeux"* "Land of our Forefathers" (1992)

Mocker swallowtail butterfly mimics other species of butterfly.

TONGA

FLAG RATIO: 1:2 USE: National/Civil DATE ADOPTED: 1875 LAST MODIFIED: 1875

Tonga's flag with its **red cross** in the **white canton** and a monochrome **red field** is full of Christian symbolism. The original design was white with a red cross but was changed to avoid confusion with the flag of the International Red Cross. The red cross represents Jesus Christ. The red field symbolizes the blood Jesus shed to save the world.

HISTORY

Tonga is a **South Pacific** island with the last remaining **Polynesian** monarchy. The archipelago consists of *c*.170 islands, only 36 of which are inhabited. The three main groups of islands are **Tongatapu**, **Ha'apai**, and **Vava'u**. **Captain James Cook** visited Tonga three times between 1773 and 1777. He named Tonga the "**Friendly Islands**" because of the warm welcome he received from the islanders. In 1849 King **George Tupou I** united the kingdom, ending more than 50 years of **civil war**. In the 19th century, **Wesleyan missionaries** converted the indigenous population to **Christianity**. Tonga was a **British protectorate** from 1900 to 1970. King **Tupou V** oversaw the transition from feudal rule to a parliamentary democracy in 2010. He was succeeded by his brother, **George Tupou VI**, in 2012.

AREA 250 sq mi (650 sq km)

POPULATION 106,000

CAPITAL Nuku'alofa

GOVERNMENT Constitutional monarchy

ETHNIC GROUPS Tongan 98%, other Polynesian and European 2%

LANGUAGES English, Tongan (both official)

RELIGIONS Wesleyan 41%, Church of Tonga 10%, Roman Catholic 16%, Mormon 14%, Baha'i 3%, Assemblies of God 2%

MOTTO "*Koe 'Otua mo Tonga ko hoku Tofi'a*" "God and Tonga are my Inheritance"

NATIONAL ANTHEM (DATE) "*Koe Fasi Oe Tu'i Oe Otu Tonga*" "National Anthem of Tonga" (1874)

Tau'olunga *is a traditional ceremonial dance performed by Tongan women.*

TRINIDAD AND TOBAGO

FLAG RATIO: 3:5   USE: National/Civil   DATE ADOPTED: 1962   LAST MODIFIED: 1962

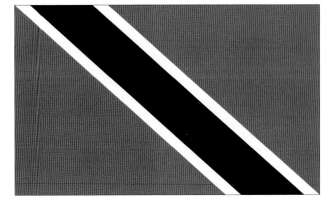

An Independence Committee designed Trinidad and Tobago's flag in 1962. The colors represent the elements of earth, water, and fire. The broad **black diagonal stripe** stands for the republic's abundant resources of oil and gas and the unity and determination of the people. The **two white diagonal stripes** symbolizes the Caribbean Sea and purity and equality. The **red field** represents the warmth of the Caribbean sun and recalls the courage and vitality of the people.

HISTORY

Christopher **Columbus** landed on Trinidad in 1498. **Spain** built the first settlement in 1532. They enslaved the indigenous **Caribs** and **Arawaks**. In 1797 **Britain** captured Trinidad. English Captain **Robert Dudley** visited the island of **Tobago** in 1596, but no colonies appeared until 1632. In 1802 Tobago became a **British** possession. Britain and Spain brought **slaves** from Africa to work on the **sugar-cane** plantations. In 1845 **Indians** arrived as **indentured labor**. In 1889 Trinidad and Tobago **united**. The islands gained **independence** in 1972, and became a republic in 1976. **Kamla Persad-Bissessar** became the islands' first woman prime minister in 2010.

AREA 2,000 sq mi (5,100 sq km)
POPULATION 1,228,000
CAPITAL Port of Spain
GOVERNMENT Multiparty republic
ETHNIC GROUPS Indian (South Asian) 40%, African 38%, mixed 21%, others
LANGUAGES English (official), Hindi, French, Spanish, Chinese
RELIGIONS Roman Catholic 26%, Hindu 23%, Anglican 8%, Baptist 7%, Pentecostal 7%, others
MOTTO "Together We Aspire, Together We Achieve"
NATIONAL ANTHEM (DATE) "Forged From The Love of Liberty" (1962)

Trinidadian artist Sybil Atteck (1911–75) painted this expressionist Fishermen.

TUNISIA

FLAG RATIO: 2:3 **USE:** National/Civil **DATE ADOPTED:** 1959 **LAST MODIFIED:** 1959

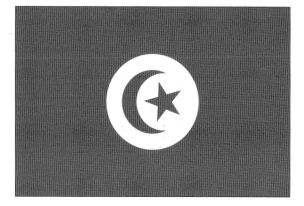

Tunisia's flag is similar to Turkey's and originated in *c*.1831, when the country was under the rule of Hassine, eighth *bey* (governor) of the Turkish Husseinite Dynasty. The **red five-pointed star** and **Osmanli (Turkish) crescent** are traditional **Islamic** symbols. The **white disk** is a stylized depiction of the sun. It symbolizes unity. The **red field** represents the blood shed in the struggle for independence. The constitution confirmed the design of the national flag in 1959.

HISTORY

In 814 BC, **Phoenician Queen Dido** founded **Carthage**. Despite **Hannibal**'s dramatic advance over the Alps, **Rome** defeated Carthage in the **Punic Wars** (249–146 BC). In 46 BC, Carthage became part of the Roman province of **Tripolitania**. In AD 640, the **Arabs** invaded. The **Berbers** converted to **Islam** and adopted **Arabic** as the main language. In 670 **Oqba Ibn Nafaa** founded **Kairouan**, a center of Islamic study. The **Hafsids** ruled from 1230 to 1574, when Spain's capture of **Tunis** led to the intervention of the **Ottoman Empire**. **Turkish** *beys* governed from 1612 to 1957. The **Husseinite dynasty** reigned from 1705 to 1881. Pirate attacks led to the **Tripolitan War** (1801–05) with the United States. In 1881 **France** invaded and Tunisia became a **protectorate** (1883). It was a major battleground in **World War II**. In 1956 Tunisia gained **independence**. In 1957, it became a **republic**. **Zine el Abidine Ben Ali** was president from 1987 to 2011 when he stepped down in response to protests, sparking off the "Arab Spring."

AREA 63,200 sq mi (164,000 sq km)

POPULATION 10,629,000

CAPITAL Tunis

GOVERNMENT Multiparty republic

ETHNIC GROUPS Arab 98%, European 1%

LANGUAGES Arabic (official), French

RELIGIONS Islam 98%, Christianity 1%, others

MOTTO "*Liberté, Ordre, Justice*" "Freedom, Order, Justice"

NATIONAL ANTHEM (DATE) "*Himat Al Hima*" "Defenders of the Homeland" (1987)

Tunisian *artisanal design marking the National Day of Sahara Tourism.*

TURKEY

FLAG RATIO: 2:3 USE: National/Civil DATE ADOPTED: 1936 LAST MODIFIED: 1936

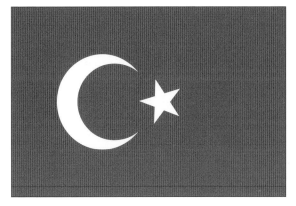

Turkey's flag is nicknamed *Ay Yildiz* (Moon Star). The **crescent moon** and **five-pointed star** are traditional **Islamic** symbols, but their association with Turkey may predate Islam. The moon was the symbol of Diana, the patron goddess of Byzantium (now Istanbul). In 330 Emperor Constantine renamed the city Constantinople after himself, dedicating it to the Virgin Mary whose symbol is the star. In legend, Sultan Murad II adopted the symbols after seeing a reflection of the moon occulting a star in pools of blood at the Battle of Kosovo (1448). The colour **red** has been associated with the Ottomans since the birth of the Empire in the late 13th century. In 1793 Sultan Selim III adopted a red naval flag with a crescent and star. The five-pointed version of the star dates from *c*.1844.

HISTORY

In 330 Emperor Constantine made **Constantinople** (now Istanbul) capital of the **Roman Empire**. In 398 it became capital of the **Byzantine Empire**. The **Seljuks** introduced **Islam** in the 11th century. In 1435 **Muhammad II** captured Constantinople, which became capital of the **Ottoman Empire**. The rule of **Sultan Mehmed VI** was overthrown by Mustafa Kemal (**Atatürk**). In 1923 Turkey became a **republic**. Atatürk created a **secular** state. **Ismet Inönü** was president from 1938 to 1950. In 1974 Turkey invaded **Northern Cyprus**. Conflict with the **Kurdistan Workers' Party** (PKK) in southeast Turkey began in 1984. Election wins for the Islamist Justice and Development Party in 2002 led to tensions with secularists.

Floral *motif on a Paçalik dress, worn by a bride on the day after her wedding.*

AREA 299,000 sq mi (775,000 sq km)
POPULATION 78,786,000
CAPITAL Ankara
GOVERNMENT Multiparty republic
ETHNIC GROUPS Turkish 80%, Kurdish 20%
LANGUAGES Turkish (official), Kurdish, Arabic
RELIGIONS Islam (mainly Sunni Muslim) 99%
NATIONAL ANTHEM (DATE) *"Istiklâl Marsi"*
"March of Independence" (1921)

201

TURKMENISTAN

FLAG RATIO: 1:2 **USE:** National/Civil **DATE ADOPTED:** 1992 **LAST MODIFIED:** 1997

Turkmenistan adopted its present flag upon gaining independence in 1992. The **white crescent moon** and **stars** are **Islamic** symbols. **Green** is the conventional color of Islam. On the hoist of the flag is a **red vertical stripe** with **carpet designs** (*guls*) from each of the five provinces: Dashoguz, Ahal, Lebap, Balkan, and Mary. The crescent moon stands for hope and a clear future. The **five stars** represent the provinces. In 1997 President Niyazov added **two olive branches** to the bottom of the stripe to mark Turkmenistan's policy of permanent neutrality and to symbolize peace.

HISTORY

The **Kara Kum** desert covers almost 90% of Turkmenistan. In the 500s BC, it became part of the **Persian Empire**. **Arabs** invaded in the 8th century, introducing **Islam**. **Turkmens** migrated to the area in the 10th century. In the 11th century **Merv** became capital of the **Seljuk Turk** lands. Part of the **Mongol** Empire of **Genghis Khan** in the 13th century, **Tamerlane** conquered it in the 14th century and founded the **Timurid dynasty**. The **Uzbeks** gained control in the 16th century. In 1881 **Russia** finally overcame fierce resistance. Turkmenistan became part of **Russian Turkistan** in 1899. In 1925 it became a republic of the **Soviet Union**. In 1991 it gained **independence**. **Saparmurad Niyazov** was President from 1990 to 2006 and was succeeded by **Kurbanguly Berdymuhamedov**.

AREA 188,000 sq mi (488,000 sq km)
POPULATION 4,998,000
CAPITAL Ashkhabad
GOVERNMENT Single-party republic
ETHNIC GROUPS Turkmen 85%, Uzbek 5%, Russian 4%, others
LANGUAGES Turkmen (official), Russian, Uzbek
RELIGIONS Islam 89%, Eastern Orthodox 9%
NATIONAL ANTHEM (DATE) *"Garashciiz Bitarap Turkmenistaniin Devlet Gimni"* "Independent, Neutral, Turkmenistan State Anthem" (1997)

The ram's horn (kotchak) *is a common and ancient motif of Turkmen nomads.*

TUVALU

FLAG RATIO: 1:2 USE: National/Civil DATE ADOPTED: 1978 LAST MODIFIED: 1997

Tuvalu adopted a national flag upon gaining independence from Britain in 1978. The **Union Jack** recalls British colonial rule and the islands' membership of the Commonwealth. The **nine five-pointed yellow stars** roughly correspond to the position of the nine islands of the archipelago. The **light blue** field represents the surrounding Pacific Ocean. In 1995 Tuvalu introduced a new flag of red, white, and blue stripes with a chevron. It removed the Union Jack and had only eight stars. (In Tuvaluan, "Tuvalu" means "group of eight" – originally only eight coral atolls were inhabited.) In 1997, after nationwide protests, Tuvalu reverted to the original design.

HISTORY

Spanish navigator **Alvaro de Mendaña** sighted the island of **Nui** in 1568, and the island of **Niulakita** on a return voyage in 1595. In 1819 British Captain **Arent De Peyster** discovered **Nukufetau** and **Funafuti**, which he named **Ellice Island** after the owner of his ship. Between 1850 and 1880, the population fell from *c.*20,000 to 3000 mainly because Europeans abducted workers for other Pacific plantations. In 1892 **Britain** assumed control, and Tuvalu was subsequently administered with the nearby Gilbert Islands (now **Kiribati**). In 1978 Tuvalu gained **independence**. It faces demands to become a republic.

AREA 10 sq mi (30 sq km)
POPULATION 11,000
CAPITAL Fongafale
GOVERNMENT Constitutional monarchy
ETHNIC GROUPS Polynesian 97%
LANGUAGES Tuvaluan, English
RELIGIONS Church of Tuvalu (Congregationalist) 97%, Seventh-Day Adventist 1%, Baha'i 1%
NATIONAL MOTTO "*Maaka te atua, karinea te vea; matakusi te atua, fakamamalu ki te tupu*" "Honor all men, love the brotherhood, fear God, honor the king"
NATIONAL ANTHEM (DATE) "*Tuvalu mo te Atua*" "Tuvalu for the Almighty" (1912)

Fatele is the national dance of Tuvalu. Women dance to a pokih *drum rhythm.*

UGANDA

FLAG RATIO: 2:3 USE: National/Civil DATE ADOPTED: 1962 LAST MODIFIED: 1962

U ganda's flag consists of **six horizontal stripes** of black, yellow and red, the original colors of the Ugandan People's Congress. **Black** represents the African people. **Yellow** stands for the abundant sunshine, and **red** represents brotherhood. At the center of the flag is a **white disk** with a **crested crane**. The crested crane, Uganda's national bird, faces the hoist and stands on one leg, symbolizing Uganda's progress. Its plumage includes the national colors.

HISTORY

In *c*.1500, the **Lwo** formed the Kingdoms of **Buganda** and **Bunyoro** in southwest Uganda. In 1862 British explorer **John** **Speke** became the first European to reach Buganda. **Sir Henry Stanley** soon followed. In 1894 Uganda became a **British Protectorate**. Britain encouraged **Asian** settlers. Uganda gained **independence** in 1962. **Milton Obote** of the Ugandan People's Congress (UPC) was the first prime minister. In 1971 **Idi Amin** led a military coup. Amin's **dictatorship** murdered more than 250,000 Ugandans. In 1979 Tanzania helped overthrow Amin, and Obote returned to power. Another military **coup** toppled Obote in 1985. The Lords Resistance Army began a rebellion in the north in 1987. Multiparty democracy was reintroduced in 2005.

AREA 93,100 sq mi (241,000 sq km)
POPULATION 34,612,000
CAPITAL Kampala
GOVERNMENT Republic
ETHNIC GROUPS Baganda 17%, Ankole 8%, Basogo 8%, Iteso 8%, Bakiga 7%, Langi 6%, Rwanda 6%, Bagisu 5%, Acholi 4%, Lugbara 4% and others
LANGUAGES English, Swahili (both official), Ganda
RELIGIONS Roman Catholic 33%, Protestant 33%, traditional beliefs 18%, Islam 16%
MOTTO "For God and My Country"
NATIONAL ANTHEM (DATE) "Pearl of Africa" (1962)

The Karamojong *live in the Karamoja region, northeast Uganda.*

FLAG RATIO: 2:3   USE: National/Civil   DATE ADOPTED: 1918   REINTRODUCED: 1991

Ukraine's flag consists of **two broad horizontal stripes** of **azure** and **yellow**. Apparently, azure and yellow were the colors of Kievan Rus, the first **Slavic** state founded in AD 882. The **azure** symbolizes the sky, mountains, and streams of Ukraine. **Yellow** represents its golden fields. In 1848 the Ruthenian Council adopted a flag with a golden lion rampant on a blue field. In 1918, Ukraine declared independence and adopted the present flag. From 1949 to 1990, Ukraine's flag featured bands of red and blue with the Soviet hammer and sickle symbol. In 1991 Ukraine reintroduced the 1918 flag.

HISTORY

Ukraine was the heart of the medieval state of **Kievan Rus**. In 1569 Ukraine became part of **Poland-Lithuania**. In 1648 the **Cossacks** overthrew Polish rule, but submitted to **Russia** in 1654. In the first two partitions of Poland (1772, 1793), Russia gained eastern Ukraine and Austria acquired the west. Ukraine was briefly **independent** after World War I, but in 1922 the east became part of the **Soviet Union**. In 1923 **Galicia**, western Ukraine, fell to Poland. In 1939 the Soviet Union held all of it. In 1991 Ukraine became **independent**. **Leonid Kravchuk** was the first president. The "**Orange Revolution**" of 2005 resulted in a west-fragile leaning coalition. Former prime minister **Victor Yanukovych** of the Party of the Regions became president in 2010. Several prominent opposition members were imprisoned for fraud.

Trio of musicians *in national dress from Chernihivshchyna region, northern Ukraine.*

AREA 233,000 sq mi (604,000 sq km)
POPULATION 45,135,000
CAPITAL Kiev
GOVERNMENT Multiparty republic
ETHNIC GROUPS Ukranian 78%, Russian 17%, Belarusian, Moldovan, Bulgarian, Hungarian, Polish
LANGUAGES Ukranian (official), Russian
RELIGIONS Mainly Ukranian Orthodox
NATIONAL ANTHEM (DATE) *"Shche ne vmerla Ukraina"* "Ukraine Has Not Yet Perished" (1917)

UNITED ARAB EMIRATES

FLAG RATIO: 1:2 **USE:** National **DATE ADOPTED:** 1971 **LAST MODIFIED:** 1971

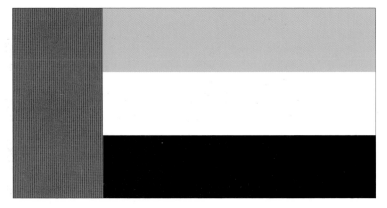

The flag of the United Arab Emirates (UAE) has three **green, white** and **black horizontal stripes** and a **red vertical stripe** at the hoist. Six of the seven members of the federation have their own **state flag** – all of which are red and white; Fujairah uses the UAE flag as its state flag. Until the 19th century, the Gulf Emirates had **monochrome red** flags. In 1820 the Emirates signed the General Maritime Treaty with the United Kingdom, placing a white stripe on their flags to differentiate them from pirate ships. The UAE's flag has the **Pan-Arab** colors. Green represents the fertility of its land, black stands for its abundance of oil, and white represents neutrality.

HISTORY

In the Middle Ages, much of the UAE was part of the Kingdom of **Hormuz**. Portugal dominated the region from 1498 to 1633. The **Qawasim** tribe fought against **British** colonialism until 1820, when a truce gave Britain control of the defense and foreign policy of nine sheikhdoms (the **Trucial States**). The **Bani Yas Bedouins** dominated the interior. In 1971 British troops left the Gulf and the six sheikhdoms of **Abu Dhabi, Dubai, Ajman, Fujairah, Sharjah,** and **Umm al-Qaiwain** federated to form the UAE. **Sheikh Zayed bin Sultan Al Nahyan** became President. **Ras al-Khaimah** joined the UAE in 1972.

AREA 32,300 sq mi (83,600 sq km)
POPULATION 5,149,000
CAPITAL Abu Dhabi
GOVERNMENT Federation of Sheikdoms
ETHNIC GROUPS South Asian 50%, other Arab and Iranian 23%, Emirati 19%
LANGUAGES Arabic (official), Persian, English, Hindi, Urdu
RELIGIONS Muslim 96% (Shi'a 16%), others
NATIONAL ANTHEM (DATE) *"Ishy Bilady"* "Long Live my Nation" (1971)

In 1996 Sheikh Zayed celebrated 30 years as ruler of Abu Dhabi.

UNITED KINGDOM

FLAG RATIO: 1:2 USE: National/Civil DATE ADOPTED: 1606 LAST MODIFIED: 1801

Officially called the "Union Flag", but commonly known as the "Union Jack", the flag of the United Kingdom consists of the **three crosses** of the patron saints. **Saint Andrew**, patron saint of Scotland, has a **white diagonal cross** set on a **blue background**. **Saint George**, patron saint of England, has a **red cross** on a **white field**. **Saint Patrick**, patron saint of Ireland, has a **red diagonal cross** on a **white background**. Soon after James VI of Scotland became King of England in 1601, the flag of Great Britain joined the crosses of Saint George and Saint Andrew. In 1801 Ireland became part of the United Kingdom and the red diagonal cross was added to the flag.

HISTORY

Britain emerged from the **Seven Years' War** (1756–63) as the world's leading imperial power, but soon lost the **United States** in the **American Revolution** (1775–83). Britain was the birthplace of the **Industrial Revolution**. The reign of **Victoria** saw the resurgence of the **British Empire**. **World War I** (1914–18) cost more than 750,000 British lives. In 1922 southern Ireland gained independence; the UK became known as the United Kingdom of Great Britain and **Northern Ireland**. **Winston Churchill** led Britain through **World War II** (1939–45), which claimed more than 420,000 British lives. In 1947 **India** became independent and the British Empire gradually dismantled. Scotland and Wales gained their own parliaments.

***The Great Exhibition**, London, displayed the world's first double-decker bus in 1851.*

AREA 93,400 sq mi (242,000 sq km)
POPULATION 62,698,000
CAPITAL London
GOVERNMENT Constitutional monarchy
ETHNIC GROUPS English 82%, Scottish 10%, Irish 2%, Welsh 2%, Ulster 2%, West Indian, Indian, Pakistani, others
LANGUAGES English (official), Welsh, Gaelic
RELIGIONS Christianity, Islam, Sikhism, Hinduism, Judaism
NATIONAL ANTHEM (DATE) "God Save the Queen" (1745)

UNITED STATES OF AMERICA

FLAG RATIO: 10:19 **USE:** National/Civil **DATE ADOPTED:** 1771 **LAST MODIFIED:** 1960

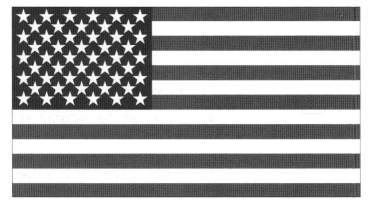

In legend, **Betsy Ross** designed the "**Stars and Stripes**" flag of the United States in 1776. In fact, it was probably designed by **Francis Hopkinson**. In 1777 the Continental Congress passed a Flag Act, which stated that the flag have "13 stripes, alternate red and white; that the union be 13 stars, white in a blue field." The stars and stripes represented the original 13 Colonies. In 1795, after Vermont and Kentucky joined the Union, the flag acquired two more stripes and stars. In 1818 a new act provided for **13 stripes** and one star for each state, to be added to the flag on the Fourth of July following the admission of each new state. There

have been 27 amendments. The last was in 1960, when Hawaii joined the union, making a total of **50 stars**.

HISTORY

In 1492 **Christopher Columbus** discovered the Americas. **Spain** built the first European settlement at **St. Augustine**, Florida, in 1565. In 1607 the **British** founded **Jamestown**, Virginia. **Puritans** founded **Plymouth Colony** in 1620. The **American Revolution** (1775–83) ended British rule. **George Washington** was the first president. **Abraham Lincoln** guided the Union to victory in the **Civil War** (1861–65). **Franklin D. Roosevelt** led the US into World War II. The country ended the 20th century as the world's dominant economic and military power.

AREA 3,718,000 sq mi (9,629,000 sq km)
POPULATION 313,232,000
CAPITAL Washington, DC
GOVERNMENT Federal republic
ETHNIC GROUPS White 77%, African American 13%, Asian 4%, Amerindian 2%, others
LANGUAGES English (official), Spanish, more than 30 others
RELIGIONS Protestant 56%, Roman Catholic 28%, Islam 2%, Judaism 2%
NATIONAL MOTTO "In God We Trust"
NATIONAL ANTHEM (DATE) "The Star-Spangled Banner" (1931)

Firemen raise the flag at "Ground Zero," after the attacks on September 11, 2001.

URUGUAY

FLAG RATIO: 2:3   USE: National/Civil   DATE ADOPTED: 1828   LAST MODIFIED: 1830

Uruguay's flag has **nine horizontal stripes** alternately **white** (top and bottom) and **blue**. On a white square on the upper hoist is a **yellow sun** bearing a **human face** with **16 rays** alternately straight and wavy. Like many other nations in South America, Uruguay adopted blue and white colors in homage to **Argentina**, the first South American nation to gain independence. The pattern recalls the design of the United States flag. The nine stripes represent the original nine provinces of Uruguay. The sun symbol also appears on Argentina's flag. It is called the "**Sun of May**" in honor of the sun shining through the clouds above Buenos Aires on May 25, 1810, when Argentine rebels overthrew the Spanish Viceroy. It is an ancient **Inca** symbol.

HISTORY

In 1516 Spanish explorer **Juan Díaz de Solís** reached Uruguay. The native **Charrúa** resisted Spanish settlement until 1624. In 1777 Uruguay became part of the Spanish Viceroyalty of **Río de la Plata**. **José Gervais Artigas** led the **revolt** that overthrew the Spanish in 1814. In 1821 **Brazil** annexed the country. Uruguay achieved **independence** in 1828. The **Blancos** and the **Colorados** fought a **civil war** from 1836 to 1872. Uruguay joined Brazil and Argentina in the **War of the Triple Alliance** (1865–70) against Paraguay. From 1973 Uruguay was governed by a brutal military **dictatorship**, but returned to democracy in 1985.

AREA 67,600 sq mi (175,000 sq km)
POPULATION 3,309,000
CAPITAL Montevideo
GOVERNMENT Multiparty republic
ETHNIC GROUPS White 88%, Mestizo 8%, Mulatto or Black 4%
LANGUAGES Spanish (official)
RELIGIONS Roman Catholic 66%, Protestant 2%, Judaism 1%
NATIONAL ANTHEM (DATE) *"Orientales, la Patria o la tumba!"* "Uruguayans, the Fatherland or Death!" (1845)

The Spanish founded the neighborhood of Cordon, Montevideo, south Uruguay, in 1750.

UZBEKISTAN

FLAG RATIO: 1:2 **USE:** National/Civil **DATE ADOPTED:** 1991 **LAST MODIFIED:** 1991

Uzbekistan's national flag consists of **three horizontal bands** of **blue**, **white**, and **green**, and **two** thin **horizontal red stripes** either side of the middle white band. The **white crescent-moon** in the upper hoist is a traditional symbol of Islam and represents the rebirth of the nation. The **12 white stars** next to the moon recall the 12 signs of the zodiac. Blue stands for water and the eternal sky. Red represents life. White symbolizes peace, and green denotes nature.

HISTORY

Uzbekistan lies on the ancient **Silk Road**. In the 7th and 8th centuries the Arab Caliphate conquered Central Asia and introduced **Islam**. In the 10th century, **Ismail Samani** made **Bukhara** capital of the **Samanid dynasty**. In 1220 **Mongol** Emperor **Genghis Khan** laid waste to the region. In the 14th century **Tamelane** ruled a great empire from **Samarkand**. **Turkic Uzbek** people conquered the **Timurid** lands in the 16th century. In the 19th century the khanates of Bukhara, **Khiva** and **Kokand** joined the **Russian Empire**. Uzbekistan became a leading producer of **cotton** and a large **railroad** network developed. Communists came to power after the Russian Revolution (1917) and Uzbekistan became a republic of the **Soviet Union** in 1924. In 1966 an earthquake hit the capital, **Tashkent**. In 1991 Uzbekistan gained **independence** with **Islam Karimov** as President. Politics has been characterized by instability and severe repression by the state.

AREA 173,000 sq mi (447,000 sq km)
POPULATION 28,129,000
CAPITAL Tashkent
GOVERNMENT Socialist republic
ETHNIC GROUPS Uzbek 80%, Russian 5%, Tajik 5%, Kazakh 3%, Tatar 2%, Kara-Kalpak 2%
LANGUAGES Uzbek (official), Russian
RELIGIONS Islam 88%, Eastern Orthodox 9%
NATIONAL ANTHEM (DATE) Untitled (1992)

Uzbekistan's state emblem has the "Humo bird" of happiness at its center.

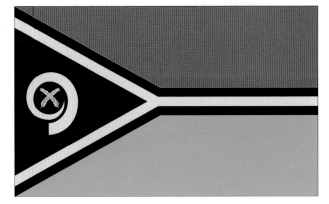

The **yellow "Y"** design at the center of the national flag is a stylized representation of the geographical distribution of the islands of Vanuatu. The **pig's tusk** and **crossed namele fern leaves** in the **black triangle** are traditional Vanuatan symbols. They symbolize prosperity and peace respectively. The **red band** symbolizes unity through blood. The **green band** represents Vanuatu's fertile agricultural land. Black stands for the Melanesian people, and yellow denotes sunshine and the Christian faith of Vanuatu's people. Prime Minister Walter Lini added black and yellow **fimbriations** to Malon Kalontas' design to emphasize the black triangle.

HISTORY

The earliest-known settlement was on **Malo Island**, where **Melanesian** pottery at least 4000 years old was unearthed. Portuguese explorer **Pedro Fernandez de Queiros** landed on **Espiritu Santo** in 1606. **Louis de Bougainville** rediscovered the islands in 1768, and **James Cook** mapped them in 1774, naming them **New Hebrides. England** and **France** settled the islands in the early 1800s. Europeans brought disease, violence and slave running, which devastated the native population. Governed jointly by France and Britain from 1906, Vanuatu became an **independent republic** in 1980. The early 21st century saw unprecedented economic growth.

Vanuatu's Pacific waters are rich in fish such as marlin, tuna, mahi mahi, and wahoo.

AREA 4,700 sq mi (12,200 sq km)
POPULATION 225,000
CAPITAL Port-Vila
GOVERNMENT Multiparty republic
ETHNIC GROUPS Melanesian 92%
LANGUAGES English, French (both official), pidgin (Bislama or Bichelama)
RELIGIONS Presbyterian 37%, Roman Catholic 15%, Anglican 15%, Seventh-Day Adventist 6%
NATIONAL ANTHEM (DATE) *"Yumi, Yumi, Yumi"* "We, We, We" (1980)

211

VATICAN CITY

FLAG RATIO: 1:1 USE: Civil DATE ADOPTED: 1929 LAST MODIFIED: 1929

Vatican City and Switzerland are the only nations with **square** flags. The Vatican's flag is **bicolor** with **vertical yellow** and **white stripes**. On the white stripe is the 14th-century **coat of arms**. The arms include the **crossed papal keys**. The **golden key** alludes to the power of the kingdom of heaven; the **silver key** represents the spiritual authority of the papacy on Earth. The mechanisms are turned toward the heavens and the grips toward the Earth. The cord that binds the keys symbolizes the bond between the two powers. The keys are crowned by the **papal tiara**, which is formed by three crowns representing the triple power of the pope as father of kings, governor of the world, and vicar of Christ.

AREA 0.44 sq km (0.17 sq mi)
POPULATION 1,000
CAPITAL (POPULATION) Vatican City
GOVERNMENT Ecclesiastical pontificate
ETHNIC GROUPS Italians, Swiss, other
LANGUAGES Latin (official), Italian, French
RELIGIONS Roman Catholic 100%
NATIONAL ANTHEM (DATE) "*Inno e Marcia Pontificale*" "Pontifical Hymn and March" (1950)

HISTORY

Vatican City is the smallest independent sovereign state, existing as a walled enclave within the city of **Rome**. It is the home of the papacy and an independent base for the **Holy See**, the governing body of the **Roman Catholic Church**. According to tradition, **Saint Peter** was the first Bishop of Rome and the first church was built on the site of his tomb in 326. Popes ruled much of the Italian peninsula until the 19th century, when the new **Kingdom of Italy** seized many of the **Papal States**. In 1870 Italy annexed the city of Rome. Italy confirmed the Vatican's independence in the **Lateran Treaty** (1929).

The crossed keys are the symbol of Saint Peter, keeper of the keys to heaven.

VENEZUELA

FLAG RATIO: 2:3 USE: National DATE ADOPTED: 1930 LAST MODIFIED: 1954

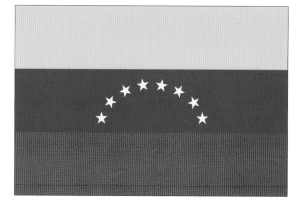

In 1806 revolutionary Francisco de Miranda hoisted a flag of **yellow, blue,** and **red horizontal stripes**. Ecuador and Colombia have the same tricolor, but Venezuela's stripes are of **equal width**. The **eight white stars** were added in 1817 to represent the eight provinces that had declared themselves independent from Spanish rule: Caracas, Cumana, Barinas, Barcelona, Margarita, Merida, and Tujillo. In 1930 the stars were arranged in an **arc**. In 1954 the **state flag** added the **coat of arms** to the upper hoist. Yellow represents the wealth of the land. Blue stands for the sea separating Venezuela from Spain, and red symbolizes the blood shed in the struggle for independence.

HISTORY

The indigenous inhabitants of Venezuela were the **Arawak** and **Carib**. In 1498 **Christopher Columbus** became the first European to sight the region now known as Venezuela. Venezuela became part of the Spanish administrative area of **New Granada**. In the late 18th century, **Francisco de Miranda** led uprisings against Spanish rule. In 1821 **Simón Bolívar** liberated Venezuela and it became part of **Greater Colombia**. In 1830 it gained **independence**. Dictator **Antonio Guzmán Blanco** ruled from 1870 to 1888. **Juan Vicente Gómez** was President from 1908 to 1935. **Oil** was discovered in 1918. From 1945 to 1948 **Rómulo Betancourt** led a junta, and served as civilian president from 1959 to 1964. In 1999 it took the title **"Bolivarian Republic"** under **Hugo Chavez**.

Mujeres macoa moliendo maiz Bs.**100**

Venezuela

ARMITANO 1996

Women *from Macoa, northeast Venezuela, grinding maize.*

AREA 352,000 sq mi (912,000 sq km)
POPULATION 27,636,000
CAPITAL Caracas
GOVERNMENT Federal republic
ETHNIC GROUPS Spanish, Italian, Portuguese, Arab, German, African, indigenous people
LANGUAGES Spanish (official), indigenous dialects
RELIGIONS Roman Catholic 96%
NATIONAL ANTHEM (DATE) *"Gloria al Bravo Pueblo"* "Glory to the Brave People" (1881)

213

VIETNAM

FLAG RATIO: 2:3   USE: National   DATE ADOPTED: 1955   LAST MODIFIED: 1955

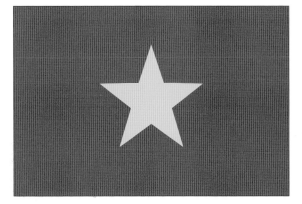

Resistance groups first adopted Vietnam's flag in the liberation struggle against Japan in World War II. The **star** can be seen either as the star of communism, with the **five points** representing the groups who helped build socialism in Vietnam (farmers, workers, intellectuals, youths, and soldiers) or as a representation of the North Star. **Red** is the color of communism, luck, and happiness.

HISTORY

In 111 BC China seized Vietnam, naming it **Annam**. In AD 939 it gained independence. In 1558 the north broke away as **Tonkin**. In 1802 **Nguyen** Emperor **Gia Long** reunited it as the Empire of Vietnam. In 1887 Vietnam became part of **French Indochina**. Japan conquered it during **World War II**. In 1954 France withdrew, and Vietnam split into **North Vietnam** with a communist regime (led by **Ho Chi Minh**) and **South Vietnam** (under **Bao Dai**). In 1955 Bao Dai was deposed and **Ngo Dinh Diem** was elected. The **United States** became embroiled in the **Vietnam War** (1954–75), which claimed about 1.5 million Vietnamese and around 50,000 US lives. In 1976 the reunited Vietnam became a socialist republic under **Pham Van Dong**. From the late 1980s, the government pursued economic liberalization. A securities trading center opened in Ho Chi Minh City in 2000.

AREA 128,000 sq mi (332,000 sq km)
POPULATION 90,549,000
CAPITAL Hanoi
GOVERNMENT Socialist republic
ETHNIC GROUPS Vietnamese 87%, Chinese, Hmong, Thai, Khmer, Cham, mountain groups
LANGUAGES Vietnamese (official), English, French, Chinese, Khmer, mountain languages
RELIGIONS Buddhism, Christianity, indigenous beliefs
NATIONAL ANTHEM (DATE) *"Tien quan ca"* "March to the Front" (1976)

Vietnamese women sometimes wear beautiful, traditional long velvet dresses.

YEMEN

FLAG RATIO: 2:3 USE: National/Civil DATE ADOPTED: 1990 LAST MODIFIED: 1990

Yemen adopted its present **tricolor** flag of **red, white,** and **black** horizontal **stripes** in 1990, when North and South Yemen united. The colors derive from the **Pan-Arab** revolt by Hussein ibn Ali in 1916. The flag of North Yemen had a green star on the middle stripe, while South Yemen's had a red star on a blue triangle on the hoist. **Black** represents Yemen's colonial past. **White** symbolizes its bright future, and **red** stands for blood shed in the struggle for liberation.

HISTORY

From 759 to 100 BC, the kingdom of **Sheba** flourished in southern Yemen. **Islam** arrived in AD 628, and the **Rassite dynasty** of the **Zaidi sect** established a theocratic state that lasted until 1962. In 1517 Yemen became part of the **Ottoman Empire**. It remained under Turkish control until 1918. In 1839 the British captured **Aden**. In 1937 Britain formed the **Aden Protectorate**. From 1958 to 1961 Yemen was part of the **United Arab Republic** (with Egypt and Syria). In 1962 a military coup overthrew the monarchy and created the **Yemen Arab Republic**. **Civil war ensued**. In 1967 the National Liberation Front forced the British to withdraw from Aden and founded the **People's Republic of South Yemen**. In 1970 Marxists won the war in South Yemen and renamed it the **People's Democratic Republic of Yemen**. In 1990 the two Yemens merged. **Ali Abdullah Saleh** became president and remained in power until the "Arab Spring" protests of 2011.

Bronze statue *of Maadi Karib (800 BC) from the Awwam Temple in Marib, central Yemen.*

AREA 204,000 sq mi (528,000 sq km)
POPULATION 24,133,000
CAPITAL Sana'
GOVERNMENT Multiparty republic
ETHNIC GROUPS Predominantly Arab
LANGUAGES Arabic (official)
RELIGIONS Islam
NATIONAL ANTHEM (DATE) "United Republic" (1990)

215

ZAMBIA

FLAG RATIO: 2:3 USE: National/Civil DATE ADOPTED: 1964 LAST MODIFIED: 1996

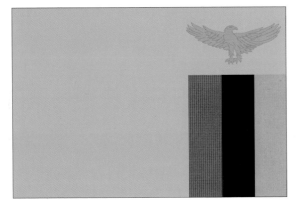

Zambia's flag consists of a **green field** with a **flying eagle** on the **top fly** and a **tricolor** of **red**, **black** and **orange vertical stripes** on the **bottom fly**. The colors appear to derive from the United Nationalist Independence Party (UNIP), which led the struggle against British colonialism. Red represents the blood shed in the struggle for freedom. Black stands for Zambia's people. Orange symbolizes Zambia's mineral wealth, and green denotes its natural resources. The eagle represents freedom.

HISTORY

In *c*.800 **Bantu speakers** migrated to Zambia. In 1855 **David Livingstone** became the first European to see Victoria Falls. In 1890 the British South Africa Company, managed by **Cecil Rhodes**, made treaties with local chiefs. The area divided into North-West and North-East **Rhodesia**. In 1911 the two regions joined to form **Northern Rhodesia**. In 1953 Britain established the Federation of **Rhodesia** (including present-day Zambia and **Zimbabwe**) and Nyasaland (now **Malawi**). In 1963, after a nationwide campaign of civil disobedience, the federation was dissolved. In 1964, Northern Rhodesia gained **independence** as the republic of **Zambia**. Multiparty democracy was introduced in 1991.

AREA 291,000 sq mi (753,000 sq km)
POPULATION 13,881,000
CAPITAL Lusaka
GOVERNMENT Multiparty republic
ETHNIC GROUPS Native African (Bemba, Tonga, Maravi/Nyanja)
LANGUAGES English (official), Bemba, Kaonda
RELIGIONS Christianity 70%, Islam, Hinduism
NATIONAL MOTTO "One Zambia, One Nation"
NATIONAL ANTHEM (DATE) *"Lumbanyeni Zambia"* "Stand and Sing of Zambia, Proud and Free" (1961)

Zambian traditional tribal hunter with shield and staff.

216

FLAG RATIO: 1:2 USE: National/Civil DATE ADOPTED: 1980 LAST MODIFIED: 1980

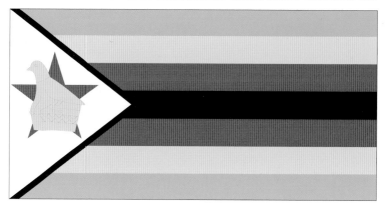

Zimbabwe's flag derives from the colors of the ruling Zimbabwe African National Union-Patriotic Front (ZANU-PF). It has **seven horizontal stripes**: **two tribands** of the **Pan-African** colors of **green**, **yellow** and **red** are separated by a **black stripe**. Green represents Zimbabwe's fertile land. Yellow stands for its mineral wealth. Red symbolizes the blood shed in the colonial struggle, and black represents its majority population. On the hoist is a **white triangle** symbolizing peace and progress. It contains a stylized depiction of a **soapstone bird** (found at Great Zimbabwe) against a **red star**. The star represents internationalism and the socialist origins of ZANU-PF.

HISTORY

By 1200 the **Shona** formed a kingdom based around **Great Zimbabwe**. In 1889 the British South Africa Company began to exploit Zimbabwe's mineral wealth. The area became **Southern Rhodesia in 1896**. In 1953 it federated with Northern Rhodesia (now **Zambia**) and Nyasaland (**Malawi**). In 1965 Ian Smith declared independence from **Britain**. In 1980, after a struggle against the white-minority regime, **Robert Mugabe** became prime minister. Increasing political repression brought international condemnation. In 2008, Mugabe's ZANU-PF party agreed a power-sharing deal with the opposition Movement for Democratic Change.

The chipendani is a plucked single-stringed mouth bow of the Shona people.

AREA 151,000 sq mi (12,200 sq km)
POPULATION 12,084,000
CAPITAL Harare
GOVERNMENT Multiparty republic
ETHNIC GROUPS Shona 82%, Ndebele 14%, other African groups 2%, mixed and Asian 1%
LANGUAGES English (official), Shona, Ndebele
RELIGIONS Christianity, traditional beliefs
NATIONAL MOTTO Unity, Freedom, Work"
NATIONAL ANTHEM (DATE) *"Kalibusiswe Ilizwe leZimbabwe"* "Blessed Be the Land of Zimbabwe" (1994)

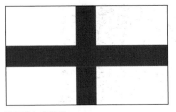

ENGLAND
Ratio : 3:5
Flag Name : Saint George's Cross

SCOTLAND
Ratio : 3:5
Flag Name : Saint Andrew's Saltire

WALES
Ratio : 3:5
Flag Name : *Y Ddraig Goch* (The Red Dragon)

ALDERNEY
Ratio : 3:5
Date Adopted : 1906

GUERNSEY
Ratio : 2:3
Date Adopted : 1985

ISLE OF MAN
Ratio : 1:2
Date Adopted : 1971

JERSEY
Ratio : 3:5
Date Adopted : 1981

SARK
Ratio : 3:5
Date Adopted : 1938

ALABAMA

Statehood :   December 14, 1819
Nickname :   The Heart of Dixie
State motto :   We dare defend our rights

ALASKA

Statehood :   January 3, 1959
Nickname :   The Last Frontier
State motto :   North to the future

ARIZONA

Statehood :   February 14, 1912
Nickname :   The Grand Canyon State
State motto :   God enriches

ARKANSAS

Statehood :   June 15, 1836
Nickname :   The Land of Opportunity
State motto :   The people rule

CALIFORNIA

Statehood :   September 9, 1850
Nickname :   The Golden State
State motto :   *Eureka*!

COLORADO

Statehood :   August 1, 1876
Nickname :   The Centennial State
State motto :   Nothing without providence

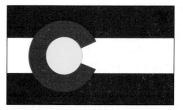

CONNECTICUT

Statehood :   January 9, 1788
Nickname :   Constitution State
State motto :   He who transplanted still sustains

DELAWARE

Statehood :   December 7, 1787
Nickname :   The First State
State motto :   Liberty and independence

FLORIDA

Statehood : March 3, 1845
Nickname : Sunshine State
State motto : In God we trust

GEORGIA

Statehood : January 2, 1788
Nickname : Empire state of the South
State motto : Wisdom, justice and moderation

HAWAII

Statehood : August 21, 1959
Nickname : Aloha state
State motto : The life of the land is perpetuated in righteousness

IDAHO

Statehood : July 3, 1890
Nickname : Gem state
State motto : It is forever

ILLINOIS

Statehood : December 3, 1818
Nickname : Prairie state
State motto : State sovereignty, national union

INDIANA

Statehood : December 11, 1816
Nickname : Hoosier state
State motto : Crossroads of America

IOWA

Statehood : December 28, 1846
Nickname : Hawkeye state
State motto : Our liberties we prize and our rights we will maintain

KANSAS

Statehood : January 29, 1861
Nickname : Sunflower state
State motto : To the stars through difficulties

KENTUCKY

STATEHOOD : June 1, 1792
NICKNAME : Bluegrass state
STATE MOTTO : United we stand, divided we fall

LOUISIANA

STATEHOOD : April 30, 1812
NICKNAME : Pelican State
STATE MOTTO : Union, Justice and Confidence

MAINE

STATEHOOD : March 15, 1820
NICKNAME : Pine Tree State
STATE MOTTO : I direct

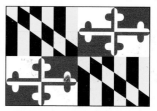

MARYLAND

STATEHOOD : April 28, 1788
NICKNAME : Old Line State, Free State
STATE MOTTO : Manly deeds, womanly words

MASSACHUSETTS

STATEHOOD : February 6, 1788
NICKNAME : Bay State
STATE MOTTO : By the sword we seek peace, but peace only under liberty

MICHIGAN

STATEHOOD : January 26, 1837
NICKNAME : Wolverine State
STATE MOTTO : If you seek a pleasant peninsula, look around you

MINNESOTA

STATEHOOD : May 11, 1858
NICKNAME : Gopher State
STATE MOTTO : Star of the North

MISSISSIPPI

STATEHOOD : December 10, 1817
NICKNAME : Magnolia State
STATE MOTTO : By valor and arms

221

MISSOURI

STATEHOOD : August 10, 1821
NICKNAME : 'Show me' State
STATE MOTTO : The welfare of the people shall be the supreme law

MONTANA

STATEHOOD : November 8, 1889
NICKNAME : Treasure State
STATE MOTTO : Gold and silver

NEBRASKA

STATEHOOD : March 1, 1867
NICKNAME : The Cornhusker State
STATE MOTTO : Equality before the law

NEVADA

STATEHOOD : October 31, 1864
NICKNAME : The Silver State
STATE MOTTO : All for our country

NEW HAMPSHIRE

STATEHOOD : June 21, 1788
NICKNAME : The Granite State
STATE MOTTO : Live free or die

NEW JERSEY

STATEHOOD : December 18, 1787
NICKNAME : The Garden State
STATE MOTTO : Liberty and prosperity

NEW MEXICO

STATEHOOD : January 16, 1912
NICKNAME : The Land of Enchantment
STATE MOTTO : It grows as it goes

NEW YORK

STATEHOOD : July 26, 1788
NICKNAME : The Empire State
STATE MOTTO : Ever upward

NORTH CAROLINA

STATEHOOD : November 21, 1789
NICKNAME : The Tar Heel State
STATE MOTTO : To be, rather than to seem

NORTH DAKOTA

STATEHOOD : November 2, 1889
NICKNAME : The Flickertail State
STATE MOTTO : Liberty and union, now and forever, one and inseparable

OHIO

STATEHOOD : March 1, 1803
NICKNAME : The Buckeye State
STATE MOTTO : With God, all things are possible

OKLAHOMA

STATEHOOD : November 16, 1907
NICKNAME : The Sooner State
STATE MOTTO : Labor conquers all things

OREGON

STATEHOOD : February 14, 1859
NICKNAME : The Beaver State
STATE MOTTO : She flies with her own wings

PENNSYLVANIA

STATEHOOD : December 12, 1787
NICKNAME : The Keystone State
STATE MOTTO : Virtue, liberty and independence

RHODE ISLAND

STATEHOOD : May 29, 1790
NICKNAME : Ocean State
STATE MOTTO : Hope

SOUTH CAROLINA

STATEHOOD : May 23, 1788
NICKNAME : The Palmetto State
STATE MOTTO : Prepared in mind and resources

SOUTH DAKOTA

STATEHOOD : November 2, 1889
NICKNAME : The Sunshine State
STATE MOTTO : Under God the people rule

TENNESSEE

STATEHOOD : June 1, 1796
NICKNAME : The Volunteer State
STATE MOTTO : Agriculture and commerce

TEXAS

STATEHOOD : December 29, 1845
NICKNAME : The Lone Star State
STATE MOTTO : Friendship

UTAH

STATEHOOD : January 4, 1896
NICKNAME : The Beehive State
STATE MOTTO : Industry

VERMONT

STATEHOOD : March 4, 1791
NICKNAME : The Green Mountain State
STATE MOTTO : Freedom and unity

VIRGINIA

STATEHOOD : June 25, 1788
NICKNAME : Old Dominion
STATE MOTTO : Thus always to tyrants

WEST VIRGINIA

STATEHOOD : June 20, 1863
NICKNAME : The Mountain State
STATE MOTTO : Mountaineers are always free

WASHINGTON

STATEHOOD : November 11, 1889
NICKNAME : The Evergreen State
STATE MOTTO : *Alki* (Native American for 'by and by')

WISCONSIN

STATEHOOD :   May 29, 1848
NICKNAME :   The Badger State
STATE MOTTO :   Forward

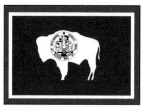

WYOMING

STATEHOOD :   July 10, 1890
NICKNAME :   The Equality State
STATE MOTTO :   Equal rights

ROVINCE FLAGS OF CANADA

ALBERTA

RATIO :   1:2
DATE ADOPTED : 1968

BRITISH COLUMBIA

RATIO :   3:5
DATE ADOPTED : 1960

MANITOBA

RATIO :   1:2
DATE ADOPTED : 1966

NEW BRUNSWICK

RATIO :   5:8
DATE ADOPTED : 1965

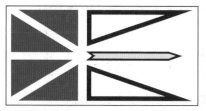

NEWFOUNDLAND & LABRADOR

RATIO :   1:2
DATE ADOPTED : 1980

NORTHWEST TERRITORIES
RATIO :   1:2
DATE ADOPTED : 1969

NOVA SCOTIA
RATIO :   3:4
DATE ADOPTED : 1929

NUNAVUT
RATIO :   9:16
DATE ADOPTED : 1999

ONTARIO
RATIO :   1:2
DATE ADOPTED : 1965

PRINCE EDWARD ISLAND
RATIO :   2:3
DATE ADOPTED : 1964

QUÉBEC
RATIO :   2:3
DATE ADOPTED : 1948

SASKATCHEWAN
RATIO :   1:2
DATE ADOPTED : 1964

YUKON
RATIO :   1:2
DATE ADOPTED : 1967

AUSTRALIA CAPITAL TERRITORY
Ratio : 1:2
Date Adopted : 1993

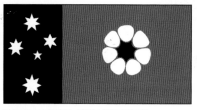

NORTHERN TERRITORY
Ratio : 1:2
Date Adopted : 1978

NEW SOUTH WALES
Ratio : 1:2
Date Adopted : 1876

QUEENSLAND
Ratio : 1:2
Date Adopted : 1876
Last Amended : 1953

SOUTH AUSTRALIA
Ratio : 1:2
Date Adopted : 1904

TASMANIA
Ratio : 1:2
Date Adopted : 1875
Last Amended : 1975

VICTORIA
Ratio : 1:2
Date Adopted : 1870
Last Amended : 1953

WESTERN AUSTRALIA
Ratio : 1:2
Date Adopted : 1953

INTERNATIONAL ORGANIZATION FLAGS

ARAB LEAGUE
Ratio : 1:2
Date Adopted : 1955

ASEAN
Full Name : Association of South-East Asian Nations
Ratio : 1:2
Date Adopted : 1955

CARICOM
Full Name : Caribbean Community
Ratio : 2:3
Date Adopted : 1983

CIS
Full Name : Commonwealth of Independent States
Ratio : 1:2
Date Adopted : 1996

COMMONWEALTH OF NATIONS
Ratio : 1:2
Date Adopted : 1976

EU
Full Name : European Union
Ratio : 2:3
Date Adopted : 1955 (by the Council of Europe)

NATO
Full Name : North Atlantic Treaty Organization
Ratio : 3:4
Date Adopted : 1953

OAS
Full Name : Organization of American States
Ratio : 2:3
Date Adopted : 1961 (last amended 1991)

INTERNATIONAL ORGANIZATION FLAGS

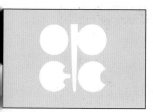

OPEC
Full Name : Organization of Petroleum Exporting Countries
Ratio : 3:5
Date Adopted : 1970

AU
Full Name : African Union
Ratio : 2:3
Date Adopted : 1970 (by Organization of African Unity)

OLYMPIC MOVEMENT
Full Name : International Olympic Committee (IOC)
Ratio : 2:3
Date Adopted : 1913

RED CRESCENT
Ratio : 1:1
Date Adopted : 1876

RED CROSS
Ratio : 1:1
Date Adopted : 1864

PACIFIC COMMUNITY
Full Name : Secretariat of the Pacific Community (SPC)
Ratio : 7:10
Date Adopted : 1999

UN
Full Name : United Nations
Ratio : 2:3
Date Adopted : 1947

WEU
Full Name : Western European Union
Ratio : 2:3
Date Adopted : 1993

SIGNAL FLAGS *ALPHABET*

A - *ALPHA*
Diver below (when stationary);
I am undergoing a speed trial

B - *BRAVO*
I am taking on or discharging
explosives

C - *CHARLIE*
Yes (affirmative)

D - *DELTA*
Keep clear, maneuvring with
difficulty

E - *ECHO*
Altering course to starboard

F - *FOXTROT*
Disabled, communicate
with me

G - *GOLF*
I require a pilot

H - *HOTEL*
I have a pilot on board

I - *INDIA*
I am altering my course to
port

J - *JULIETT*
I am going to send a message
by semaphore

K - *KILO*
You should stop your vessel
instantly

L - *LIMA*
Stop, I have something
important to communicate

M - *MIKE*
I have a doctor on board

N - *NOVEMBER*
No (negative)

O - *OSCAR*
Man overboard

P - *PAPA (BLUE PETER)*
All aboard, ship is about to sail
(At sea) Your lights are out

Q - *QUEBEC*
My vessel is healthy and I
request free pratique

R - *ROMEO*
The way is off my ship. You
may feel your way past me

S - *SIERRA*
My engines are going astern

T - *TANGO*
Do not pass ahead of me

U - *UNIFORM*
You are running into danger

V - *VICTOR*
I require assistance
(not distress)

W - *WHISKY*
I require medical assistance

X - *X-RAY*
Stop your intentions, watch
for my signals

Y - *YANKEE*
I am dragging anchor

Z - *ZULU*
I require a tug

A+E I must abandon vessel
C+J Do you require assistance?
C+N Unable to give assistance
J+ I Are you aground?
J+L Risk of going aground
J+W I have sprung a leak
K+N I cannot take you in tow
K+N+1 I cannot take you in tow,
but will report you and ask for
immediate assistance

L+N Light (name follows) has
been extinguished
L+O Not in my correct position
L+R Bar is not dangerous
L+S Bar is dangerous
M+F Course to reach me is ...
M+G You should steer course...
N+C I am in distress
N+F You are running into danger
N+G You are in dangerous positio

1

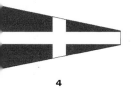

2

3

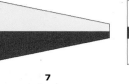

4

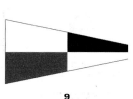

5

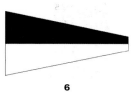

6

7

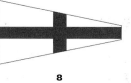

8

9

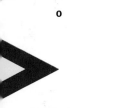

0

NUMERIC PENNANTS

A numeral is added to general messages to provide variation in meaning, to ask or answer a question, or to supplement the basic message.

FIRST REPEATER
Repeats the upper flag or pennant of a hoist.

SECOND REPEATER
Repeats the second flag or pennant of a hoist.

THIRD REPEATER
Repeats the third flag or pennant of a hoist.

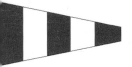

ANSWERING PENNANT

ANSWERING PENNANT

The answering pennant is used as a decimal point when sending numeric data. Close up (top of mast), the receiving vessel indicates she understands the hoist.
At the end of the signal, it indicates that the message is complete.

At dip (half-mast), hoisted by receiving vessel as each hoist of the transmitting ship is seen.

NATIONAL FLAG DAYS

Afghanistan — Apr 27
Albania — Jan 11, Apr 7*, Nov 29
Algeria — Jul 5§, Nov 1
Andorra — Sep 8
Angola — Nov 11§
Antigua and Barbuda — Apr 27*, Nov 1
Argentina — Apr 2, May 25, Jun 20*, Jul 9§, Jul 25*, Aug 17, Oct 12
Armenia — Apr 7, Apr 24, May 28, Sep 20§
Australia — Jan 26, Apr 25, May 22*, Aug 20, Sep 3*
Austria — May 1*, Oct 26§
Azerbaijan — May 28, Aug 30§
Bahamas — Jul 9§, Oct 12
Bahrain — Dec 16
Bangladesh — Feb 25*, Mar 26§, Dec 16§
Barbados — Nov 30
Belarus — Jul 27§
Belgium — Jan 23* Jul 21§, Oct 4§, Nov 11, Nov 15
Belize — May 9, Sep 10, Sep 20§, Nov 19
Benin — Aug 1§, Nov 16*, Nov 30
Bhutan — Nov 11
Bolivia — Jul 16, Aug 6§, Nov 30*
Bosnia and Herzegovina — Apr 5§, May 4*
Botswana — Jul 20, Sep 30§
Brazil — Apr 21, Apr 22, Sep 7§, Nov 15, Nov 19*
Brunei — Feb 23§, May 31, Jul 16
Bulgaria — Feb 6, Mar 3§, May 24, Sep 9, Nov 7
Burkina Faso — Aug 4§
Burma — Jan 4§, Feb 12, Mar 2, Mar 27, Jul 19
Burundi — Jul 1§
Cambodia — Apr 17§, Nov 9§
Cameroon — Jan 1§, Feb 11, May 20, Aug 12
Canada — Feb 15*, Apr 17, Jul 1, Oct 18, Nov 11
Cape Verde — Jan 20, Jul 5§, Sep 12, Sep 25*
Central African Republic — Aug 13§, Dec 1
Chad — Jun 7, Aug 11§, Nov 6*, Nov 26
Chile — May 21, Sep 18§, Oct 12, Oct 18*
China — May 4, Jun 1, Oct 1
Colombia — Jul 20§, Aug 7, Oct 12, Nov 11, Nov 26*
Comoros — May 13, Jul 6§
Congo — Jul 31, Aug 14§
Congo, Democratic Republic of — Jun 24, Jun 30§, Nov 17, Nov 21*
Costa Rica — Apr 11, Sep 15§, Oct 12, Oct 21*
Côte d'Ivoire — Aug 7§
Croatia — Jan 6, May 9, May 30, Jun 22, Aug 5, Aug 15, Nov 1
Cuba — Jan 1, May 20§, Oct 27
Cyprus — Mar 25, Apr 1, Oct 1§
Czech Republic — May 8, Jun 5, Jul 6, Oct 28
Denmark — Mar 28, Apr 9, Apr 16, Apr 27, Apr 29, May 5, May 26, Jun 5, Jun 7, Jun 11, Jun 15
Djibouti — Jun 27§

Dominica — Nov 3§, Nov 9*
Dominican Republic — Feb 27§, Aug 16, Nov 6*
East Timor — May 20§
Ecuador — May 24, Jul 24, Aug 10§, Oct 9, Oct 12, Nov 3
Egypt — Feb 28§, Apr 25, May 2, Jun 18, Jul 23, Oct 24
El Salvador — Sep 15§, Oct 6, Oct 12, Nov 5
Equatorial Guinea — Mar 5, Jul 7, Oct 12§
Eritrea — May 24§, Jun 20
Estonia — Feb 24§, May 12, Jun 14, Jun 23, Aug 20§, Nov 16
Ethiopia — Apr 6, May 28, Sep 12
Fiji — Jul 25, Oct 10
Finland — Feb 5, Feb 28, Apr 9, Apr 27, May 29*, Nov 6, Dec 6§
France — May 8, Jul 14, Nov 11
Gabon — Mar 12, Aug 9*, Aug 17§
Gambia — Feb 18§, Apr 24
Georgia — Mar 31§, May 26§
Germany — May 3, May 5, May 9*, May 23, Oct 3, Nov 16
Ghana — Mar 6§, Jul 1
Greece — Mar 25§, Oct 28
Grenada — Feb 7§, Mar 13, Oct 25
Guatemala — Jun 30, Sep 15§, Oct 12, Oct 20
Guinea — Apr 3, Nov 10*
Guinea-Bissau — Sep 10§, Sep 12
Guyana — Feb 23, May 26§
Haiti — Jan 1§, May 18*, Nov 17
Honduras — Jan 18*, Feb 3, Sep 15§, Oct 12, Oct 16, Oct 21, Oct 23
Hungary — Mar 15, Apr 4, Jun 16, Aug 20
Iceland — Jun 7, Jun 17, Oct 9
India — Jan 26, Aug 15§, Aug 31*, Oct 2
Indonesia — Jan 27*, Aug 17§, Sep 9
Iran — Feb 11, Apr 1
Iraq — Jul 14, Jul 17, Oct 3
Ireland — Mar 17, Oct 6
Israel — Apr 24§
Italy — Apr 25, Jun 2, Nov 4
Jamaica — May 23, Aug 5§
Japan — Jan 14, Feb 11, Apr 29, May 3, May 5, Aug 5*, Sep 15, Nov 3, Nov 23
Jordan — May 25§, Jun 10, Aug 11
Kazakstan — Oct 25
Kenya — Jun 1, Oct 20, Dec 12§
Kiribati — Jul 12§
Korea, North — Feb 16, Mar 1, Apr 15, Sep 9
Korea, South — Jan 25*, Mar 1§, Jun 6, Jul 17, Aug 15, Oct 1, Oct 3
Kosovo — Feb 17§
Kuwait — Feb 26, Sep 7*
Kyrgyzstan — Mar 3*, Aug 31§
Laos — Jan 6, Jan 20, Jun 1, Jul 19§, Aug 23
Latvia — May 12, Nov 18
Lebanon — Nov 22§
Lesotho — Jan 20, Mar 12, Oct 17, Oct 4§
Liberia — Feb 11, Apr 7, May 14, Jul 26§, Aug 27*, Nov 29
Libya — Sep 1, Dec 24§
Liechtenstein — Feb 14, Aug 16, Sep 26, Oct 5

Lithuania — May 5, Jul 6
Luxembourg — Jun 12*, Jun 23, Sep 19
Macedonia, Former Yugoslav Rep — Jan 2§, Aug 2, Nov 16
Madagascar — Mar 29, Jun 26§, Oct 14*
Malawi — Mar 3, May 14, Jul 6§
Malaysia — Aug 31§
Maldives — Jul 26§, Nov 11
Mali — Feb 10, Mar 1*, Sep 22§, Nov 19
Malta — Mar 31§, Jun 7, Jun 29
Marshall Islands — May 1, Oct 21§
Mauritania — Apr 1*, Nov 28§
Mauritius — Mar 12§
Mexico — Feb 5, Feb 19, Feb 24*, Mar 21, May 5, Jun 1, Sep 16§, Oct 12, Oct 23, Nov 20
Micronesia, Federated States of — May 10, Nov 3§
Moldova — Aug 27§
Monaco — Jan 27, Apr 4*, Nov 19
Mongolia — Jul 11
Montenegro — May 21§, Jul 13
Morocco — Mar 2§, Mar 3, May 23, Jul 9, Aug 14, Nov 6, Nov 17*, Nov 18§
Mozambique — Feb 3, Jun 1, Jun 24§, Sep 5*, Sep 25
Namibia — Mar 21§, Aug 26, Oct 7
Nauru — Jan 31§
Nepal — Jan 11, Feb 18, Nov 7
Netherlands — Jan 19, Jan 31, Feb 19*, Apr 27, Apr 30, May 4, May 5, Jun 29, Sep 6, Dec 15
New Zealand — Feb 6, Apr 25, Jun 12*
Nicaragua — Jul 19, Sep 14, Oct 12
Niger — May 18, Aug 3§, Nov 23*, Dec 18
Nigeria — Oct 1§
Norway — Feb 21, May 8, May 17, Jun 7, Jul 4, Jul 17*, Jul 20, Jul 29, Sep 22, Dec 10
Oman — Nov 18
Pakistan — Mar 23, Aug 14§, Sep 6, Sep 11
Palau — Mar 15, May 5, Jun 1, Jun 13*, Jul 9, Oct 1§, Oct 24
Panama — Jan 9, Jun 4*, Oct 11, Oct 12, Nov 1, Nov 4*, Nov 28§
Papua New Guinea — Sep 16§
Paraguay — May 14§, Jun 12, Aug 25, Sep 29, Nov 27*
Peru — Feb 25*, Jun 24, Jul 28§, Aug 30, Oct 8
Philippines — Feb 25, May 6, Apr 9, Jun 12§, Jul 4, Nov 30, Dec 30
Poland — May 3, Jul 22, Nov 11§
Portugal — Apr 25, Jun 10, Oct 1*, Oct 5, Dec 1§
Qatar — Sep 3§
Romania — Aug 23
Russia — Feb 23, May 9, Jun 12, Nov 7
Rwanda — Jan 28, Apr 7, Jul 1§, Jul 5, Sep 25
Saint Kitts and Nevis — Sep 19§
Saint Lucia — Jan 22, Feb 22§, Mar 1*
Saint Vincent and the Grenadines — Jan 22, Oct 27§
Samoa — Jan 1§, Sep 5
San Marino — Feb 5§, Sep 4

São Tome and Príncipe — Jul 12§, Sep 6
Saudi Arabia — Sep 23
Senegal — Apr 4§, Jul 14
Serbia — Apr 27, Jul 4, Nov 29
Seychelles — Jun 5, Jun 29§
Sierra Leone — Apr 19
Singapore — Aug 9§
Slovak Republic — Aug 29, Sep 1
Slovenia — Feb 8, Apr 27, Jun 24§, Oct 29, Dec 26§
Solomon Islands — Jul 7§, Nov 18*
Somalia — Jun 26§, Jul 1§, Oct 21*
South Africa — Mar 21, Apr 27, May 10, May 31§, Jun 16, Aug 9, Sep 24
South Sudan — Jul 9§
Spain — Apr 22, Jul 25, Aug 29*, Oct 12, Oct 15
Sri Lanka — Feb 4§, May 22, Oct 20*, Oct 22
Sudan — Jan 1§, Apr 6, May 25, Jun 30
Suriname — Jul 1, Jul 22, Nov 25§
Swaziland — Apr 19, Apr 25*, Aug 1, Sep 6§
Sweden — Jan 28, Mar 12, Apr 30*, May 18, Jun 6*, Jun 14, Aug 8, Nov 6, Dec 10, Dec 23
Switzerland — Jan 2
Syria — Mar 8, Apr 17§
Taiwan — Mar 12, Mar 29, Sep 28*, Oct 10, Oct 25, Oct 28*, Oct 29, Nov 12
Tajikistan — Sep 9§
Tanzania — Jan 12, Apr 26, Apr 30*, Jul 7
Thailand — Apr 6, May 5, Sep 28*
Togo — Jan 13, Apr 27§
Tonga — Apr 25, May 4, Jun 4, Nov 4
Trinidad and Tobago — May 24, Jun 19, Aug 5, Sep 24, Nov 10
Tunisia — Jan 18, Mar 20§, Mar 21, Apr 9, Jul 25, Aug 3§, Oct 15, Nov 7
Turkey — Apr 23§, May 19, Jun 5*, Aug 30, Oct 29, Nov 10
Turkmenistan — Feb 19*, Oct 27§
Tuvalu — Oct 1§
Uganda — Apr 11, May 27, Oct 9§
Ukraine — May 9, Aug 24§
United Arab Emirates — Dec 2
United Kingdom — Feb 6, Feb 19, Mar 10, Apr 21, Jun 2, Jun 10, Aug 4, Aug 15, Aug 20, Nov 5, Nov 11
United States of America — Jan 15, Feb 12, May 22, Jun 14*, Jul 4, Sep 17, Oct 21, Oct 27, Nov 11
Uruguay — Apr 19, May 18, Jun 19, Jul 18, Aug 25§, Oct 12
Uzbekistan — Sep 1§, Oct 11*
Vanuatu — Mar 5, Jul 30, Oct 5, Nov 25
Vatican — Feb 11§, May 18, Oct 22
Venezuela — Mar 12*, Apr 19, Jun 24, Jul 5§, Oct 12
Vietnam — Apr 30, May 19, Sep 2, Nov 30*
Yemen — May 22, Sep 26, Oct 14, Nov 30§
Zambia — Mar 19, Oct 24
Zimbabwe — Apr 18§, Aug 11